"As a correspondent for NBC News, Soboroff was among the first to report on the Trump administration's family separation policy; here, he digs deeper into its roots and consequences." —*New York Times Book Review,* "New & Notable"

"Jacob Soboroff zooms in on President Trump and his administration's decision to separate children from their parents as a deterrent to border crossers. In doing so, he illuminates how, in the face of congressional inaction, a cadre of presidential advisers can introduce policies with shocking, unintended consequences. . . . With the immediacy of cable news, Soboroff attempts to reconstruct the quiet run-up to the public acknowledgment of the policy, including one official's efforts to destroy the internal list of separated parents and children. He interweaves this reporting with his own on-the-ground work as one of the first journalists to enter detention facilities holding the separated children. And he follows Juan and José, a Guatemalan father and son seeking asylum who are swept into the maw of the separation machine. . . . Soboroff, who acknowledges that he came to the story late, offers generous recognition to fellow journalists and the advocates who saw the looming crisis well before he did. . . . Ultimately, the reporter is the protagonist, providing the book's strength and emotional core." —Laura Wides-Muñoz, *Washington Post*

"Jacob Soboroff's excellent reporting at the border helped shine a light on Trump's cruel family separation policy. His new book, *Separated,* is a sobering account of what he saw and the human toll of the Trump agenda." —Julián Castro

"Fantastic. . . . Serves as a blueprint, honestly, for everything that we are seeing now in the pandemic, everything wrong with this administration, it's all right there in black and white. . . . The book is fantastic, the reporting is fantastic."

—Chris Hayes

"Jacob Soboroff, an award-winning NBC correspondent, delves deep into the Trump's administration's systematic family separation practice. It's a bleak but necessary read about why this inhumane policy is allowed to happen in America."   —*Cosmopolitan*, "Best Nonfiction Books of 2020"

"A thorough account. . . . *Separated* takes a well-deserved place among the multiple accounts of the Trump administration's machinations as one journalist's up-close view of an extremely painful moment in the nation's history."

—*Texas Observer*

"An expansive, complex, and multi-layered story about the immigration crisis and the policy that separates families seeking asylum in the United States."   —Texas Public Radio

"Jacob Soboroff was among the first American civilians to witness what family separation looked like. . . . In *Separated* Soboroff chronicles the crossed wires and cold calculation that fostered America's most glaring humanitarian crisis in recent memory. It's a chronological account of his own reporting at the border interwoven with accounts of the efforts of career government professionals who worked to block or advance the zero-tolerance immigration policy used to justify family separation. Most affectingly, the book is also a portrait of a Guatemalan father, Juan, and his teenage son, Jose, who sought asylum in the U.S., only to be forced apart as they crossed from Mexico into Arizona."   —Forward

"A powerful and eye-opening account of Trump's separation of migrant families at the US-Mexico border. A wonderful example of political journalism."

—Marc Lamont Hill (via Twitter)

"I have relied on Jacob's relentless reporting about the Trump administration's barbaric treatment of migrant children at our border. This is a hard and necessary book. . . . Impossible to overstate the importance of Jacob Soboroff's book because it's impossible to overstate the importance of these children and their families."   —Connie Schultz (via Twitter)

"The details Jacob Soboroff uncovered are demoralizing. The government deliberations coupled with the painful personal stories of parents who lost kids and Jacob's own reporting journey make this book a must-read."

—Katy Tur (via Twitter)

"Phenomenal. Please read it."   —Andrew Zimmern (via Twitter)

"Jacob Soboroff has done A LOT of very good work on [immigration policy]. I hope you will buy his book and educate yourself on the horrors Donald Trump inflicted on so many innocent families and children."

—Don Winslow, author of *The Border* (via Twitter)

"An important and disturbing book."

—Errol Morris (via Twitter)

"Add Jacob Soboroff's *Separated: Inside an American Tragedy* to the library of essential reading about the administration of the 45th president of the United States. . . . The story *Separated* tells is massive in scope; in its later pages, a government official confides that the administration's family separation policy caused 'the greatest human rights catastrophe in my lifetime' within the United States. Soboroff scales it to human size by grounding his clear-eyed, sometimes self-deprecating reporting in two parallel tracks: his personal journey of discovery of what was happening, and the wrenching experience of a father and son, Juan and 14-year-old José, who had sought asylum here from death threats in Petén, Guatemala. That brings narrative clarity and some dramatic tension to coverage of policy deliberations and agency politics."

—*Pasadena Weekly*

"To experience the pain and anger many suburban voters felt about Trump's policy of ripping children from the arms of their asylum-seeking parents along the southern border, I'd recommend *Separated: Inside an American Tragedy* by Jacob Soboroff."
—Eugene Robinson, *Washington Post*

"Harrowing and deeply informed. . . . An impassioned, essential account of 'one of the most shameful chapters in modern American history."
—*Publishers Weekly*

"Piercing. . . . Consistently affecting and haunting. . . . A book of justifiably righteous indignation at—and condemnation of—a monstrous program."
—*Kirkus Reviews*

"[A] captivating account, which deftly weaves together the political and the personal."
—*Library Journal*

"A blistering report on the Trump administration's family-separation policies."
—*America* magazine

"Critically important. . . . Soboroff offers the chilling history of our changing immigration policy, one highly political decision after another, made to create the effective deterrence the President demanded. . . . We all can benefit from reading Jacob Soboroff's *Separated*."
—Berkshire Edge

Separated

Separated

INSIDE AN AMERICAN TRAGEDY

JACOB SOBOROFF

CUSTOM
HOUSE

HarperCollins books may be purchased for educational, business, or sales promotional use. For information, please email the Special Markets Department at SPsales@harpercollins.com.

A hardcover edition of this book was published in 2020 by Custom House, an imprint of William Morrow.

FIRST CUSTOM HOUSE PAPERBACK EDITION PUBLISHED 2021.

Designed by Elina Cohen

Library of Congress Cataloging-in-Publication Data has been applied for.

ISBN 978-0-06-299220-8

21 22 23 24 25 LSC 10 9 8 7 6 5 4 3 2 1

FOR NICOLE, NOAH, AND LUCIA

CONTENTS

FAMILY SEPARATION AND REUNIFICATION: TIMELINE OF KEY EVENTS   xiii

AUTHOR'S NOTE: "FACTS ON THE GROUND"   xvii

PROLOGUE: *"They Were Going to Kill Us"*   1

PART ONE

CHAPTER ONE: *"I Just Couldn't Do That"*   11

CHAPTER TWO: *"I Don't Have Those Numbers"*   27

CHAPTER THREE: *"A Significant Increase"*   33

CHAPTER FOUR: *"Very, Very Worried"*   93

CHAPTER FIVE: *"Get Rid of the List"*   139

PART TWO

CHAPTER SIX: *"These Kids Are Incarcerated"*   193

CHAPTER SEVEN: *"They're Cages"*   229

CHAPTER EIGHT: *"No Way to Link"*   253

PART THREE

CHAPTER NINE: *"Shocks the Conscience"*   285

CHAPTER TEN: *"Made-for-TV Drama"*   307

CONTENTS

CHAPTER ELEVEN: *"It Hurts in My Heart"*   321

CHAPTER TWELVE: *"We Know That He Is a Good Person"*   341

EPILOGUE: *"The Greatest Human-Rights
Catastrophe of My Lifetime"*   351

AFTERWORD TO THE PAPERBACK EDITION: *"It's Criminal"*   369

ACKNOWLEDGMENTS   381

NOTES ON SOURCING   387

INDEX   403

Family Separation and Reunification: Timeline of Key Events

March 2017

DHS Secretary states publicly that DHS might separate families who enter the United States without authorization; weeks later, he announces DHS will not pursue the policy.

April 2017

Attorney General issues memorandum prioritizing prosecution of immigration offenses.

July 2017

El Paso sector of CBP implements policies resulting in increased family separations.

February 2018

Ms. L v. ICE lawsuit is filed.

April 2018

Attorney General issues memorandum instituting zero-tolerance policy at DOJ.

May 2018

DHS adopts zero-tolerance; the Attorney General publicly announces the policy's implementation at DOJ and DHS.

June 2018

President Trump issues Executive Order directing DHS to detain migrant families together.

June 2018

Court orders Federal Government to cease most family separations and reunite eligible families.

July 2018

HHS identifies 2,654 separated children under *Ms. L v. ICE.*

December 2018

After multiple revisions, HHS reports a new total of 2,737 separated children under *Ms. L v. ICE.*

March 2019

Court expands the *Ms. L* class to include parents who entered the United States on or after July 1, 2017, with children from whom they were separated.

October 2019

HHS identifies an additional 1,556 separated children under the expanded *Ms. L* class.

Source: HHS Office of Inspector General analysis of memoranda, court filings, and other public documents, 2019.

I am an unlikely eyewitness to one of the most shameful chapters in modern American history. The Trump administration's deliberate and systematic separation of thousands of migrant children from their parents was, according to humanitarian groups and child welfare experts, an unparalleled abuse of the human rights of children. The American Academy of Pediatrics says the practice will leave thousands of kids traumatized for life. I was there to see it myself, though I didn't expect to be and, as a journalist, almost missed the story entirely. What I saw now is forever seared into my memory.

Though the Trump administration had been carrying out widespread family separations at the border for more than a year, the horror separated families endured set in for me personally on the thirteenth day of June 2018. I could feel the thickness of the air as soon as I walked off our United Airlines flight at the tiny Brownsville South Padre Island International Airport in South Texas, the early summer steam of the Rio Grande Valley sneaking in between the weak seal connecting the jet bridge and the plane. The gray marine layer that draped my hometown of Los Angeles when I took off no longer seemed worth complaining about as sweat started dripping down my back.

As producer Aarne Heikkila and I headed up the ramp, I pulled off the sweatshirt I flew in, my T-shirt now sticking to my skin even as we made our way through the air-conditioned terminal toting our carry-ons. I'm probably going to get sick, I thought to myself. We headed past the baggage claim, out the doors, under a row of palm trees, and across a small parking lot to pick up our rented minivan.

We had rushed to Brownsville, not far from where the Rio Grande meets the Gulf of Mexico, after being invited by a Trump administration official to tour what is known as Casa Padre with several other journalists. Its name reflected the street it was on, meant to honor the Spanish priest who, in 1804, established the first permanent settlement on the southern tip of a nearby island. Literally translated, it means Father's House. We'd soon learn how regrettably misnamed the facility was.

The 250,000-square-foot former Walmart—what we were told was a "shelter"—was holding nearly fifteen hundred migrant boys, ten to seventeen years old, hundreds of whom had been separated from their parents as a direct result of Donald Trump's zero tolerance immigration policy. By then the existence and execution of Trump's family separations had been widely reported, but no journalist had seen the realities from the inside. I was anxious.

On the four-mile drive from the airport, I asked Aarne to pull over at a Walgreens so I could run inside to buy a car charger for my laptop. I figured it was going to be a long night and we'd be waiting in the car in between live shots. I paced the aisles looking for one. No luck, but I grabbed a little blue notebook (no cameras would be allowed inside), some dry shampoo (I'm a TV reporter with curly hair about to do a live shot in ninety-degree humidity), and a cold Gatorade (for mysterious reasons the yellow flavor calms my nerves). Aarne picked up a bag of almonds, like he always does when we're on assignment.

We paid and were on our way. In minutes I'd bear witness to the reality that our country, under the direction of President Donald Trump, was ripping parents and children apart. Casa Padre would become the scene of international breaking news later that night.

IT HAS NOW been two years since I walked into Casa Padre with that Walgreens notebook. After its pages were filled with four different stories, it lived on my desk at home for months, a reminder of the tragedy it had helped me document.

In late 2018, as my wife, son, and I were moving out of our rental and into our first home, I put the "memo book," as it says on the front in big bold type, in a bag with other valuable possessions and brought it to a storage locker. A year later, as I began writing this book, I went and dug the bag out from under boxes of Christmas decorations. With my iPhone flashlight I found the notebook at the bottom of the bag. Holding it in my hand for the first time in months made my heart race. The reporting inside, by President Trump's own admission, contributed to his ending systematic family separations. "I didn't like the sight or the feeling of families being separated," the president said while signing the executive order that stopped the policy he had claimed days earlier did not exist.

The notebook burned in my hand. Inside the five-by-ten-foot storage unit, surrounded by camping equipment and a baby-changing table and a pendant lamp that was gathering dust, I sat on a stool and flipped open its tiny cover to the first page of spiral-bound lined paper. If someone else found these fifty pages of chicken scratch they'd have no idea what they were looking at. I barely needed to read a word to bring back the sights and sounds and feelings of being there.

> As of
> Friday June 8—11,214 migrants
> in UAC [Unaccompanied Alien Children] program—avg length
> 56 days

Translation: the U.S. government was overwhelmed by an influx of kids—many of whom couldn't be released because their parents could not be found. I kept going, stopping again on the sixth page.

> kids everywhere
> oreos
> applesauce
> smile at them—they "feel like animals in a cage being looked at"

I recognized those details as among the first I revealed when I walked outside Casa Padre to a TV camera and told my MSNBC colleague, anchor Chris Hayes, and the world what I saw inside.

"This place is called a shelter, but effectively these kids are incarcerated."

A monitor was set up to the side of the camera, and I could see the breaking news banner at the bottom of the

screen. It read NBC NEWS TOURS IMMIGRANT CHILD DETEN-
TION CENTER. The notebook now in my hands was then
tucked in my pocket, during the first live national report
about the conditions of separated children in government
custody.

I brought it with me days later when, on Father's Day, I
toured the Ursula Border Patrol Central Processing Station,
not far away in McAllen, Texas, where more children were
separated from their parents than anywhere else on the border. There they shut families into what a Border Patrol agent
told me were "pods," a generous description. My notes hastily
captured what I learned.

> Child could
> get moved even
> If parent
> back in a day

The Trump administration was potentially "creating thousands of immigrant orphans," as a former acting director of
Immigration and Customs Enforcement put it, by deporting
separated parents before they were given a chance to reunite.
When I closed my notebook that day in South Texas, I walked
outside and again detailed on national TV what I saw: "People
in here are locked up in cages, essentially what look like animal
kennels. I don't know any other way to describe it."

I still don't. I can't recall why, but I left a few pages in
the middle of the notebook blank until I took notes during
my first phone call with Lindsay Toczylowski, the lawyer who
represented a separated three-year-old who, she said, "started
climbing up on the table" in court. On that call, she clued

me in to the Trump administration's lack of a plan to reunite families.

> Everyone has been
> told nothing about
> next steps

Toczylowski later introduced me to one of the parents she was describing at the time, Juan, who alleged he was coerced into signing away the right to reunify with his son, José. Their story appears throughout this book. I've spent hours with them recounting details of their almost five-month-long separation, a living nightmare in which, in his words, the United States government "treated us like animals, like dogs." At their request I've changed their names to ones they picked, in order to protect themselves and their family from the danger they told me (and the United States government) they were fleeing. The image on the cover was taken near the location where they crossed into the United States before being separated, nearly a decade before they arrived together.

The final pages of my notebook became home to what I saw and learned inside the San Diego courtroom where a federal judge ordered the Trump administration to reunite separated families. That case, brought by the American Civil Liberties Union (ACLU), is still ongoing today. At the time, Sarah Fabian, the government lawyer who later became famous for arguing migrant kids don't need blankets or toothbrushes, called in to the hearing and was asked to provide a number of separated family members facing deportation.

Fabian! Latest #'s
Executable 1,000!

Two exclamation points. At the time it all felt noteworthy. I did not plan or expect to be there, at the heart of it all, when the nation finally noticed the American government was systematically separating migrant families in unprecedented numbers.

Since the summer of 2017, the Trump administration has taken *at least* 5,556 kids from their parents. But still today, nobody knows for sure exactly how many families have been separated. In February 2020, the United States Government Accountability Office noted, "it is unclear the extent to which Border Patrol has accurate records of separated [families] in its data system." Scarce few of their stories have been told. Most will never be. There are families who were quickly put back together, and children who were, as predicted, permanently orphaned. My one little blue notebook could never do all their stories justice, nor is this book an attempt to. I encourage you to seek out, read, and learn about what happened from as many sources as you can.

That first report from outside Casa Padre went viral, my tweets from outside the shelter before and after my tour amassing tens of millions of impressions and tens of thousands of retweets, even before I went to sleep that evening. Tens of thousands of new people started following me on Twitter that night. Maybe you were one of them. Many of those new followers tweet me with links and leads and questions to this day.

As I continued covering family separations and the fallout, I obsessively tracked the number of children the Trump administration was reuniting and those it deemed "ineligible" for reunification by routinely checking PACER, the online documents portal of the federal court system, for any status updates posted by the government or the ACLU. Every time I posted the latest court-ordered update about the number of separated children still in U.S. custody, I received a social media signal boost from people around the world who invested time and energy in following the details of what was happening. Without them, this story would not have received the attention it did, long after most national reporters left the border, nor would this book be possible.

After having missed the slow-motion lead-up to this disaster, I became fixated on the policy and how it shattered so many lives. To those who have spent far longer than I have chronicling or experiencing life along the border, the answer was obvious: family separations were an extreme extension of decades of harsh policies aimed at keeping Mexican and Central American migrants from entering the United States, at a time when racists and xenophobes said they felt emboldened by the commander in chief. But why was its implementation, according to healthcare professionals, so needlessly cruel? Why was its ending so astonishingly sloppy? And why were its ramifications so ill-considered? Finding the answers to those questions is why I decided to write this book.

What follows is my attempt to fill in the blanks that I did not understand in real time. I started by revisiting my notes, as well as my public reporting, seeking to retrace my steps over two years. I pored through hundreds of pages of documents, obtained by myself and others, including NGOs doggedly filing public records requests. Still more files have been made publicly available through investigations by inspectors general and Congress. To contextualize these documents, I spoke with dozens of sources, from those responsible for considering, implementing, then unwinding the policy, to others who were caught in its crosshairs. I heard from people who participated in and experienced the policy on the border, and some of those who directed it from Washington, including, at times, from inside the White House itself.

What I have now unequivocally learned is that the Trump administration's family separation policy was an avoidable catastrophe made worse by people who could have made it better at multiple inflection points, which I'll share with you here in a series of pivotal moments presented as scenes. The dialogue you'll read in these pages is reconstructed, when I was present, to the best of my memory or using recordings made as part of my reporting. Where I was not a firsthand witness or participant, I rely on the retelling of moments by sources who were, cross-referencing their version of events with others who were present or had knowledge of what transpired when possible. Some of those sources considered my reporting adversarial at the time the policy was carried out, but agreed to speak with me to share important details with the goal of providing an accurate historical record of events. Indeed, certain individuals may have an alternate motivation: to ascribe blame to someone other than themselves, which is why I cast such a broad net in reporting the details in this book.

My mentor and producer Mitch Koss has always pushed me to report the facts on the ground before anything else—and they form the basis of this story: where I was, what I experienced, who I met, and how I came to believe that *separated* defines not just the Trump administration's act of seizing children and breaking apart families. For Juan, José, and thousands more just like them, the word describes a deep understanding of physical and mental pain—an unspeakable horror they were made to endure. For many others, including, for a time, myself, it describes the opposite: an inability to comprehend how Donald Trump's self-inflicted American tragedy was able to happen. The existence of both of those realities is only reconciled by facing the truth about our country—and ourselves.

Separated

"They Were Going to Kill Us"

Mugging for the camera, the twelve-year-old with his hair slicked back, sporting cool sunglasses, and wearing an oversize T-shirt, reminded me of myself as a preteen, eager to hang around my dad when he was busy working. The boy, José, was standing in front of a wall filled with products in the small convenience store his family owned and operated in Petén, Guatemala. It was there that his dad, Juan, snapped a photo of his son, which he showed to me proudly three years later. When José wasn't there or at school, you could likely find him kicking a soccer ball around the large field with patchy grass below his family's single-story home.

They were both born in Petén, a region slightly bigger than Maryland bordering Belize to the east and Mexico to the north. Making up one-third of the landmass of the country, Petén is the largest of Guatemala's twenty-two departments, though only 3 percent of the nation's population lives there.

When the photo was taken, José was the eldest of three children. His baby sisters were seven and one, and their mom, María, watched over them closely as the de facto head of their household while Juan, his dad, worked. Juan was one of five children, and José's grandmother and aunts and uncle were never far away, they explained.

Across the field and up a pathway made of stone was their home. At the top of the ramp were the five archways framing the outside of their house. To the left, a covered parking space where Juan kept the family's pickup truck, and to the right, a detached kitchen where meals were made and family celebrations centered. Their life and lifestyle was, he would tell you, well-off compared to many of their neighbors because Juan worked hard to make it so.

It was no surprise José wanted to hang around his dad's shop. He had only spent half his life together with his father. Juan was thirty-five but had first left for the United States himself when he was twenty-three, two years after his boy was born. He went to provide income for his family, returning in 2008. In 2010, he left again, this time staying away for longer, coming home in 2014.

They lived a short drive from Aeropuerto Internacional Mundo Maya, an airport that services tourists coming from around the world to explore the region's spectacular Maya ruins, the remains of the Americas' extraordinary ancient civilization that rivaled classical Greece and Rome in sophistication. Juan's journeys to the United States never started or ended there. Rather, Juan would pay a smuggler, or coyote, to help him navigate the journey north through Mexico and into the United States illegally, sneaking across the border both times in Arizona.

"They didn't catch me," he told me in English over a rib-eye steak in October 2019, José sitting close by his side. He shrugged his shoulders and cracked a half-smile.

When my great-great-grandparents arrived in the United States from Poland and Russia, I imagine they expressed a similar sense of guarded relief, one embedded in the disparate American story—a quilted patchwork of displacement and migration, journeys on ships forced and voluntary, treks on land to seek opportunity and survival, and eventually by planes carrying refugees, students, and entrepreneurs alike. Over generations, it produced a singular American identity shaped in equal parts by pain and hope, the place that represented a new and better life, while often betraying the trust of those who dared to believe in it. Juan and José are now a part of that story.

If Juan had flown to or from the United States on his earliest journey, he would have looked out the window to see breathtaking views of the lush terrain around his home stretching to the horizon. But by the time Juan snapped the photo of José in his store, his son quickly approaching his five-foot, two-inch frame, that landscape was transforming.

"Aeropuertos clandestinos," he whispered, as if anyone hearing him inside a D.C.-area steakhouse chain would notice or care.

Juan typed a phrase into YouTube—*narcos aterrizando en peten*—and slid me his smartphone across the table. The search results revealed what he would have seen from the sky: far more airports and runways down below than any official map or navigational chart would show, a symptom of the region's critical location for transnational criminal organizations—cartels—moving drugs through the country, into Mexico and into the bodies of American consumers. Because of this, Petén had become home to some of Guatemala's highest homicide rates.

Juan was living in fear of the narco-traffickers who terrorized his community. In the spring of 2018, he had sold his car, which in turn was sold to someone else. One day in late April his brother called him and said that drug traffickers had gotten a hold of the car and wanted him to sign paperwork claiming he had given ownership to them. If not, the message was relayed, they would kill José. Juan was able to ask the narcos for a delay, but every day that month, he was "afraid they were going to kill us."

As he told me the story, Juan started to wring his hands together at the table, looking downward. He crunched the white starched napkin with his fingers, pausing to take a deep breath. He looked at me, holding back tears and shaking his head, thinking not only about the fear he experienced at home—but also the consequences his decision to flee Guatemala set in motion for him and his son. He didn't say another word. That night, after I called an Uber and dropped him and José off at their apartment, Juan cried as he thought about what happened to him and José. He texted me to let me know.

On May 15, 2018, unaware that the Trump administration was systematically ripping parents away from children to punish illegal border crossers, and to escape the brutal end so many others in Petén had suffered, Juan and José said goodbye to their family, and to María, now pregnant with José's third sister and Juan's fourth child, and left their pueblo for the United States, heading north like the drugs funding the narcos in their homeland.

After a risky two-week, two-thousand-mile journey, Juan made it to the Arizona border for the third time, his son's first. When they saw the border, relief passed through them: they believed they'd survived—together—one of the most dangerous passageways on earth. They had worried daily about the hazards they faced as they passed through cartel-held territory: extortion, kidnapping, and murder. But they'd made it. Though apprehensive about what life held in store over the dividing line, José knew he had his father.

Within a matter of days, on the side of the U.S.–Mexico border they believed represented safety and security, they would be forced apart from one another, unable to even say good-bye.

PART ONE

"Ana" fled her abusive partner in Mexico with three U.S. citizen children and two non–U.S. citizen children, three-year-old Odalys and two-year-old Rosie. After arriving at a U.S. port of entry (in 2016), Ana and her children were detained and processed by Customs and Border Protection (CBP) officials. Ana unsuccessfully attempted to flee the processing office to return to Mexico with Odalys and Rosie. The ICE report stated that the three U.S. citizen children were taken from their mother by officials because they were at risk of child endangerment. The report based this assessment on the assertion that when Ana was fleeing from the agents, she picked up Rosie and grabbed Odalys by the arm. CBP claims that Ana dragged Odalys a little and her face was scraped in the process. Odalys and Rosie were also taken from Ana as a result and were placed in Office of Refugee Resettlement (ORR) custody. There were no potential sponsors identified for Rosie and Odalys. The placement of their older siblings who have U.S. citizenship was never communicated to ORR, nor was information provided to ORR about how to contact Ana. After Lutheran Immigration and Refugee Service (LIRS) providers contacted Ana, they came to the conclusion that it was not in the best interests of the children to be separated from their mother and LIRS advocated for Ana's release from ICE custody so Odalys and Rosie could be reunified with their mother.

—LUTHERAN IMMIGRATION AND REFUGEE SERVICE

CHAPTER ONE

"I Just Couldn't Do That"

April 8, 2016

"The special interests in D.C. who have controlled our political process for forty years, they don't care about you!" a balding young man screamed from the podium in a Colorado Springs, Colorado, ballroom. He had yet to master the fine art of modulating the volume of one's own voice.

"They don't care about your family, and they don't care about your security!"

My eyes grew wide as I shot a look at Aarne, my producer.

"Who the fuck is this dude? I cannot believe *this* is the guy Trump sent here to win over delegates," I said. At stake was the mantle of leader of the free world.

This gathering felt like a bizarro Fourth of July parade had been crammed into a single, too-small room. Tensions were rising. Earlier in the day, after noticing the MSNBC logo on the microphone I was holding during live reports, an extremely large man threatened to fight me and later invited me to give him oral sex.

Welcome to the Colorado Republican Party district conventions, taking place in the city that is the rapidly beating heart of American evangelical Christianity.

"That's Stephen Miller," a local said to me, identifying the guy behind the podium, his five o'clock shadow seemingly filling in by the second.

I was here to cover this unusual display of democracy, because the Republican Party was in the middle of a hotly contested primary election, in which 1,237 delegates would be needed to clinch the party's nomination and the chance to take on either Hillary Clinton or Bernie Sanders.

Colorado, like several other states, was home to a cache of "unbound" delegates who could cast their vote for whichever candidate they wanted come July at the national party's convention in Cleveland, potentially helping Donald Trump put a lock on the nomination or causing him to come up short.

The purpose of this madhouse event was to elect those delegates. The outcome would be determined without a primary election, or caucus, or any actual will of the electorate. Without a single voter backing them, the thirty-plus delegates who would emerge from here after this weekend would end up being among the most influential political figures in the United States.

Here in the twilight zone of American politics, Stephen Miller went on to tell the story of Kate Steinle, killed in San Francisco by a "five-time deported illegal immigrant." He cited Donald Trump's recent endorsement by the thousands of Border Patrol agents (which was actually the eleven-member executive committee of the Border Patrol Union) as evidence that his candidate would stop tragedies like Steinle's death.

"What a psycho," I felt comfortable saying aloud. "He thinks he's going to win over anyone here?"

Several hours later, after hourly live reports on MSNBC in which I attempted to count every delegate, naming names even the most obsessed cable news viewer had never heard before, like Kendal Unruh and Joel Crank, I got word *The Rachel Maddow Show* requested to have me on her broadcast in prime time—a first for me since I started at MSNBC less than a year earlier.

Not long before seven in the evening local time, I put in my custom earpiece, and in the other ear jammed tissue paper to block out the chatting and clinking silverware behind me. My pulse racing, I could hear our network's star start her show.

"Happy Friday," she started. "There's lots going on to-night."

Rachel began her legendary "A-block" as she always does, taking her time while discussing Bernie Sanders's campaign and its strength at competing in caucuses—a skill that had kept his candidacy alive against Hillary Clinton's juggernaut.

Next, she pivoted to the Republican race, unsettled by novice Trump's surprisingly strong showing against establishment favorite Jeb Bush in the early presidential contests. She dissected the battle to win the required number of delegates in the Republican primary, pointing out that no candidate had a lock on the process.

Underscoring how up in the air the moment was, Rachel brought up the rumors that House Speaker Paul Ryan might jump into the Republican presidential primary.

After a commercial break, she was back in my ear, and the control room was telling me to get ready. My heart pounded.

"Turns out the Donald Trump for President campaign is terrible at this," Maddow said of the campaign's political strategy. "Colorado has been a case study at just how terrible they are at it. And tonight, just within the last hour we have learned that Donald Trump, who before today had already lost eighteen of eighteen possible Colorado delegates to Ted Cruz, just in this past hour we have learned that Donald Trump has just lost three more. Which means that in all of Colorado's congressional districts the Trump campaign has gone oh-for-twenty-one. Ted Cruz has won all of the delegates on offer in Colorado thus far. Which means Ted Cruz has won another state. NBC News is calling Colorado tonight for Ted Cruz."

The red breaking news banner appeared at the bottom of the screen, and the text stretching across it switched to NBC NEWS: CRUZ WINS COLORADO. With that she introduced me, the self-proclaimed "Delegate Hunter" of MSNBC, running from state to state to see what Republican would clinch the nomination—if any—before the July convention in Cleveland.

"Jacob," she asked, "what happened here? It sounded like the Trump campaign set itself on fire and couldn't find a pool of water to put it out."

"I guess the official sports terminology would be an oh-fer, Rachel, oh-for-everything, for Donald Trump here," I said in a whisper worthy of a golf broadcaster as attendees munched on a hotel dinner behind me.

On the one hand, Maddow and I were both right. Cruz delegates succeeded in skunking Trump in Colorado, and as I told her that night, the Trump campaign seemed to have egg on its face, and more important, the nomination and the 1,237 delegates needed to clinch seemed at risk.

Of course, we were both dead wrong about Trump's campaign prospects. Another truth emerged on that ballroom floor in Colorado Springs: Trump, while a savant on messaging, was unable to muster any organizational discipline. If Trump and Miller couldn't secure their own party's delegates despite strong support from voters, how would they fare in the dirty work of implementing policies like the ones Stephen Miller was shouting about if they were to take the White House?

July 18, 2016

"You're blocking the aisle, get out of the way!"

That's not what you want screamed at you by a delegate to the Republican National Convention when you're reporting live on nationwide television.

"Thanks," I said while turning away from the camera to look directly at the heckler, a goateed middle-aged man dressed head to toe in Republican red, another stick microphone grasped firmly in my hand.

Pivoting back to the lens, an embarrassed smirk creeping across my face, I tossed back to Steve Kornacki, who was anchoring his four o'clock afternoon hour on MSNBC from New York. "That's what you go through here, Steve, on the convention floor."

Life wasn't at all glamorous on the campaign trail and in the middle of the madness at Quicken Loans Arena. Getting chewed out as millions watched was low on the drama scale, compared to what would transpire between pro- and anti-Trump factions at the convention.

"You're clear, thanks, Jacob," the producer told me in my ear.

I pulled out my IFB, those coiled earpieces you see newscasters wear, and couldn't help but shake my head and laugh. I was surrounded by cowboy hats, a bespectacled and curly-haired sore thumb among the Texas delegation. A group, no doubt, that had a keen interest in what presumptive nominee Donald Trump would have to say in the days ahead about his signature campaign promise: a border wall with Mexico. Texas is home to two-thirds of the border with our neighbor to the south—more than twelve hundred of the nineteen hundred miles stretching between the Pacific Ocean and the Gulf of Mexico.

Sure enough, Trump delivered. "We are going to build a great border wall to stop illegal immigration," he bellowed a few days later toward the end of his acceptance speech as I watched from the convention floor, "to stop the gangs and the violence, and to stop the drugs from pouring into our communities."

Trump turned to the policy that roiled the blood of people like Stephen Miller.

"By ending catch-and-release on the border, we will stop the cycle of human smuggling and violence. Illegal border crossings will go down. Peace will be restored."

I rolled my eyes dismissively, oblivious to how deadly serious those words, and the motivation underlying them, would be to the lives of tens of thousands in the years to come. Trump finished his speech and an avalanche of red, white, and blue balloons fell from the ceiling. The control room in New York cut to a shot of me as I playfully punched them away, looking more like a kid on a playground than a journalist contemplating the GOP nominee's just-stated intent to radically reshape the American immigration system.

DON'T GET ME wrong: I was keenly tracking Trump's border policy. But only because his perception of what happened at the U.S.–Mexico boundary was so different from the realities I had experienced on the ground.

At the time, I would occasionally file an immigration-related piece, usually through a human-interest lens. In late May, ahead of the conventions, I had traveled to a section of the border near San Diego where there was no fencing or wall. Standing there with Border Patrol agent Wendi Lee, I wondered why they wouldn't want Trump's proposed wall here, at a place where the dividing line between Tijuana and California wasn't even a line in the sand we were standing on.

"We manage with what we have," she told me.

In Las Vegas, I rode bikes with a young undocumented immigrant "Dreamer" who, brought to the United States by her parents as a young child, was now canvassing for Hillary Clinton. Another Dreamer I met was campaigning on the campus of the University of Nevada, Las Vegas for Bernie Sanders. Both were engaged in politics despite neither being able to vote. In Phoenix, I went inside Sheriff Joe Arpaio's tent city and met inmates living outside in scorching heat because I wanted to understand the man who said he was the original Trump.

"It's crazy," one man locked up for driving under the influence said to me about Trump's rhetoric while lying on his stomach from the top bunk. Clutching a pink pillow provided by the Maricopa County Sheriff's Department, he admitted he was undocumented and was worried about getting deported as a result of his crime. "Everybody makes mistakes."

After Trump's shocking victory in the November general election, mass deportations were a distinct possibility. He had, after all, talked of a "deportation force" that would round up and remove all eleven million undocumented immigrants living in the United States. We wouldn't need to wait to find out what mass deportations looked like: President Obama had already deported more people than any other president.

As it happened, I had met some of those who were swept up in Obama's mass deportations.

I first crossed the border as a journalist in the spring of 2014 while working for a little-known cable channel called Pivot, backed by the same people who made Al Gore's Oscar-winning documentary about climate change. Driving a hand-me-down Volvo, I navigated the border crossing between San Diego and Tijuana and negotiated my way through roundabouts and street vendors.

"This is the definition of a clusterfuck," I said to the late Jim Downs, my executive producer, who was filming me with a handheld camcorder. I said that partially because I had blown by the sign indicating we were at the last exit before heading into Mexico, where we were supposed to meet our colleagues, and now found ourselves clueless about where to go in a country we weren't supposed to be in.

Jim was a wild man, a kid in a grown-up's body who was obsessed with video games and cats and adventure. Two years later, he would die the way he lived—pursuing a good story, literally, after falling off a cliff while riding an ATV chasing bears in Alaska for a television program.

Downs was adamant we show the truth about what was happening on the ground, buying a pitch from veteran producer Mitch Koss, who was hired by Downs on my suggestion. Mitch, who had spent his career traveling around the world with young correspondents at Channel One and Current TV, was waiting for us on the U.S. side of the border I had just driven past.

Once we ultimately crossed together, I learned a lesson that would prove relevant in the Trump era. Mass deportations weren't a threat under Obama; they were a reality easily visible by driving minutes past the international boundary to the Casa del Migrante shelter, which housed not only migrants heading north from Mexico and Central America, but countless Mexicans who had spent nearly their entire lives in the United States before being deported by the Obama administration.

In 2016, before Trump was inaugurated, Mitch and I headed back down to Tijuana, this time as MSNBC employees, having been hired together in 2015, now accompanied by an actual NBC News team, not our rag-tag Pivot group. Back in the same spot, it was easy to find deportees who grew up in the same Southern California county I did, but were now stuck living in Mexico for a variety of reasons, including nonviolent crimes. Most of the people I met sounded exactly like I did, too, so much so that Obama's deportations had provided a stimulus to one industry in particular in Mexico: call centers staffed with deportees for American companies. At a massive warehouse in an industrial area of the city, I visited one company taking calls for a U.S. auto parts company. At a cubicle, I met a young woman, hair pulled back in a ponytail, who told me she had worked for the United States Postal Service, paid taxes, and left her two young U.S. citizen children behind when she was deported from Oregon.

"They know I'm in a waiting process for a visa. They know I'm just waiting," she told me through tears. "They're patient."

WHETHER IT WAS fear of mass deportations, an economy struggling to recover from the Great Recession, or something else, apprehensions of migrants attempting to cross into the United States illegally dropped to and remained near all-time lows throughout the Obama presidency. It was an administration that grappled, particularly in its first term, with a political strategy of looking tough on the border while attempting to court the growing influence of Latino voters by providing a pathway to citizenship for the millions of undocumented immigrants living in the United States. At the White House, senior-level staff members met regularly with the agencies responsible for carrying out immigration policy: the Department of Homeland Security, the law enforcement operators on the border and the interior; the Department of Health and Human Services, the caregivers of unaccompanied migrant children; and the Department of Justice, the enforcers of the law.

Multiple times during Obama's two terms—in 2011, 2014, and 2016—relative quiet at the border was interrupted by what was referred to as a "surge" in unaccompanied migrant children and families, most fleeing Central America. In response to overcrowded conditions in Border Patrol stations, pictures of which were eventually leaked (by future Trump advisor Steve Bannon's Breitbart, believe it or not, an outlet not particularly known for humanitarianism), the administration set up temporary "soft-sided" tent facilities on military bases in Texas, Oklahoma, California, and Florida, where officials from HHS looked after the refugee children until they could be placed with a sponsor, usually family members already in the country. Families were kept together until they were released.

"I encouraged our people to bring to me all legally available options for dealing with the border," President Obama's second and final secretary of homeland security, Jeh Johnson, explained to me after I met him one recent morning.

During the 2014 surge, Secretary Johnson and other high-level Homeland Security officials gathered at DHS's Nebraska Avenue Complex (the NAC, as they call it) for an immigration all-hands-on-deck meeting. Gil Kerlikowske, the commissioner of Customs and Border Protection, his deputy Kevin McAleenan, and Tom Homan, the head of Immigration and Customs Enforcement, were there.

As a way to avoid these border pileups and stop the flow of young migrants coming to the United States, in Obama's second term, some in the administration had advocated for indefinitely detaining migrant families until their immigration cases were adjudicated. Otherwise stated, the Obama administration proposed ending "catch and release," the paroling of undocumented migrants who illegally entered the country while they waited for their court cases. Candidate Trump would later champion this same position from the stage at the Republican National Convention.

The Obama administration opened family detention centers in 2014. The ACLU successfully fought them in court, the organization arguing the centers violated a settlement agreement known as *Flores*, a case named for a young migrant indefinitely (and illegally) detained in Los Angeles in the 1980s. Obama's migrant families would need to be released from detention within twenty days.

Indefinite detention wasn't the only deterrence policy the Obama administration considered. Another, more extreme idea was floated: charging parents who traveled with children with the federal crime of illegally entering the country, necessitating the separation of families, resulting in children going into the care of HHS and adults into the custody of the Department of Justice.

"I just couldn't do that," Secretary Johnson told me.

But the idea didn't die at the NAC.

In the White House Situation Room, Cecilia Muñoz, President Obama's director of the Domestic Policy Council, convened one of many regularly scheduled meetings to address the surge in unaccompanied migrant children and families coming to the United States. She considered the meetings a hub where officials from all relevant agencies, including DHS, HHS, the State Department, and DOJ, would gather to consider policy options to slow the migration flow. When family separations were raised, a spirited discussion ensued but "after five minutes," she recalled, the idea died. If it ever made it all the way to President Obama, Muñoz said, it would have been in a memo to let him know why the idea was deemed to be a bad one.

By late 2016, as the Obama administration was dealing with another migration surge, data shows Border Patrol agents on the ground were carrying out separations anyway. In September, James "Jim" De La Cruz, senior field specialist at the Department of Health and Human Services' Office of Refugee Resettlement, sent a list of procedures for the release of a family after separation by the Department of Homeland Security, including instructions for reunification. De La Cruz made clear in his email that he was not a fan of the policy.

"Please consider these items a work in progress with changes to come," he wrote as a disclaimer. "The best that could happen is for the OFO to stop the practice of family separation."

OFO, the Office of Field Operations, the folks who wear the blue uniforms at customs at the airport and land ports of entry on our borders with Mexico and Canada, did not stop the alarming practice. One hundred and twelve were separated, by De La Cruz's count, between October and December of 2016, as the Obama administration was winding down and Trump was getting ready to move in.

···

I am a citizen of Brazil and am seeking asylum in the United States. When I came to the United States, I passed my initial asylum interview ("credible fear interview") and am now in immigration proceedings before an immigration judge to seek asylum.

Although I was seeking asylum, I was convicted of the misdemeanor of entering the country illegally. When a border guard approached me a few feet after I entered the country [on August 26, 2017], I explained I was seeking asylum. I was still prosecuted. I spent 25 days in jail for the misdemeanor.

After my jail sentence, I was sent on September 22, 2017, to an immigration detention center in Texas called the El Paso Processing Center and transferred to the West Texas Detention Facility, also known as Sierra Blanca. I have been in that detention center since that date. I am attempting to proceed with my asylum claim from detention.

My biological son, J., is 14 and came with me from Brazil. He is also seeking asylum.

When I was sent to jail for my conviction, my son was taken from me and sent to a facility in Chicago.

I know that the jail did not allow children to stay with their parents. But I have now [been] out of jail and have been in immigration detention since September 22, 2017. I am desperate to be reunited with my son. I would like to be released with my son so we can live with friends in the United States while we pursue our asylum cases. But if we cannot be released, I would like us to be detained together.

I worry about J. constantly and don't know when I will see him. We have talked on the phone only a [sic] five or six times since he was taken away from me.

I know that J. is having a very hard time detained all by himself without me. He is only a 14-year-old boy in a strange country and needs his parent.

I hope I can be with my son very soon. I miss him and am scared for him.

I declare under the penalty of perjury under the laws of the United States of America that the foregoing is true and correct, based on my personal knowledge. Executed in Sierra Blanca, Texas, on March, 7, 2018.

—DECLARATION OF MS. C.

MS. L V. ICE

CHAPTER TWO

"I Don't Have Those Numbers"

January 20, 2017

"You can kind of see people way down there in the distance, but it's a bit lonely out here at the moment," I told Mika Brzezinski on Inauguration Day, smiling awkwardly while reporting live on Morning Joe.

The Capitol Building and the stage where Trump would soon walk out were just over a mile away, and in between us lay lots of white plastic floor mats, with barely a soul on them. If you want proof Donald Trump didn't have the largest, biggest, best inauguration crowd ever, I'm your man. I got the plum assignment of covering the inauguration of President Donald J. Trump—from the farthest possible position along the National Mall. The way, way back near where the press tent was built, to accommodate a massive crowd. And there wasn't one.

"When President Obama was inaugurated the crowd stretched all the way down to the Washington Monument. That was 1.8 million folks. We'll see how many people show up today."

And with that, I threw to commercial break. A lonely correspondent in a sea of nobody at the inauguration of the forty-fifth president of the United States of America. Where

I was standing, company never came. After a few more live shots, and a few more people showed up (that back area never was packed, as the satellite imagery confirmed) I gave back my stick mic, pulled out my earpiece, and started walking back toward our hotel. As we left the Mall, we walked with protestors, who for the most part were peaceful. More protesters were preparing to show up in the same place, at the same time, the following morning for the Women's March, an event organized to take place globally in resistance to the Trump presidency.

One of them was a career employee at the U.S. Department of Health and Human Services who would, weeks later, march again, this time against Trump's plans to ban Muslims from entering the United States and to build a border wall. That official was not the lone government employee marching discretely in opposition to the new president. The State Department, too, was informally represented.

The HHS official described knowing people who became "physically sick when Trump was elected. I was absolutely terrified about what he would do."

This type of opposition to President Trump's stated immigration policies wasn't surprising: to many career officials across the government, Trump's xenophobic campaign rhetoric was great cause for concern. Just short of the Trump administration's one month anniversary, that rhetoric became reality amongst those caring for migrant children seeking refuge in the United States.

February 14, 2017

A Valentine's Day meeting had been convened in the fourth floor suite of acting U.S. Customs and Border Protection

Commissioner, Kevin McAleenan, and on the agenda was ending the practice known as "catch and release." Only twenty-five days into the Trump administration, and they were hitting the ground running. But what would that mean?

That question was front of mind as Commander Jonathan White walked into the Ronald Reagan Building and International Trade Center in Washington, D.C., the federal building that doubles as a wedding venue and event space but also is the headquarters of U.S. Customs and Border Protection, where decisions affecting the fate of millions are made.

White, a Bic-bald career officer of the U.S. Public Health Service Commissioned Corps—the small army of thousands of federal government healthcare workers—was now serving his third presidential administration from inside the department of Health and Human Services. A clinical social worker and emergency manager by education, he was now overseeing refugee programs for the United States federal government as the Deputy Director of the Office of Refugee Resettlement's Unaccompanied Alien Children Program within HHS's Administration for Children and Families. White's colleagues describe him as a man of unimpeachable integrity, with unparalleled devotion to the health and well-being of the children he served. Amongst the small, tight-knit group of career officials at ORR, that was the rule, not the exception.

It was with that value set that Jim De La Cruz, White's subordinate at ORR, had the previous year bemoaned the limited practice, under the Obama administration, of family separations to colleagues. White and others were about to find out if the Trump administration's Department of Homeland Security would be expanding the policy to match the president's tough talk on the campaign trail, and now that he was in the White House.

They sat around the conference table, joined by McAleenan and representatives from other relevant government stakeholders including the Department of Justice's Executive Office of Immigration Review, U.S. Citizenship and Immigration Services, Immigration and Customs Enforcement, and the policy shop at the Department of Homeland Security.

It was so early in the administration that around the country, walls in offices just like this one were still missing photos of the newly inaugurated President Trump and Vice President Pence, as is customary at the seven thousand different federal installations worldwide. At the Department of Homeland Security, Trump and Pence's photos would soon hang next to that of General John Kelly, the new secretary of the Department of Homeland Security, confirmed by a vote of 88-11 on the first day of the Trump administration.

Twenty days earlier, the officials in the room had been tasked with a massive overhaul of the nation's immigration system in the form of an executive order issued by the president. The directive, titled "Border Security and Immigration Enforcement Improvements," was President Trump's way of signaling he was getting right to work on his signature campaign issue, ending undocumented migration to the United States. In the order, he specifically tasked the government with ending "catch and release."

> Sec. 6. Detention for Illegal Entry. The Secretary shall immediately take all appropriate actions to ensure the detention of aliens apprehended for violations of

immigration law pending the outcome of their removal proceedings or their removal from the country to the extent permitted by law. The Secretary shall issue new policy guidance to all Department of Homeland Security personnel regarding the appropriate and consistent use of lawful detention authority under the INA, including the termination of the practice commonly known as "catch and release," whereby aliens are routinely released in the United States shortly after their apprehension for violations of immigration law.

"One policy option for implementation of [ending] catch and release that was discussed was referral of minors as part of family units as unaccompanied alien children to ORR," Commander White recalled later in congressional testimony about the Valentine's Day meeting.

Translation from government-speak: in order to end the "catch and release" of undocumented adults who arrived with minor children, their kids would be separated, classified as "unaccompanied" (even though they arrived with their family), and transferred to ORR, where they would be sheltered as refugees while their parents went through the United States criminal justice system. The thought was that word of the separations happening would deter other migrants from coming at all.

"If we go this route, we need to be ready," is how one former DHS official in the room later described the discussion of family separation to me.

Several attendees characterized the mood as celebratory among law-enforcement officials advocating for harsher immigration policies.

"You should buy rubber stamps for your immigration judges

that say 'denied' because that's what they're going to be doing from here on out," an ICE official joked.

The display shook some of those at the table who were used to these gatherings being productive interagency conversations during the Obama administration.

"For those of us who were looking how to institute good governance around immigration it was a turning point for all of us—like, this is a new day," a former government official who was present told me. "Our voice is not what's going to be echoed in this chamber. Half of us left very shell-shocked."

Commander White kept stoic through the meeting despite mounting concern as the idea of systematically separating parents and children to deter others from coming to the United States was raised. This was the same proposal that career ORR employees had opposed when it was considered during the Obama administration.

"We need a white paper for our secretary," another ORR official present said, attempting to stall, referring to Tom Price, the secretary of the Department of Health and Human Services, a physician and former congressman from Georgia, who, she believed, would ultimately have to sign off on what could potentially be thousands of children taken from their parents.

Not long after the meeting concluded and what was proposed inside the Reagan Building was shared amongst ORR staff, the whispers began.

"They're going to the Hague and I'm not going to testify for them," the same ORR employee repeated regularly of Trump administration political appointees pushing the policy. The consequences would be disastrous, and obvious: human rights abuses; running out of beds; violations of international laws and treaties; problems with communication between parents and children; and prohibitive expenses. To stop potential family separations, those in ORR would have to rely on "tricks and mind games to stop" those who would try to execute separations.

Commander White was more diplomatic about it, at least publicly in the aftermath of the policy, when he confirmed the Valentine's Day meeting took place.

"On a number of occasions, I and my colleagues made recommendations raising concerns not only about what that would mean for children, but also what it would mean for the capacity of the program," he said.

A former DHS official in the room that day remembered any potential pushback differently.

"Nobody warned of the impact on children."

February 16, 2017

One of President Trump's stated goals of his immigration agenda—and part of the underlying rationale for a deterrence-based family separation policy—was stopping what he said was "the single-biggest problem" along the southwest border: drugs coming in and killing Americans.

Trump was right about one thing: it didn't take long to see multiple kilos of hard narcotics after I showed up in a wool jacket at the southern border one frigid morning less than three weeks after the inauguration. The "packages" of the deadly drug were wrapped in plastic, about the size of a mini football that would still be too big for my then one-year-old son to wrap his hands around and throw. When sliced open with a knife, the white powdery substance was instantly visible. I took a step back to avoid inhaling any residue of what could be the drug fentanyl, fueling the most deadly drug overdose crisis in American history. This is the part of the story I knew the president and his advisors wanted people to understand: *what* was coming across the border. But based on the way he talked about it, I assumed he'd rather not know *where* I was.

The San Ysidro Port of Entry is the largest land border crossing in the world. Tens of thousands of cars and hundreds of thousands of human beings make their way between Tijuana and San Diego on a daily basis. So do an untold volume of narcotics—more than anywhere else along the entire southern border. As President Trump continued to make the case for his big, beautiful border wall, I was curious if it would do what he said: stop drugs from "pouring across" the southwest border. At least here, the answer was no way. Most hard narcotics come through legal ports of entry, like this one, and today was no exception.

Given candidate and now President Trump's rhetoric, I asked Sidney Aki, the Customs and Border Protection official who oversees San Ysidro, what the biggest threat coming across at San Ysidro was. Standing in between hundreds of cars streaming into the United States—many daily commuters heading to work or school—he explained where the real challenge along the border was.

"It's everything. We're looking at everyone. We're looking at illegal narcotics. Heroin. Methamphetamine. Cocaine. Fentanyl. All entering the borders."

"That's one of your agents that stands out here specialized to look for suspicious activity?"

"Correct." But the primary screening lanes, where we were standing, isn't where most of the hard narcotics are found, he explained. Aki took me into what is known as "secondary screening," a place where motorists suspected of wrongdoing are moved for a closer look by CBP agents, the same men and women in the blue uniforms who might stamp your passport after you returned from an international trip. Within minutes, that's where we saw the giant load.

An excited dog that looked like a German shepherd was alerting its handler that the gray Chevy sedan with California plates might have drugs inside. It was right. The vehicle was pulled into yet a third location, where I watched multiple CBP agents tear apart the car. I'm probably the last person you want to change your tire or oil or even your windshield fluid, but that day I learned what a cowl is. The agents tore open the upper part of the engine below the windshield and inside they found what the man driving the car, now in handcuffs in a separate room, was smuggling. One after another they pulled out nearly thirty of those football-sized packages of what, after being sliced open and field tested, turned out to be methamphetamine.

"Is that a normal load?" I asked Pete Flores, the director of all field operations for CBP in the San Diego sector, who had joined us as we filmed.

"For us, hard narcotics are trending. Particularly heroin and methamphetamine. Packages are getting a little bit smaller for us. The number of them have increased obviously because the packaging is smaller in order to put them into deeper concealment into the vehicles."

"Is this all you're going to get today?"

"I would say if I were a betting person, no. This wouldn't be all that we get today. I would say we could get up to another five, six loads today and that wouldn't be abnormal for us."

"Why if you're a cartel do you want to send drugs like this

through a legal port of entry where you could cross with your passport?"

"On a yearly basis we're going to deal with seventy-five million travelers coming across the border. Drug smugglers feel there are opportunities to mix in with the general population who are generally compliant with what the laws are."

"So, translation," I interpreted, "they think they can sneak it by you."

"Right," Flores admitted.

Evidence directly contradicting what President Trump had been saying was right in front of my eyes: most hard narcotics were not coming through unwalled areas, they were entering through legal ports of entry, just like this one. None more so than right here between San Diego and Tijuana.

That begged a question: If Mexican cartels were smuggling drugs mostly in places you had to show your passport, who *was* crossing in between the ports—where there were no walls—or trying to get around the ones that did exist? Mostly, it was Central American family members looking to seek asylum. It was a group now in the crosshairs of the Trump administration.

March 6, 2017

"Rollout!"

It was five in the evening on the dot. Wolf Blitzer's familiar voice punched through a car speaker over CNN's satellite radio network.

"President Trump quietly takes another try at a travel ban, this time leaving Iraq off the list of targeted countries and exempting U.S. green card and visa holders. Will the White

House face a new legal battle and more protests? I'll speak live to the secretary of homeland security, John Kelly."

At least one official driving home from the Office of Refugee Resettlement was listening live.

This should be interesting.

Three days earlier a Reuters reporter named Julia Edwards Ainsley broke publicly what staffers at ORR had been hearing since the Valentine's Day meeting at CBP: the Trump administration was revisiting the rejected Obama-era family separation proposal and was now considering systematically separating migrant kids from their parents. In a major scoop, Ainsley, citing three government officials, wrote that wide-scale separations "to deter mothers from migrating to the United States with their children" had been in the works even before the still-unreported Valentine's Day meeting.

> Two of the officials were briefed on the proposal at a Feb. 2 town hall for asylum officers by U.S. Citizenship and Immigration Services asylum chief John Lafferty.
>
> A third DHS official said the department is actively considering separating women from their children but has not made a decision.

Now, Kelly, the man who would ultimately be responsible for operationally putting any separation policy in place, was about to be on national television.

What is he going to say?

At ten after the hour Blitzer addressed Kelly. "General, Mr. Secretary, thanks for joining us and thanks for your military service as well."

They spent seven minutes talking about the justification (or lack thereof, as Blitzer made clear as he pressed Kelly) for banning travelers from mostly Muslim-majority nations from the United States, until at seventeen minutes into the show they addressed family separations.

"Let me get to some other sensitive Homeland Security issues while I have you," Blitzer began. "Are you, the Department of Homeland Security, considering a new initiative that would separate children from their parents if they tried to enter the United States illegally?"

Here we go.

"Let me start by saying I would do almost anything to deter," Kelly said, admitting right off the bat his goal was frightening people away from the United States, "the people from Central America to getting on this very, very dangerous network that brings them up through Mexico into the United States. And I would underline that the Mexicans are after this network in the same way we are. It's extremely dangerous. I wouldn't say one hundred percent but certainly in the high ninety percent and this is by the social service organizations that inform me from Central America that the vast majority of the young women, all women, are sexually abused along this—"

"Let, let me . . ." Blitzer cut him off, sensing Kelly was evading the question.

"My point is . . ."

"Let me just be precise."

"Right," Kelly replied.

"If you get some young kids who manage to sneak into the United States with their parents, are Department of Homeland Security personnel going to separate the children from their moms and dads?"

"We have tremendous experience in dealing with unaccompanied minors," Kelly said. "We turn them over to HHS, and they do a very, very good job of either putting them in kind of foster care or linking them up with parents or family members in the United States."

And then, finally, Kelly admitted it.

"Yes, I am considering, in order to deter more movement along this terribly dangerous network, I am considering exactly that. They will be well cared for as we deal with their parents."

Wow.

What was until this point a publicly unconfirmed secret was now confirmed by the top government official responsible for carrying it out.

He blew the whistle on himself.

Blitzer kept pressing Kelly.

"You understand how that looks to the average person who is, you know . . ."

"It's more important to me, Wolf, to try to keep people off this awful network."

The ORR official—one of many who would ultimately bear the burden of caring for separated children—kept driving home, uncertain of what might happen next.

March 10, 2017

Days later, in Los Angeles, I was on my way to learn more about how immigration enforcement was already tearing families apart. But not because I caught Secretary Kelly's interview. If I did—and I don't remember—it was only a passing glance. I was headed to South El Monte, where, on this night, the Catholic Church was training undocumented immigrants already in the United States how to avoid deportation.

Producer Mitch Koss had worked out our access. "They're training people how not to get deported! It will be very vivid," he pitched to me in a way that would sound terrifying to many reporters. I trusted him. Mitch had pioneered a free-flowing style of reporting with two young reporters in the nineties—CNN's Anderson Cooper and Lisa Ling—that valued real-time and on-camera explorations of situations. Basically, he taught them, and now me, how to unlearn what most TV reporters are schooled to do: go places and actually look around instead of just showing up to use a location as a backdrop for an interview. He taught me how to be a reporter.

By the time I got to Epiphany Catholic Church—Iglesia Católica de la Epifania—Mitch and our team were there waiting in the dark parking lot outside the church, illuminated by a large neon white cross atop the façade, and under it, blue and yellow light emanating from six panels of stained glass. We were filming a story for the *Today* show.

"Hey fellas," I said out the window as I rolled up.

Having been bar mitzvahed exactly thirty miles from here, I'm not exactly an expert in who shows up for Friday night mass—but it didn't seem like the normal crowd to me milling about in front. Young kids—what looked like middle and high schoolers—were hanging around outside, as parents went in.

An eight-and-a-half by eleven-inch sheet of paper with a printed message, in Spanish, with the seal of the Los Angeles Archdiocese up top, greeted those entering: "Preparing Your Family for an Encounter with Immigration."

Inside I met the representative the archbishop had sent that night, Lucy Boutte. Petite and gray-haired, the outreach coordinator would be giving the presentation, as she had at other churches throughout Los Angeles, based on an official fifty-plus page document. Before she went in I had a question for her.

"How many people are at risk of an encounter with ICE?"

She looked down, then up at me through her thin rectangle-shaped glasses. She lifted up her left arm, squeezing her fist into a ball and pulling it back toward her face, purposefully drawing my attention to the brown skin on her wrist.

"Anybody that looks like *this* is at risk. Because they're stopping everybody."

"That's a lot of people in Los Angeles," I said to her, immediately realizing I had asked a stupid question with an obvious answer.

"Tell me about it," she replied.

We walked inside the sanctuary, and not long after the seven o'clock service began, Boutte and other representatives from the archdiocese—the largest in the nation and home to one million undocumented people, many of whom were raising American children—made their way to the front of the room, acting out a raid by Immigration and Customs Enforcement as if it were a school play.

"Open the door, this is ICE!" shouted a man into a microphone, as a group stood behind an invisible door.

Boutte jumped up, waving her arms in the air in between the man and the family, to stop the scene and explain that they did not have to open the door, because under the U.S. Constitution, ICE does not have the right to enter without a judicial warrant. Dozens of parishioners watched from the pews, following along with "Know Your Rights" paperwork handed out to them in Spanish and English.

As the training continued, I walked back out front, and met Anna Cordova, a thirteen-year-old wearing her hair in a ponytail, who came to the church with her family to know what to do if the moment they all feared happened. Anna is a U.S. citizen; her parents are not.

"You're thirteen. Why did you show up here?"

"It's difficult to picture a life, without . . ." She trailed off, collecting her thoughts, her braces shining in the neon and stained-glass light.

"Your life," she continued. "You know, my mom and dad have always been here for me. And they're literally the world to me and I wouldn't like to imagine the world without them."

"You came here tonight to learn what?"

"To learn what happens when someone gets deported, and how to hide or talk your way out of it."

Three days after meeting Anna at her church's training session, she invited me back to South El Monte to meet her undocumented mom and siblings. We piled in their white minivan, me in the way-back in between her little brother and sister, behind two others in the middle row, to get a tour of her neighborhood. She explained that rumors of roadside checkpoints were driving fear.

From the shotgun seat, acting as a tour guide, Anna explained, "The checkpoint is like two streetlights from here," and she and her mom both pointed to the right.

"Up that way?" I asked.

"Yeah," they said in unison.

"And so what does that do? How do people feel? What are people saying?"

"We don't come out; that's why we're kind of you know, in our shells," Anna said while pushing her fists together mimicking a shell closing.

"You stay home?"

"Yes," they again said together.

"We stay home," Anna said, with a sigh.

THE FOLLOWING MORNING, March 14, I met with the archbishop of Los Angeles, José H. Gomez, in the courtyard of the massive Cathedral of Our Lady of the Angels in downtown Los Angeles. He had just taken off his choir cassock, what I thought was called a robe, and his miter, the bishop hat, after finishing a service inside. Under it, he was wearing a black suit with his clerical collar and a cross the size of a piece of toast.

"It's a beautiful church," he mused, as we walked outside under the modern structure, completed in 2002 to replace the Cathedral of Saint Vibiana, which was badly damaged in the 1994 Northridge Earthquake.

I brought with me the fifty-page document that informed Lucy Boutte's presentation and asked him why they were going from church to church preparing families for immigration enforcement.

"I have been talking about stopping the deportation for a long time. Because it's breaking families. And it's destroying the lives of people."

"Do you see what you're doing here in Los Angeles as a conflict with the Trump administration?"

"We've been doing this for a long time, as I said, before with the Obama administration and now with the Trump administration. Because we want the undocumented people to really be a part of our society."

"You think the pope would like this plan?" I wondered aloud, waving the antideportation document.

Gomez laughed. "I'm sure that he does. I've talked to him several times. He's always encouraging me to help people. Whatever they need."

Candidate Trump had promised a "deportation force" to my colleagues on *Morning Joe,* and the specter of widescale ICE raids now had to be a top concern to the one million undocumented people in Los Angeles. Breaking families apart, as the archbishop pointed out, was not new in a city with more Mexicans and Central Americans than anywhere else in the country, but now they were the stated target of the man in the Oval Office.

With so much concern over "interior removals," as ICE refers to them, neither the archbishop, nor the pope, nor myself understood that another way of breaking families apart—at the border itself—was in the works.

April 11, 2017

The stage had been set for family separation. After President Trump issued the executive order calling for the end of "catch and release" on the fifth day of his presidency, then homeland security Secretary John Kelly revealed on CNN that he was considering the policy, the legal framework needed to be put into place. In a three page memo, Attorney General Jeff Sessions, the former boss of Stephen Miller, now a senior advisor to President Trump, laid out his case for criminalizing immigration violations, historically treated as a civil offense.

It is a high priority of the Department of Justice to establish lawfulness in our immigration system. While
dramatic progress has been made at the border in recent months, much remains to be done. It is critical
that our work focus on criminal cases that will further
reduce illegality. Consistent and vigorous enforcement
of key laws will disrupt organizations and deter un-
lawful conduct. I ask that you increase your efforts in
this area making the following immigration offenses
higher priorities. Further guidance and support of
executing this priority—including an updated memorandum on charging for all criminal cases—will be
forthcoming.

In the memo Sessions cited statute after statute for which
migrants could be charged for crossing the border illegally:
entering for the first time, entering after previously being deported, identity theft, assaulting a law enforcement officer.
He directed prosecutors, at sentencing, to seek "judicial orders of removal," or deportation, and each federal district to
set up a "Border Security Coordinator" to oversee investigations and prosecutions and report back to Washington.

This was the same Jeff Sessions who, in a publicly broadcast conversation with Steve Bannon in 2015, before both
were members of the Trump administration, praised a racist
1924 law intended, by its authors' own admission, to end "in-
discriminate acceptance of all races" as "good for America."

Now he had the power of the U.S. Department of Justice
to fix what he saw as "a big problem," what Bannon called a
"war" to preserve what Sessions believed was about "classical
American values."

July 4, 2017

As two fighter jets screamed across the Los Angeles skyline in celebration of Independence Day, my one-year-old son blurted something that sounded like "airplane" if you said it with a mouth full of marshmallows.

That same day, back in Washington, D.C., Commander Jonathan White, known to dress in his perfectly pressed and decorated officer's uniform, was planning ahead. In a memo to his colleagues in the Office of Refugee Resettlement (which I'm sure they appreciated receiving on a federal holiday), White delivered a regularly scheduled update on the status of unaccompanied migrant children in the custody of the United States of America. These types of updates were necessary, as he and the small team he worked with within the Administration for Children and Families, within the Department of Health and Human Services, had learned the hard way during the Obama administration.

The surges of unaccompanied children in 2011, 2014, and 2016 caught ORR flat-footed, and when there was not enough shelter space available, thousands of children piled up in Border Patrol stations until the government could find a place for them to be cared for while they waited for what was usually a family member already living in the United States to be vetted and pick them up.

Under a new presidential administration with a new set of potential immigration enforcement priorities, White worried available bed space could quickly evaporate. He outlined six factors that could contribute to a sudden surge, but there was one that would send numbers skyrocketing and shelters overflowing with nearly ten thousand more children sent into his care than projections for current levels—what he called the "DHS Deterrence" model, which had two parts. The first was already operational, and it was designed to stop children from coming to the United States because their undocumented relatives would be scared away from picking them up once they made it to safety.

> **DHS immigration enforcement actions may adversely affect discharge rate.** DHS has launched a national "[Unaccompanied Alien Children] Sponsor Initiative," which involves contacting sponsors of UAC who are without legal status, interviewing them, and in some cases taking them into custody, issuing criminal charges against them, or issuing Notices to Appear. Effects of this initiative upon readiness of individuals to step forward as sponsors are expected to result in significant increases in length of stay and decline in discharge rate.

The other part of the deterrence model, White noted, would have similar effects, but wasn't yet launched: family separations.

> This ["UAC Sponsor Initiative"] step would represent one-half of the DHS policy changes necessary to fulfill the "DHS Deterrence" scenario model (since family unit separations are not yet being implemented). ORR is currently reviewing that model to determine if it should be refined to current policy realities.

47

Commander White's insistence that "family unit separations are not yet being implemented" turned out to be wishful thinking.

August 15, 2017

As most career employees walked out of the Department of Health and Human Services for the day into eighty-degree heat and humidity, one stayed behind, dropping a massive clue about the fate of thousands of migrant children in Commander Jonathan White's email inbox.

"We have received 27 separations over the last 7 days. The majority of these referrals seem to be coming from El Paso and Phoenix," a staffer at the Office of Refugee Resettlement's Division of Unaccompanied Children Operations explained.

White had requested the information about what his briefer called "a breakdown of the trends seen in [child] separations from parents as identified by DHS at the time of referral, both this week and across the last few months."

If White and like-minded colleagues were going to prove—and somehow stop—the Trump administration's practice of what he had heard they might do as early as Valentine's Day—separating families and children for no other reason than to deter others from coming to the United States—he would need the evidence. Separations had always happened, but historically separations from parents only occurred when the safety and security of children were at risk. If there was a case to be made, it would be in the data White was now looking at.

The numbers said that in April, May, June, and July between ten and forty-four children were taken from their parents at the border each month—between 1 and 2 percent of overall referrals from the Department of Homeland Security, which was detaining the families. The children were sent to White's colleagues at ORR, who would ultimately care for the children once they were taken from their parents. The percentage of those separations that were due to the civil infraction of entering the United States illegally—not safety concerns for the children or a criminal offense—was only between 13 and 30 percent during those months.

August was only half over, but the data for the month told another story. In only half as many days—between the first of the month and the day before Commander White received this email—thirty-seven children had been separated and a whopping 54 percent of them were separated only because of the way they crossed the border. No danger. No illness. No threat. Two separate times in the last week alone, eight kids were taken from their parents in one day.

A separation surge was happening.

But there was an even more damning bit of information in the email. In order to prove separations were happening for no other reason than crossing the border illegally, the government would need to keep track of all separations. On that front, White's briefer did not have good news. The government was separating children and parents and losing track of who they were and where they went.

"I understand from the field that they are discovering more

separations that were not reported in the initial referral—I don't have those numbers."

Almost five hours after the email was sent, White acknowledged receipt of the shocking information with a simple reply.

"Thank you!"

I am a citizen of Kyrgyzstan and am seeking asylum in the United States. When I came to the United States, I passed my initial asylum interview ("credible fear interview"), and am now in immigration proceedings before an immigration judge to seek asylum. I am currently detained in the Otay Mesa Detention Facility.

I came to the United States on or around October 18, 2017, with my biological son, T.U., who is thirteen years old. He is also from Kyrgyzstan and seeking asylum.

When we came to the United States, we sought admission at the San Ysidro Port of Entry, and we said that we wanted to seek asylum.

A few days later, I was told that I was going to be separated from my son. I suffer from high blood pressure and felt as though I was having a heart attack. I was not able to ask why they were separating my son from me and did not know what to do. I feel like I was in shock and do not remember what happened next or even how I got to the detention center after that. All I can remember is how much my son and I were both crying as they took him away. I do not recall anyone questioning whether I am really his biological father or whether I was a danger to him or abusive in any way. I even had my son's birth certificate proving I am his father.

I was sent to the Otay Mesa Detention Center on or around October 23, 2017. I learned that my son was sent to a facility in Chicago.

It has been about six months since I last saw my son. We speak over the phone once a week for about ten minutes. It is not enough. The last time we spoke, it sounded like he had been *crying. I worry about him constantly. He is just a boy in a strange land with no parents or relatives with him. He needs me.*

I feel like this separation is causing T.U. great harm. He sounds depressed and each time I speak with him over the phone, he talks less and less. This separation is tearing me apart inside. T.U. is only thirteen years old and I should be with him to comfort and protect him.

I hope I can be reunited with my son very soon. I miss him and I want to be with him to tell him everything will be all right. I am so scared about how this separation is affecting him.

I declare under the penalty of perjury under the laws of the United States of America that the foregoing is true and correct, based on my personal knowledge. Executed in San Diego, California, on April 18, 2018.

—DECLARATION OF MR. U.

MS. L V. ICE

CHAPTER THREE

"A Significant Increase"

September 8, 2017

Commander Jonathan White spent his career working to put the "best interests" of his clients first—the first principle of social work—and he suspected the Trump administration was planning to do the exact opposite in separating migrant families. From the moment John Kelly—who was promoted to Trump's chief of staff in July 2017—admitted he was considering family separations as a way to deter migration to the United States, White had been doing everything he could to keep track of the policy's development and implementation. If separations happened, like it was suggested they should on Valentine's Day in the fourth floor suite at Customs and Border Protection headquarters, it would be unprecedented, and the children taken from their parents would end up in his care, housed in one of the roughly one hundred shelters for unaccompanied migrant children run by the Office of Refugee Resettlement within the U.S. Department of Health and Human Services. Neither he nor his colleagues were ready.

In the early hours of the morning, White noticed a report by Julia Ainsley, who had left Reuters to join NBC News, that

Immigration and Customs Enforcement was poised to conduct the largest raid on undocumented immigrants in American history. Dubbed "Operation Mega," it would target for deportation 8,400 undocumented migrants who were living in the United States illegally—precisely the terror the Catholic Church was preparing for in Los Angeles.

ICE wouldn't confirm Ainsley's reporting and issued the standard denial that the agency was "not able to speculate about potential future targeted enforcement actions." This didn't sit well with White, who emailed Scott Lloyd, the boyish Trump-appointed thirty-eight-year-old director of ORR.

Lloyd, who before being tapped by Trump worked as an attorney for the Catholic fraternal organization Knights of Columbus and in the Bush administration's health and human services department, had never resettled refugees before taking the ORR role in March 2017. He had, however, advocated vociferously against abortions in his previous jobs, and he would continue to at ORR. Lloyd was White's boss. But White felt it was Lloyd who would need guidance for the day ahead.

> I'm betting tomorrow that ICE leadership will want to talk to you about their planned Operation Mega, which is expected to net thousands of undocumented immigrants in what everyone is discussing (the NGOs have been all abuzz and tonight it's even in the mainstream news) to be the largest immigration enforcement action in modern history. If it comes up, our biggest request, I think, should be this: Please don't separate minors from family units and refer them to us.

"Family unit" is the term the Department of Homeland Security, under which the Border Patrol and ICE are situated, uses to describe children together with biological parents or legal guardians. White was intimately familiar with the terminology. In 2012, 2014, and again in 2016 his agency ran out of bed space when surges of unaccompanied migrant children and families—mostly from Central America—showed up at the southern border.

Because of the backlog, young children were literally piling up in Border Patrol stations, sleeping in the squalor of jail facilities built decades earlier when most border crossers were Mexican men looking for seasonal work. In response to images of the conditions being released, the Obama administration had opened temporary facilities to house the children on military bases in Oklahoma, Texas, and California. Back then, families weren't Commander White's responsibility—they would go into ICE custody and be held at controversial family detention centers or be paroled into communities where they likely had family members. But now the Trump administration was suggesting that families would be broken apart, parents would be prosecuted and jailed, and their children would be taken away and placed into the system operated by Commander White. Without proper planning, that would surely overwhelm the ORR system, if not break it entirely, he believed.

Later that day, Ainsley followed up on her initial report with an update: ICE was calling off the raid. For White, bullet dodged. He would not have to rely on Lloyd to protect the migrant children in their care and custody. But it wasn't because of the political pressure that White had told his boss was building.

"Due to the current weather situation in Florida and other potentially impacted areas, along with the ongoing recovery in Texas, U.S. Immigration and Customs Enforcement (ICE) had already reviewed all upcoming operations and has adjusted accordingly," spokeswoman Sarah Rodriguez told Ainsley, referring to Hurricane Irma bearing down on Miami and the aftermath of Hurricane Harvey in Houston.

"There is currently no coordinated nationwide operation planned at this time. The priority in the affected areas should remain focused on life-saving and life-sustaining activities."

BY THE TIME Ainsley received the statement from ICE, Irma was a category 5 mega-storm tracking directly for Florida's east coast, but Boca Raton mayor Susan Haynie wasn't worried about residents who hadn't yet stocked up on supplies.

"Well, they have time this morning," she said live on MSNBC. The banner at the bottom of the TV said Irma was 281 miles southeast of Nassau, Bahamas, and packing a wind speed of 150 miles per hour—potentially catastrophic. "The weather here is still beautiful."

The screen was divided into a "triple box" showing empty shelves at a local supermarket, thousands of cars evacuating on Interstate 75, and the surf churning on South Beach, nature's advance warning that something was brewing offshore.

One thousand miles to the north, in Washington, D.C., those images were playing live on television monitors as Tom Price, the secretary of Health and Human Services, received a briefing from aides about HHS's readiness for Irma. Also there were Dr. Robert Kadlec, Price's assistant secretary for preparedness and response, the life-saving arm of HHS known as ASPR, and Kadlec's chief of staff, Chris Meekins, who was across the room behind a bank of computer monitors in the room known as the Secretary's Operations Center, or SOC.

Kadlec and Meekins were ready for this moment: in a natural disaster, ASPR is tasked with preparing for and recovering from public health emergencies.

"If you want doctors, nurses, paramedics to be able to supplement what's needed in given communities there, that's ASPR's job," Meekins later said about his role on a *Politico* podcast.

That afternoon in the SOC, my face materialized on the TV screen playing MSNBC. At seven minutes before three o'clock, I reported live from the back of an ambulance as we bounced around the emergency vehicle on our way to conduct wellness checks on elderly residents.

From there, we rebased our coverage to the western part of the state, where we spent days chasing Irma's hard left turn. We ultimately rode out the storm in Naples, where I performed the time-honored and ridiculous tradition of dodging terra-cotta tiles on live television as she made a direct hit. When Irma passed, we emerged unscathed, but in the darkness of the next morning, veteran camera operator Dana Roecker and I discovered our rental Suburban did not. Its roof had been split in two by a projectile palm tree.

Though dozens were killed as a result of the storm, the worst-case scenario projections reviewed in the SOC never materialized. ASPR would refocus a plethora of other urgent threats including but not limited to a global outbreak.

"I can't talk about the lists I might see," Meekins presciently told reporter Dan Diamond more than a year before COVID-19 exploded worldwide. "What I will say is the H7N9 strain of the flu pandemic that is circulating in China is a great threat and I think could be a real problem going forward."

While, temporarily at least, Kadlec's and Meekins's fears were assuaged, Commander White's were not. He was prescient, too. Across the street from the SOC, at ORR headquarters, White saw a disaster of another sort barreling toward HHS like a superstorm or global health emergency.

Within months, they would all be in the SOC together as it would again become operational for a disaster, this time the man-made one that Commander White was worried about: family separations.

September 27, 2017

Inside the Department of Health and Human Services, some in the small D.C. headquarters of the division caring for migrant children were starting to feel like they had a second job: sleuthing.

Employees of the Office of Refugee Resettlement were talking and they suspected, based on data and anecdotal reports trickling in, that the Trump administration would follow through on then-homeland security secretary, now White House chief of staff, John Kelly's threat to separate families to scare others away from coming to the United States. Kelly had quickly backed away from the policy after he announced its consideration in March, but evidence continued to pile up.

Still, nobody could say for sure. Pinning down whether or

not widescale separations were happening, where they were happening, and who was ordering them wasn't easy.

"We had to be detectives," I was told, "just to be able to answer the question: Are these legitimate separations or for deterrence?"

By fall, it did not take much effort for pieces of the puzzle to begin to fall into place regularly. Something was happening. Word made its way back quickly to ORR after a meeting about migration with members of the White House on an unseasonably hot fall Wednesday.

In an air-conditioned room in a Washington, D.C., law firm as temperatures outside broke ninety, Trump administration officials talked obliquely about their plans for migrants coming to the United States.

That evening, Commander Jonathan White received an email about the meeting from an ORR colleague who was there and overheard them.

> *DHS Policy is working on a family separation policy again, to send all children to ORR. They don't understand that ORR has its own obligations and these types of cases often end up with parent repatriated and kid in our care for months pending home studies, international legal issues, etc.*
>
> *I will try to get some info unless you and Scott already have it.*

White wrote back four hours later, in the early hours of Thursday morning.

> *No I definitely will need all the info you can find.*

Later that day, Commander White scheduled a meeting between one and two in the afternoon. The subject: "Find out about separation policy." Answers, for any non-political inside ORR, would not be easy to come by.

"On the occasions that I raised it," White said later during congressional testimony, "I was advised that there was no policy that would result in the separation of children and parents."

"We always knew," one of White's ORR colleagues told me, "we were dealing in an environment [where] people wouldn't acknowledge what we knew was happening."

October 11, 2017

Homestead, Florida, dodged a bullet when Hurricane Irma rolled through. The city had been devastated by Hurricane Andrew twenty-five years earlier, but damage this time around wasn't as severe. Local reports documented avocado harvests that were cut short and landscaping palm tree orchards that were blown into chaos, but fears of tens of thousands of displaced residents never materialized.

The farms would eventually recover, and repairs were under way to the roof of the airplane hangar belonging to the 125th Detachment of the Florida Air National Guard on the Homestead Air Reserve Base, home to the F-15 fighter jets that would shake the neighborhoods below on their way out and over the Everglades for training flights. Around the corner from the air reserve base, the Homestead temporary shelter for migrant kids, on the property of the U.S. Department of Labor's former Job Corps site, survived, too.

Homestead, as it is known for short, was first opened in

the summer of 2016, during the Obama administration, as an overflow facility for the thousands of migrant children arriving unaccompanied in the United States. Shelters all across the country were at or near capacity, and the temporary facility—operated by a private company, not a nonprofit like most ORR shelters—provided a pressure relief valve for the system.

When Donald Trump was elected, numbers of all migrants—including children—crossing the southern border illegally dropped precipitously. Trump officials proudly boasted about the "Trump effect"—migrants staying home because of fear about his tough talk. In April 2016, 48,511 people were taken into custody at the southern border. In April 2017, only 15,798 were—an unheard-of low. ORR shelters that had been packed sat nearly empty that month, and Homestead discharged its last migrant child.

Now, ten months into the Trump administration and with no significant change to border policy, migrants and the smugglers who helped them were calling the president's bluff. Numbers began to tick upward, but still remained shy of the record lows set during the Obama administration.

Understanding this, and with the specter of family separations on the horizon, Commander Jonathan White, thinking like the emergency manager he was, wanted to prepare. That meant making sure there were enough beds to care for a sudden surge, like he had seen three times during the Obama administration, of migrant children coming into his custody. He drafted a memo for Trump-appointed ORR director Scott Lloyd to send to his superior, another Trump appointee and former George W. Bush administration official, Steve Wagner, the acting assistant secretary for children and families.

White and Lloyd did not see eye to eye, particularly

around the issue of abortions for girls and young women in the custody of ORR. Lloyd, a devout Catholic and then the father of seven children, instituted a policy soon after his appointment in early 2017 that mandated any migrant girl seeking an abortion would require his direct approval, and White found it reprehensible. As the policy was argued in court, White continued to work closely with Lloyd, attempting to prepare for the family separation policy he feared was coming.

Lloyd sent the memo to Wagner, making White's case why both should advocate for the Trump administration to again prepare to use the facility.

> In FY 2018, there are multiple threats which could trigger a requirement for temporary influx shelter, of which the key threats are:
>
> • Rapid growth in referrals due to increased migration of UAC across Southwest border;
>
> • Policy or operational change at DHS resulting in rapid growth in referrals (e.g., separation of children from Family Units for designation as UAC) or decline in discharges (e.g., enforcement actions against sponsors);
>
> • Natural disaster, major grantee issue, or other unplanned event resulting in a sudden or rapid loss of existing permanent shelter capacity;
>
> Any of these threats could cause ORR to exceed the 85% capacity target faster than additional bed capacity could be added.

Though the memo cited three factors that would cause Homestead to be called into service, it's not difficult to deduce the reason it was written.

Natural disaster? Unlikely. If a natural disaster were to strike, Homestead itself could also be a primary target, as it was during Irma.

Increased migration? Maybe. Numbers were starting to trend back upward after all-time lows due to President Trump's harsh rhetoric.

Policy or operational change? Bingo. In drafting the memo, White finally memorialized what could create a man-made backup at ORR shelters scattered throughout the country. One reason would be increased scrutiny of "sponsors," family members or friends of the unaccompanied migrant children who arrived in the United States by themselves, some of whom may be undocumented. That alone would slow the discharge rate of children from the shelter system. But the other option was the potential policy that had all of ORR talking: family separations.

If they needed the facility, which could house thousands of children at any given time, it wouldn't take long, Lloyd wrote to Wagner in the memo.

"ORR has assessed and validated the site to be logistically suitable for activation to receive UAC within 30–45 days if required."

October 13, 2017

"What are we looking at?"

"There are a total of eight prototypes," said Roy Villareal, the Border Patrol deputy chief of the San Diego sector, dressed in a green uniform with short shirtsleeves on this chilly morning. "Four of which are constructed out of concrete, and four that are constructed out of alternate material."

"These are pretty tall!"

"They are. Eighteen to thirty feet tall."

Villareal and I were in Otay Mesa, California—six miles east of the San Ysidro Port of Entry, where I saw all that meth busted six months earlier. It's here, on a stretch of land in between the two existing border fences—the original six- or seven-foot one made out of temporary steel aircraft runways used during the Vietnam War, and the secondary fence, a much larger wall, maybe eighteen or so feet and made of metal mesh—that President Trump's border wall prototypes were taking shape. Villareal was touring me here, and President Trump had found the money to build these prototypes, despite the fact that crossings across the country were on track to be as low as ever without his wall.

"Will this lower the numbers even further?"

"It's hard to gauge," Villareal says. "There's always going to be some form of crime or, in this case, illegal migration. Can we do our job better? Absolutely. And I think that these walls are going to contribute towards that."

Fair enough, I think. A big drop in the number of people crossing in this area—what is known as the San Diego sector—coincided with the building of the fencing in the Clinton and Bush administrations.

"So currently we have just under seven hundred miles of fencing along the border. We don't have any intentions of fencing off the entire southwest border. It's not necessary," Villareal told me.

At least he's being honest.

"So what happens now?" I ask. "Does the president come out here and literally say . . ." I pause briefly, preparing my best Trump impression while turning toward a tan-color prototype, half white bollard on bottom and half white sheets on top, ". . . 'Ohhhkayyy, I like that one.' "

"We're going to test it for the breachability. For the subterranean aspect. Can we dig under it? Can we cut through it? Can we scale over it?"

Before either of us knew it, I heard producer Aarne Heikkila tell me to look up. He fired up the camera he was holding, a Canon 5D, and zoomed in to see Border Patrol agents on horseback riding up to a family who had climbed over the short primary fence and dropped into the United States.

"What happened?" I shouted. And then I realized. *People are crossing.*

Villareal was still standing next to me, and I kept talking.

"Looks like a small group of three people just jumped over in the middle of the day. A girl there with a pink backpack. Can you explain to me what's going on?"

I was far more excited by what I was seeing than was Villareal.

"This is a reality of everyday border enforcement. The United States is still *the* draw—the ultimate draw—for people that have dire situations where they're at. We're going to continue to witness this. It plays out on a regular basis for us."

"And it did just here, just now."

"Just now, yeah."

The family had sat down in the dirt as the agents rode up on horses. As they were being apprehended by agents on horseback, they told the Americans they wished to declare asylum. They were stood up and taken away to be booked and processed at a nearby Border Patrol station.

Just weeks later, in the same Border Patrol sector, another family declaring asylum would set off a chain reaction, ultimately affecting thousands.

November 16, 2017

Commander White's team spent October gathering a year's worth of data about the kids in their care. He now had in hand the proof to show that an increasing number of children were being taken from their parents, despite the lack of an official policy announcement by the Trump administration.

Scott Lloyd, who consistently told White that he had heard nothing from the White House about a family separation policy, had given him the go-ahead to investigate what he suspected was happening.

In a phone conversation with Lloyd, acting ICE director Thomas Homan, and Kevin McAleenan, acting commissioner of Customs and Border Protection, White explained that ORR's shelters were caring for an increased number of children who had said they were separated from their parents. At McAleenan's request, Commander White agreed to follow up with an email providing more information.

The next morning, he broke down the specifics for McAleenan, also copying Homan, who was in charge at ICE. McAleenan was present for the meeting with White in which implementing separations were first raised on Valentine's Day 2017. Also copied was Scott Lloyd.

While a small number of referrals each month have been separation cases, generally as a result of criminal apprehensions of parents accompanying [Unaccompanied Alien Child], ORR has noticed a significant increase in recent months—both in raw numbers, and in particular as a proportion of total referrals.

What Commander White was saying would have been clear to McAleenan: yes, separations had happened in the past, including during the Obama administration, but only in the limited circumstance of a family being apprehended and the parent or parents in that family committing a criminal act. Now, it appeared, more and more families were being separated for no other reason than they had crossed the border illegally, and they were being charged with the crime of illegal entry. This had never happened in a widespread fashion before.

Starting in July 2017, shelters and advocates for the children in them started to see an unusual slowdown in the time it took for unaccompanied minors to be discharged from ORR custody. The percentage of separated kids as a proportion of the total referred to HHS also was ballooning. The year before, in October 2016, the Obama administration had separated sixty children from their parents out of nearly seventy-five hundred children sent to ORR. In October 2017, ninety-one kids sent to ORR were separated out of less than three thousand cases.

Commander White attached a spreadsheet, compiled by his ORR colleague Jim De La Cruz, with individual data on each of the 170 children taken from their parents in September and October alone. Nobody outside the government, other than lawyers and service providers on the ground, had much of a clue. Not even all of the federal agencies that should have been sharing information in order to ensure the well-being of the children in their custody.

"As you can see from that data, minors separated by DHS from FMUA and declared UAC are often TAs (12 years of age and younger) and in a significant number of cases are very young (ages 1–5)," White wrote. "FMUA" means "family unit apprehensions," and "TAs" signified "tender aged," often babies, as Commander White laid out.

This was a big deal—separations for reasons other than safety and security of the child were surging, either a highly unlikely coincidence or evidence of something coordinated afoot. Either way, Commander White and his colleagues at ORR were, despite his best efforts, unprepared for a sudden surge in children placed in their custody. As he had previously, he warned the children may literally not have a place to go once separated.

> These UAC require specialized licensed beds different under state licensure law from most licensed UAC beds, and the numbers of these very young UAC resulting from separation has on some dates resulted in shortfalls of available beds licensed for very young TAs. UAC referred through separation generally have longer length of care in ORR custody than other UAC.

The message was clear, if not explicitly laid out in the email: whoever had decided to start separating these children, and wherever it was happening along the border, a lack of planning for its repercussions was breaking the system used by the federal government to safely care for children. White was blowing the whistle to the leadership responsible for the separations he was seeing.

McAleenan had to do something. The evidence White had in hand didn't look good—particularly because they were both in the room when the policy was floated weeks after Trump took office. He now owed White a response.

THAT DAY JOSÉ celebrated his fourteenth birthday in Petén, Guatemala. It was an unremarkable day.

"We didn't do anything," his dad, Juan, recalled. At the house on the hill with the arches and palm trees, a pickup truck parked on the side, across from the big field, it was quiet.

They didn't invite lots of people; it wasn't customary. José's eight- and two-year-old sisters were there and so was his mom, María. There were no signs that, six months away, the family would change forever.

"I wasn't thinking of leaving Guatemala. I was with my family, working in a business. I had a store and that took care of our family," he said.

They celebrated together, like their family always did.

José didn't know it, but his fourteenth birthday would be his last in his home country.

THE NEXT MORNING, Saturday, November 18, McAleenan received a daily summary of news articles referencing Customs and Border Protection. The third on the list was a *BuzzFeed* article about a father claiming Border Patrol agents separated him from his one-year-old son.

> *While this story has yet to be widely reported in other media outlets, it is gaining traction on Twitter since Buzzfeed first ran the article in the early morning hours.*

McAleenan forwarded the email to other officials including Carla Provost, the acting Chief of the Border Patrol.

"Do we have any info on number 3 below?" he asked.

Provost sent McAleenan's question to Gloria Chavez, the Deputy Chief of the Border Patrol's operations division.

"Going to need to know what's going on in EPT on Monday based on what you brought up yesterday," she told Chavez, referring to the El Paso sector of the agency. Chavez responded that afternoon.

"T4, Chief, let me dig over the weekend and get more info. I need to confirm a few items and make sure I interpreted it correctly."

Chavez wasn't the only one looking into what was going on in El Paso. Meanwhile, President Trump was focused on another part of his immigration agenda, and so was I.

November 22, 2017

With apprehensions along the border continuing to rise, and unable to secure funding for his "big, beautiful" border wall, President Trump and Congress became locked in a budget stalemate. Trump's bargaining chip was what he would do about his September decision stopping Deferred Action for Childhood Arrivals, DACA, the Obama-area executive action that gave protected status to the 689,000 undocumented people who were brought to the United States by their parents as children, through no fault of their own. If no deal was reached, in March of 2018 recipients would start to lose their legal status.

At first, President Trump sounded supportive of a deal.

"We're working on a plan for DACA," he said in early September before he boarded Marine One at the White House. "The wall will come later."

But a month later, a deal still hadn't materialized, and the federal government was on course for a shutdown. If no deal on DACA was reached, by March all recipients would be at risk of deportation. Since a quarter of them had U.S.-born kids, American citizens, any deportation would leave the family a choice: self-separate, leaving their children behind with family members or friends, or bring them with. In Mexico, this was not something new, so as always, we went there to see for ourselves.

Again, Mitch Koss and I drove down from Los Angeles. As you approach the border, you either get off at Camino de la Plaza, where the green freeway sign has highlighted in yellow "LAST USA EXIT," or drive into Tijuana (as I did accidentally in 2014). I exited and pulled into the parking lot to, as I'd get used to, rendezvous with the others in our NBC team. The lot was familiar to us now, as was the outlet mall across the freeway.

We all piled in the same van, the most efficient way for us to cross the border as a team without running into any unnecessary delays. For some, crossing the border like this was a daily routine. For me, it remained novel and every detail fascinating, choreographed so that we stayed on track.

We stopped at a local hotel chain to pick up our trusted

fixer, Mariana, whom Mitch met years earlier. She's a journalist herself, and in her spare time helps us out when we head to her part of the world. The story we were pursuing today was her idea.

She hopped in the car, we did the double-kiss thing, she hugged the crew, and we were off.

Fifty thousand foreign-born students attended school in the Mexican border state of Baja California. Thirty thousand of those children lived in Tijuana. The majority, the Mexican government told us, were United States citizens. We arrived at a public school Mariana had arranged for us to tour. After we were inside the gates and guided into a classroom by an administrator, I quickly understood the choice these families were making.

I was introduced to a young man about half my size, hair slicked to the side and matted down with gel. The cardigan sweater over his white polo was dark blue.

"What's your name?" I asked him.

"George," he said back right away, clearly understanding my English.

"George, Jacob. Nice to meet you. Where are you from, George?"

"I'm from Bakersfield, California."

"You're from the United States."

"Yes."

"Are you an American citizen?"

"Yes." He paused. "And Mexican. My dad was deported."

"So, how long have you lived here?"

"Just barely a year and a half."

I asked how different his life was here, compared to the United States.

"Very different. I've actually cried sometimes. I miss my friends."

George missed his friends, but he still was in the close care of his dad, George Sr., whom I met when he came to pick up his son from school. He wore a ball cap with the logo of a commercial printing chain in Southern California, and rectangular plastic glasses just like mine. His white T-shirt was tucked into his jeans, which were clinging to his skinny frame. On his feet were work boots, which he'd use after picking up George Jr. and going back to the house he was renovating.

We sat together on the staircase outside one of the classrooms, math equations painted on each stair behind us in the green, white, and red of the Mexican flag.

"So you got deported, and they followed you here?"

"Yeah, basically," he told me.

"Can I ask you what happened?"

"Yeah, I got in trouble. I was in drug trafficking."

After he served time back at home and was deported, he found his way here. We followed George and his son in their silver Toyota pickup truck to the beachfront house he was fixing up on Rosarito Beach. With a huge hotel in the distance and horseback riders going along the shore, little George rode his bike onto the sand.

His dad told him, he said, that "this is a million-dollar view."

He pointed to the waves of the Pacific Ocean crashing on the beach, the same ocean and same waves crashing a short drive to the north, separated by a steel fence jutting out into the water.

"So you would trade a million-dollar view to go back to Bakersfield?

"For a million-dollar family."

We said good-bye to the Georges, dropped off Mariana, and headed back north, waiting in the hour-long line to get through the same San Ysidro Port of Entry where I had seen government agents bust the smuggling of multiple kilos of meth in February. Back then, and again now, there was a line of humans on foot forming next to the epic queue of vehicles we were now idling in. Just like the tens of thousands of cars crossing daily, tens of thousands of people do, too—many to go to work or school or visit family and friends.

There was another line I didn't see, with another group of people I missed, too. Forming apart from the throng of daily border crossers was an entry for asylum seekers—people in flight from their home countries and seeking refuge in the United States. These individuals wouldn't have documents scanned and handed right back to them. They would be taken into the basement of the port of entry and put into cells with cinder block walls, gray linoleum floors, and metal toilets while their fates were decided.

Those who have seen the process describe it as mechanized and cold. They "pass through a chain-link gate and stand at a counter to answer questions from officers sitting behind computers. Mothers and children sit together beneath a large American flag hanging in a waiting room. Meanwhile, migrants shuffle back and forth from holding cells to the cafeteria or showers, walking in single file with their hands behind their backs," local public broadcaster KQED reported.

Twenty-one days before I unknowingly drove right over this secret jail, a Congolese mother and her daughter were separated from each other after having been detained there. They were moved to what she described as a makeshift hotel, and on what she believes was the fourth day of her detention, her daughter was taken from her, screaming. The mother was taken to an adult immigration jail in San Diego, and her daughter was sent to a "shelter" in Chicago. When she was told her daughter was in Chicago, she did not know what the word meant.

All the while, aboveground, life went on at the Las Americas Premium Outlets and at the parking lot across the freeway. Once through the border crossing and back in the States, we returned to that parking lot. I said good-bye to everyone, shook hands, hopped out of the team van, got in my car, and drove home to Los Angeles, clueless about the separated mother and daughter who would soon be engaged in a fight not just for their right to be reunited, but for thousands of others as well.

November 25, 2017

Under a perfectly sunny late-autumn sky, dozens of Border Patrol agents and other law enforcement officials gathered outside Our Lady of Guadalupe Church in El Paso to watch the body of fellow agent Rogelio Martinez placed into a hearse to be transported for burial. A local fire truck flew a giant American flag off its outstretched ladder as firefighters in blue uniforms stood at attention below. Bagpipes played. It was Thanksgiving weekend.

Agent Martinez died after what initial reports suggested was a rock striking his head; his partner was also badly injured. President Trump tweeted about the death of Agent Martinez, indicating he was murdered, despite a lack of evidence. He promised to "seek out and bring to justice those responsible" for the killing, a tragedy he implied made the case for his promised border wall, which wasn't even under construction or anywhere close to it. Months later, the FBI declared it found no evidence of an attack against Agent Martinez, giving credence to an alternate theory: he may have accidentally fallen into the roadside culvert in which he was discovered.

The lack of certainty didn't stop President Trump from using the death as political fodder to justify his border wall, but with the project—and his promise Mexico would pay for it—in jeopardy, the Trump administration pushed forward on policies that would have the same effect. This policy "wall" was one not made of steel or concrete, but of terror. The night Agent Martinez was laid to rest in El Paso, the plan Commander White suspected was under way, despite assurances otherwise, was publicly revealed to be taking place in the same city.

In a bombshell story, Lomi Kriel of the *Houston Chronicle* reported the Trump administration was following through on the policy my colleague Julia Ainsley had uncovered it was considering back in March, and, with Jim De La Cruz, Commander White documented: systematic separation of parents and children who crossed the southwest border illegally. Ripping families apart had become regular U.S. government practice, if a secret one.

The *Chronicle*, prudently, had used the word "questionable" to describe the policy in its headline. Indeed, despite Kriel's report and the insistence of her sources that family separations were happening, what exactly that looked like would be an unknown until the Trump administration acknowledged the policy, and more important, until outsiders were able to get inside government facilities to see what was actually happening for themselves.

Testimonials from child advocates and attorneys cited by Kriel were the first public documentation that separations were happening. The Trump administration was charging migrant parents of families apprehended at the border with the federal crime of illegal entry and rendering their children unaccompanied, placing them in the custody of the child refugee program run by Commander White. Kriel and the *Chronicle* were able to identify twenty-two separation cases; additionally, she reported there were dozens more cases like them, according to attorneys.

The Trump administration, while denying the policy existed, found justification in the increasing number of Central American migrants arriving to seek asylum, even though overall numbers of border crossers remained near all-time lows. The idea was "to deter" them from making the journey, as then-Secretary Kelly had explained on CNN.

Deterrence-based immigration policy was nothing new, whether it was the first wave of border fencing put into place by the Clinton administration, the creation of the Department of Homeland Security at the same time as a massive expansion of the Border Patrol by the Bush administration, or the record number of deportations by the Obama administration. The "prevention through deterrence" enforcement philosophy, an official name coined in 1994, has never stopped the most desperate from coming to the United States. Not even word of dog-kennel style cages, "la perrera," used by the Obama administration to hold a surging number of unaccompanied Central American minors in 2014, made people want to turn back.

Among these outrage-inducing immigration policies carried out over decades, unnecessarily separating families was considered uniquely reprehensible by doctors, social workers, and immigration lawyers, which quickly became apparent. Families fleeing the threats of violence, persecution, and hunger found themselves unable to find their own children, taken by the American state, even after their criminal proceedings ended.

"Parents are being denied access to their children without any due process," federal public defender Maureen Franco told Kriel. "Even the worst drug addicts still have rights to their children, but here we are just removing them without even a hearing."

Kriel found that parents could not find their children because of what U.S. magistrate judge Miguel Torres described as a "limited and often non-existent lack of information about the well-being and whereabouts of their minor children from whom they were separated at the time of their arrest." Her reporting not only uncovered what was happening, but it revealed how after separations occurred and parents were charged with crimes, reunifications with children were complicated and in some cases not happening at all.

"This is a huge problem," an assistant public defender in San Diego emailed Kriel after spending two weeks trying to locate a five-year-old child taken from her client.

The *Chronicle* had the evidence in hand, but the government was denying its own policy. Kriel reported a Customs and Border Protection lawyer as claiming the "Border Patrol does not have a blanket policy requiring the separation of family units."

Of course, that is exactly what was happening, and the evidence was now published by the *Houston Chronicle* for the world to read. The United States of America, a nation as thoroughly defined by immigration as any on earth, was deliberately breaking apart families seeking asylum here—to scare other families from coming.

Most of the separations Kriel uncovered were happening in one place, evidence that would later become critical to piecing together where and when widescale family separations began. "The practice appears particularly pronounced in west Texas," she wrote, "where Border Patrol agents at an October meeting in El Paso acknowledged they were separating families."

TWO DAYS LATER, I landed in El Paso in the late afternoon on assignment. Having missed Kriel's article entirely over the holiday weekend, I was focused on the cratering morale in the Border Patrol and was eager to learn more about the death of Agent Martinez.

You don't have to drive far outside of the city until the freeway opens up and the speed limits hit eighty; a wide and vast landscape unspools before us.

We're practically flying, with the windows down, and it's clear that Aarne, whom I've been teamed up with since covering the 2016 presidential campaign, is taking full advantage of the open road. We were going too fast, rushing out of the airport and into our rental car and off to our destination like so many times before. But we were in such a blind hurry that we missed the family separation story entirely. In fact, we were driving right by it.

Zooming past the giant Border Patrol checkpoint on Interstate 10, we carried on, en route to shoot a feature story on the failure of the Trump administration's hiring push for the agency. They were failing, in part, because potential recruits were being scared off by the prospect of the dangers of the job and, in the case of where we were headed, an extremely remote assignment.

It's just before five in the evening local time, and to my right outside the passenger window the sun looks like it's about to set into Juarez, Mexico, which is weird because I thought the sun sets to the west and not to the south. Also outside my window are fluffy white clouds and blue sky and a yellowish-orange horizon and mountains and telephone poles and low shrubs and cacti. It's all going by so fast. If you wanted to order a border sunset for a Hollywood movie, this would be it.

"The air smells different, doesn't it?" I ask Aarne.

There's not a wall out there, at least I don't think, but now there's not enough light to see for sure. And I'm not thinking about any of that anyway. I'm talking with Aarne about having a son, and when he and his wife will have a baby, and we're listening to the news on satellite radio. I've never been to this part of the border before. Where we're headed, the Big Bend sector, is as remote as you can get along the U.S.–Mexico dividing line. As we speed along, night falls on West Texas, and the murder mystery of Agent Martinez remains unsolved for a ninth day.

"You think he was killed right out here? It has to be somewhere nearby."

The sun also sets on dozens of children alone and scared and without their parents. They are out there in the darkness, invisible to us. But it's not the night that's hiding them.

We did come here to cover a border story. Just the wrong one.

SINCE DONALD TRUMP announced his presidential campaign by calling Mexicans rapists and criminals, his anti-immigrant policies have been front and center. I live in Los Angeles—a "majority-minority" city with a nearly 50 percent Latinx population—where Trump's rhetoric and policies directly affect millions of people. I didn't set out to be an immigration reporter, but it's hard to miss big stories important to immigrant communities as an Angeleno.

After I graduated college I marched, then vlogged in 2005 and 2006, respectively, at the *"Gran Marchas"*—huge protests—for comprehensive immigration reform that filled some of Los Angeles' busiest streets with seas of people. Almost a decade later, when I was working for the now-shuttered cable network Pivot, I drove my mom's station wagon to learn who was caught up in President Obama's record number of deportations and met a bunch of people who grew up in Southern California just like I did. One of my first assignments at MSNBC was to get the reactions of migrant farmworkers in California's Central Valley to the pope's visit to the United States—one man wanted Francis to "tell Trump to calm down." In between the 2016 Republican and Democratic conventions, we made the trip to a place outside of San Diego where there is no border fence, and asked the Border Patrol if they needed Trump's wall. We reported that most undocumented immigrants come by air, not the southern border; that most drugs come through ports of entry; and while visiting Trump's "big, beautiful" prototypes we watched a little girl wearing a pink backpack and her family declare asylum at the base of it after they were apprehended by officers on horseback. All that is to say if you called my cell phone on this drive and asked me if I had my finger on the pulse of immigration policy, I would have told you yes. I would have been wrong. This trip to El Paso was a prime example of how wrong I was.

WE PLANNED TO overnight in Marfa, the small West Texas desert city, where we'd meet our guide from the Border Patrol the next morning. We made it, just in time for an unexpectedly cold night, the temperatures dipping into the thirties. And we had an unexpectedly fancy dinner with Dana Roecker and Rob Colvill, the top-notch crew Aarne and I had started working with during the 2016 campaign, at Hotel Saint George, where we had booked rooms. Are we really in Texas? That night, what seemed like all night, a cargo train chugged by as I tried to sleep. My bed shook. Even the TV on with those foam earplugs stuffed in my ear canals didn't do the trick.

This is going to be a long night, I thought. And then I passed out.

The next morning, I woke up and headed downstairs for breakfast with the team, flipping through the local paper for stories about the late Agent Martinez and the mystery surrounding his death. At the same time, Border Patrol agent Javier Prieto was on his way to meet us at the Marfa Border Patrol Station, where we'd set off on a drive through mountainous windy desert roads to a place where the Rio Grande is not even a few yards wide. Multiple migrants had died trying to cross the border here over the summer. Patterns were unusual. Did he know anything about the families being separated in the sector next door? Had he separated any families himself? Those were not questions I knew to ask. And today wasn't going to be the day I figured that out.

December 3, 2017

Over two weeks after Commander Jonathan White told his own leadership and CBP Commissioner Kevin McAleenan that ORR was seeing an increase in children separated from their parents—and after the *Houston Chronicle* reported the same—McAleenan finally got back to White.

"Thanks again for this, Jonathan," he wrote White in an email asking for a password for the spreadsheet containing information about separated children White had sent him on November 17. "You should have seen a change the past 10 days or so."

McAleenan meant that he had ordered an end to a family-separation pilot program that had been taking place in the El Paso sector. McAleenan learned more about the program after asking for details on separations from Border Patrol Chief Carla Provost, who in turn had her deputy, Gloria Chavez, "dig" deeper. Data showed that during the El Paso pilot program, apprehensions of families dropped by 64 percent, which as Commander White and ORR staff suspected, they carried out between July and November.

Ready to order the end of the pilot program himself, McAleenan further pressed Provost about it.

"I know boss, I shut it down already," she told him.

Despite McAleenan's assurance to White that he would "have seen a change" regarding separations, White remained skeptical. He told colleagues as much when he forwarded McAleenan's email on December 5.

> *Sorry—meant to share this yesterday. As you know, we did some lobbying of CBP leadership on the separations issue. Kevin advises we should be seeing the numbers of separations decrease. We shall see what the future holds.*

White's intuition was right.

Less than a week later, on December 13, he received an email from an ORR colleague who had been on the phone with Gloria Chavez that day. The deputy chief had revealed the Border Patrol was still looking to expand the "prosecution of parents." But the ORR staffer reported to White that Chavez said the larger-scale policy would require the sign-off of the new secretary of homeland security, Kirstjen Nielsen, who had just assumed her post.

December 5, 2017

Kirstjen Nielsen was confirmed as President Trump's second secretary of homeland security by a vote of sixty-two to thirty-seven, ten Democrats joining Republicans in tapping her for the post responsible for the United States immigration enforcement system.

Her now former boss John Kelly left his post as DHS secretary in July to become President Trump's chief of staff, which set off a game of musical chairs. At his urging, his chief of staff at DHS and then aide in the White House, Nielsen, a former George W. Bush aide who worked on his administration's widely panned Hurricane Katrina response, was nominated as his permanent successor. Her deputy, Chad Wolf, would soon become her chief of staff at DHS.

Before Nielsen was confirmed she had to appear before the Senate Homeland Security and Governmental Affairs Committee to face questions from the U.S. senators who would decide her fate, which she did in early November. Senator Kamala Harris had intended to bring up a question about family separations, but didn't quite get to it.

"I am running out of time," California's junior senator said, "so I just want to ask you one more question. Do you agree with a policy that would expedite deportation of unaccompanied minors who are coming from those Central American countries?"

Senator Harris was referring to a goal of both the Trump administration and some in the Obama administration, to quickly deport unaccompanied Central American migrant children to deter others from coming.

"I believe in reuniting children with their families," Nielsen said, in a bizarre bit of foreshadowing.

"If their families are not here—"

Senator Harris interrupted, pointing out to Nielsen that doing so would only put them back in the same desperate circumstances they had fled in the first place.

"Well," Nielsen replied, "in that case I would certainly want to work with you to understand more about the implications."

Though Kelly, the nominee's former boss, had confirmed

on CNN nine months earlier that a family separation plan was in the works, and Lomi Kriel had confirmed it was now happening, Nielsen was asked exactly zero questions by the panel about the practice on that eighth day of November.

Senator Harris submitted in writing the questions she ran out of time to ask about family separations, and by law, Nielsen was forced to answer under oath. The responses were attached to the official transcript of Nielsen's confirmation hearing.

The Young Center for Immigrant Children's Rights has reported a dramatic increase in the number of requests for Child Advocates for children separated from parents by immigration authorities this year. For example, in New York, there has been nearly a fourfold increase in such requests as compared to the same quarter of the prior year.

1. If confirmed, will you issue written guidance to make clear that mothers are not to be separated from their children at the border?

I am not familiar with the increase cited in the question nor its causation. Should I be confirmed, I will work with Acting Commissioner McAleenan and Acting Director Homan to understand the current practice and policy and if necessary work with them to issue additional guidance.

2. What are you doing to ensure families are not being systematically separated, and if they are, what steps is the Department taking to ensure reunification and communication of separated family members?

As the nominee, I currently have no role in what you

describe. If confirmed I will review current policies to ensure DHS is not unnecessarily separating families. My understanding is that while ICE has limited-capacity family residential detention facilities to house alien family members, the separation of alien families generally occurs outside the United States when one or both parents, particularly those from countries in Central America, depart their countries and illegally enter the United States, leaving behind their children, or, the parent(s) arrange for illicit human smuggling organizations to smuggle their children into the United States. In either case, the children arriving at or between ports of entry entering the United States without their parents or legal guardians are processed as unaccompanied alien children (UAC) upon apprehension and, pursuant to the Trafficking Victims Protection Reauthorization Act (TVPRA), the Department of Health and Human Services (DHHS), not DHS, has the sole statutory authority and obligation to provide for the care and custody of such children and to seek reunification with their parents or suitable sponsors in the United States. I am aware that ICE does have an Online Detainee Locator System to help family members locate individuals in immigration custody.

3. If you are confirmed, will you report to me whether DHS is currently drafting or considering a policy to separate families at the border?

If confirmed, I commit to sharing additional policy guidance and appropriate information with Congress.

4. Will you commit to review what procedures exist when U.S. Customs and Border Protection (CBP) makes such a decision

(i.e., reviews, opportunity for parents to be represented in challenging a separation)?

I will.

The inconsistency between Nielsen's answers and the public reporting was troubling for Senator Harris, who was one of the Democrats who voted against her along with thirty-six others just days after the *Houston Chronicle* exposed the secret family separations pilot program in El Paso.

Ten days after Nielsen was sworn in, Gene Hamilton, the thirty-something counselor to Attorney General Jeff Sessions, sent a message to Nielsen's deputy, Chad Wolf, asking about the status of ten "decision memos" they had been working on during the interim tenure of Acting DHS Secretary Elaine Duke, who had ascended to the acting secretary position after John Kelly moved to the White House. These nominal memos were actually policy proposals that would require the signature of the homeland security secretary. Wolf and Hamilton had until recently been colleagues at DHS, working on policy issues first for John Kelly as senior counselor, then for Duke, and now Nielsen.

"Any new ones make it up to you yet?" Hamilton asked Wolf in a series of emails later obtained by my colleague Julia Ainsley.

"Sorry for the delay, Gene. Yes—a number of them have been signed out. We consolidated the 10 memo's into 8 and have signed out 4 of them. We're working to get the others out the door."

Hamilton was excited.

"Just let me know if I can do anything to help get them teed up!"

Just over an hour later, Wolf wrote back again, this time with an unusual request. Wolf asked Hamilton to keep "close hold" of what he was about to send. He did not even want Hamilton to forward the documents to Stephen Miller, President Trump's right hand on immigration. "I plan to once Kevin, Tom and Francis cut in on it," referring to Kevin McAleenan, the acting Customs and Border Protection commissioner; Tom Homan, the head of ICE; and Francis Cissna, the head of U.S. Citizenship and Immigration Services, which manages legal immigration in the United States.

The goal, Wolf wrote, "is to give S1 [Secretary Nielsen] an idea of what she can do right away versus actions that will take months + to implement."

The second item on his list of sixteen proposals was separating families.

> **Separate Family Units:** Announce that DHS is
> considering separating family units, placing the adults in
> adult detention, and placing the minors under the age of
> 18 in the custody of HHS as unaccompanied alien children
> (UACs) because the minors will meet the definition
> of "unaccompanied alien child," i.e., (1) has no lawful
> immigration status in the U.S.; (2) has not attained the age
> of 18; and (3) has no parent or legal guardian in the U.S.,
> or no parent or legal guardian in the U.S. is available to
> provide care and physical custody. *See* 6 USC § 279(g)
> (2). This will require close coordination with HHS, to
> ensure that sufficient capacity is available to detain the
> UACs. Advocacy groups are aware that this policy shift
> may occur and therefore are seeking to identify families
> who have been separated in order to bring a class action

lawsuit. Hence, close coordination with DOJ will also be required.

> *Status: Currently under consideration; dependent on policy determination*
>
> *Implement: Direct DHS OPA to develop messaging options*

> a. Once legal coordination between DHS, HHS and DOJ is complete, begin separating family units, as stated above.
>
> *Status: Currently under consideration; dependent on policy determination*
>
> *Implement: Secretarial memo needed for full implementation*

Eleven days after Kirstjen Nielsen was sworn in as secretary of homeland security, her staff and others inside the Trump administration were working aggressively to put a potential nationwide family separation policy in front of her—the exact scenario Senator Harris asked Nielsen to report back to her on.

Nielsen did not, nor did her staff.

Hamilton, the loyal aide to the Attorney General, was looking forward to digging into and giving comments to Wolf on potential new policies, including separations.

"Happy to," he wrote. "Have to go do pictures with the kids and can review this pm. And won't share with anyone."

I am a citizen of Honduras and came to the United States seeking asylum. I received a negative determination of my initial asylum interview ("credible fear interview"), and an immigration judge affirmed it so I have a final order of removal but have not been deported.

I came to the United States on or around February 18, 2018, with my biological son, R.Z.A.R., who is three years old. He is also from Honduras and seeking asylum.

When we came to the United States, we turned ourselves in at the border in Brownsville, Texas, and I said that I wanted to seek asylum.

Shortly after arriving, I was told that I was going to be separated from my son. There were no doubts expressed that I was my son's biological father and I have a birth certificate to show our relationship. I also had my son's vaccination records and his passport. They did not tell me that I was a danger to my son or was abusive. They told me that they had to separate me from my son because I had a prior removal order and they did not have any places to detain fathers and children.

I was sent to the South Texas Detention Center around February 19, 2018. My son was sent to an ORR facility in or near El Paso, Texas.

I have not seen him for over two months. I worry about R.Z.A.R. constantly and don't know when I will see him. We have talked on the phone several times, but I do not have many minutes and I do not always get an answer when I call.

I know that R.Z.A.R. is having a very hard time detained all by himself without me. My son has already suffered a lot because his mother disappeared about six months ago. He is too young to understand that she was taken from us, but he knows she is gone and he misses her. That has been very hard on him. He is only a three-year-old in a strange country and needs his parent.

I hope I can be with my son very soon.

I declare under penalty of perjury under the laws of the United States of America that the foregoing is true and correct, based on my personal knowledge. Executed in Pearsall, Texas, on April 25, 2018.

—DECLARATION OF MR. A.

MS. L V. ICE

CHAPTER FOUR

"*Very, Very Worried*"

January 2, 2018

The smell of marijuana was overpowering. I was surrounded by cannabis plants, easily stacked ten feet high on all sides of me. It was just before four in the morning Los Angeles time.

"Hey, Jacob, can you hear us? Jacob?"

In my ear, I could hear a voice talking to me. But I wasn't bugging out; at least I don't think I was.

"Jacob, good morning, it's Studio 1A. Can you hear us?"

"I can, good morning."

"Great, stand by for rehearsal. This is just a rehearsal."

This was the day recreational pot was legalized in California, and anyone over the age of twenty-one could buy what used to be referred to as the devil's weed without fear of getting locked up. The days of massive hauls of marijuana across the southern border had already started to taper off. With pot being grown and sold in a regulated market, the need for it to be smuggled from Mexico into the United States was fading away. Today, in between ports of entry, you were much more likely to meet a family seeking asylum crossing the border than you were a narco-trafficker, as I learned from Sidney Aki at the Port of San Ysidro. (Customs and Border Protection continually pointed to statistics indicating they were still seizing loads of pot in the Rio Grande Valley and southern Arizona, two places along the border I had not yet been but was hoping to visit soon.) My border reporting of late had been focused not on drugs, but what the consequences of deportations would mean for so called mixed-status families—those with some family members arriving undocumented with others born in the United States and receiving American citizenship—just like the Georges I met near Tijuana in November.

Twelve days after my weed live shot I was in New York City to appear on the *Today* show again, this time to share their story with the world. I walked into Studio 1A and waited in the wings, ready to sit down at the famous desk known behind the scenes as "home base," makeup applied by the pros in the basement greenroom, microphone and IFB hooked up by the techs in the corner of the studio, and blue wool suit jacket and tie freshly lint-rolled by the wardrobe department. While Al Roker ran through the national forecast, I took my seat at the table to the left of Hoda Kotb and Savannah Guthrie, directly across from Carson Daly and Craig Melvin.

"Morning, guys," I whisper while giving a little wave.

"Hey, Jacob," they say back in unison, also in TV quiet voice but a little less quiet than mine since this is their show, after all.

"All right, Al. Thank you," Guthrie says as Roker wraps up, and not missing a beat, she turns right to my story. "Now to the raging debate over immigration and a group that is left in limbo: hundreds of thousands of children born here in the United States. NBC's Jacob Soboroff is here with more on that."

"Good morning, you guys."

I tee up the segment we filmed several months before, reading my introduction off the teleprompter in front of me, careful not to get too far ahead of myself and landing on my "roll cue," the signal that tips off the control room it's time to run the taped portion of my report.

"In Mexico, it's a question they've been dealing with for years," I said, as footage began.

As the spot played, Hoda, Savannah, Al, Carson, and Craig watched in monitors placed under the glass-top table or under the cameras surrounding us. We sat there together as I, in the spot, told the story of how George Sr. had been deported for a crime, and his American citizen son, George Jr., went with him to Mexico instead of staying behind in California. It was a decision that tens of thousands of families were making, many with no criminal record at all, only the civil violation of entering the United States illegally.

There were so many kids like George that the public school system in Baja California was now teaching students English-language curriculum designed in conjunction with American teachers. The report ended with George insisting, as he had to me that day on the beach, that he would trade the "million-dollar" Mexican beach view for his "million-dollar family." The control room cued me to start again reading the teleprompter, wrapping up the spot live. Talking way too fast, I jumped in.

"There are least two hundred thousand American-born kids of Dreamers that are facing deportation. If that were to happen, every single one of those kids, they would face a situation just like George did. They gotta find a way to stay in the U.S." I said, breaking away from the teleprompter and turning to my colleagues to explain how the Georges' story overlapped with President Trump's continuing threat to end DACA. "Or, follow their parents to a foreign land. That's why these schools are teaming up—California and Mexico—to keep these kids educated and keep them in the programs so they don't feel like they're in a foreign place."

At this point, I waited to see if one of the regular cast members would have something to say, a sign the story had captured their attention, or send me off with a simple thank you. It's the TV news equivalent of Johnny Carson asking you to stick around on the couch for another segment. Guthrie jumped in.

"Well, I like how educators are trying to, you know, do their best in a difficult situation," she remarked.

"Making the best of a terrible situation," I replied, glad that what was going on at the border had resonated.

"Good story, Jacob, thank you."

And with that, I was done, and the show pivoted back to lighter fare.

"Still to come," Kotb teased, "we've got Jill's deal of the day. The best bargains on stylish winter fashion. Plus, sinless sweets."

"Thanks, guys, have a good one," I told the cast and crew as I headed off set. As I did it was hard not to think about how the world of mainstream media is so weird—pivoting from the deadly serious to the silly with almost no transition. "Switching gears" is a thing we're all trained to do, and a phrase often utilized in broadcast news.

I was grateful to the brass at *Today* and NBC News for turning to me for stories like this and putting them on the air. But is it what our audience wanted to see? In an ill-advised move I make far too often, I checked Twitter after the report aired.

"The parent broke the law by entering illegally & then continued to break the law by dealing drugs—the consequences the child is suffering are solely on the parent," one user replied.

"Send their kids back with them," said another.

Doubt washed over me. Would a story like the one I just presented make a difference in this environment? Was it getting through to the audience tuning in for the "deal of the day" that my report was about more than one father who made a serious mistake and his son living with the consequences? Insofar as I was thinking about separation as I walked away from Studio 1A, it was how some in our audience, and so many others, were separated from the reality of how immigration policy was creating thousands of "Georges," rippling through virtually every part of our country.

As I thought of others, I, too, was separated from how extreme that reality was.

A FEW HOURS after I got off the air at 30 Rock, Jennifer Podkul walked into the Mary E. Switzer Federal Building in Washington, D.C., the headquarters of the Administration for Children and Families. The grand structure looks more like a train station than a federal office complex, and a historian of architecture (or the website of the General Services Administration, which maintains the building) would tell you the style is a combination of Art Moderne and abstracted

Egyptian Revival—I looked it up. It was designed to house the National Defense Commission and the Department of War, although neither department ever moved in despite the fact the building opened before World War II.

Podkul, an immigration policy wonk, had served in the Peace Corps in Honduras before becoming the senior director for policy and advocacy at KIND—Kids in Need of Defense, a nonprofit organization founded by Microsoft and Angelina Jolie to make sure no refugee child faces court alone. She had burning questions for Commander Jonathan White and his colleagues at the Office of Refugee Resettlement. She wanted to press ORR leadership about the family separations that by all indications were happening, despite the government's repeated denials.

"Is this going to happen?" she wondered. "Or not? Is everyone prepared?"

Podkul wasn't alone in her concerns.

ORR holds a regularly scheduled stakeholders meeting with the service providers who take care of the thousands of migrant children in the custody of the federal government, both while they are detained in custody and once they're out of it. This month was different. Podkul had seen Lomi Kriel's report in the *Houston Chronicle* and, having heard some of the same anecdotal reports from lawyers she worked with, she was worried about the prospect of family separations happening on a wide scale.

Her fears were also based on years of research into the practice. Ten days *before* Donald Trump was inaugurated as the forty-fifth president of the United States, Podkul and her colleagues at KIND, along with the Women's Refugee Commission and the Lutheran Immigration and Refugee Service, published a report called "Betraying Family Values: How Immigration Policy at the United States Border is Separating Families." The report's cover featured a photo of a family of four in silhouette behind a chain link fence topped by barbed wire and looking out at a city in the distance as a helicopter flies by. It is an indictment of decades of immigration enforcement, illuminating how it has contributed to family members being separated from one another: "Over the last year, a disturbing new trend has emerged at the U.S. Border: families torn apart. As an increasing number of families migrate together to the United States, the number of documented cases of family separation has escalated."

The dozens of cases examined for the report make clear that family separations during the Obama administration were haphazard and not systematic—making tracking of families and ultimately reuniting them a challenge. Families were being separated when a child migrated with anyone other than their parent or legal guardian, including cousins, grandparents, and aunts or uncles. In addition, separations were occurring when a parent was prosecuted for illegally entering or reentering the United States (a practice that was ramped up as part of a "Consequence Delivery System" to deter families from migrating).

Between 2012 and 2017, the report explains, "the United States has seen a shift in the demographics of migrants encountered at our borders—from a majority of adult males, often from Mexico seeking employment, to families, children, grandparents, aunts, and uncles fleeing together, seeking protection in the United States, coming mostly from Central America. Tragically, U.S. Immigration enforcement policies, instead of shifting to adapt to this significant change, have continued to try forcing a square peg into a round hole, and in doing so have compounded the vulnerabilities of families and protection-seeking migrants. Instead of promoting family unity, we as a nation are breaking families apart."

There was no question, based on the cases studied, of the consequences of family separations. The practice, regardless of why it was carried out, "negatively impacts emotional and psychological development and well-being, creates security and economic difficulties, and strips the dignity of an individual and their family as a whole."

During the Obama administration, a blanket family separation policy had been considered and even discussed in the Situation Room. But it wasn't adopted. The report, a warning of sorts ahead of the Trump administration, lays out how there were actually multiple policies that resulted in family separations, and the lack of an overall federal policy to protect the well-being of those separated made it worse. Now separations were reportedly happening on a wider scale, deliberately, and Podkul feared the coming ramifications. Along with Lutheran Immigration and Refugee Service, she submitted questions to be addressed by ORR staff at the monthly meeting.

- *How is ORR preparing for the Administration's plans to separate families at the border? What kind of impact will this have on ORR and how will ORR manage a potential large increase of referrals? Has DHS consulted ORR on this policy consideration and asked to provide a child welfare perspective? (KIND/LIRS)*

Podkul went in with the philosophy that "it was like throwing spaghetti at the wall." Armed with so many questions, she assumed she would get some answers. She was in good company. The meeting agenda shows nearly every other stakeholder and service provider submitted similar questions.

- *Can ORR please share any new trends it is seeing with regard to family separation? Is ORR working to coordinate with ICE and/or DHS on family separation cases? **(CARA)***

- *USCRI has noticed an increase in family separation, particularly single fathers traveling with their young children. The fathers have been deported, leaving the children, some as young as two years old, in the care of extended family. What steps if any is ORR taking to address this issue and how can we as service providers assist when we learn during the home study process that the biological parents would like the child to return to their care in home country? **(USCRI)***

- *At the last meeting, ORR mentioned that it would look into its ability to collect information/data on children in its custody as a result of family separation due to immigration enforcement by CBP or ICE. What has ORR determined in this regard? **(WRC)***

- *Has or is ORR considering establishing a mechanism or a policy to facilitate family communication and other needs in the event of a separation? **(WRC)***

- *LIRS has found a common problem for kids seeking voluntary departure in order to reunify with their parent prior to departure is delayed court proceedings. Even when cases are expedited, the court date is often still many*

weeks away and ICE decides it cannot wait that long. Would
ORR be willing to do outreach to EOIR about expediting
these types of cases so that a child isn't separated from
a parent in ORR custody for unnecessary long periods of
time. (LIRS)

• *What is ORR's policy when ICE wants to take custody of a*
child that is in ORR care? (VERA)

The questions Podkul and her colleagues were asking
were the same ones that she had been trying to answer for
years—only now the number of children who would be affected could end up exponentially higher. While separations
could happen for a variety of reasons, what she wanted done
boiled down to a simple question she would ask the government over and over again: "Can't you make a check box?"

Podkul knew that without a way to designate that children were separated from family members in the federal government's records—none of which interacted with each other,
including relevant agencies like ORR, the Border Patrol, and
ICE—family members would lose track of one another. She
had even asked similar questions several months earlier, at
a November stakeholder meeting. All that yielded was more
questions.

"Sometimes ORR is informed at the referral point if
a child was separated from a family member," she and her
fellow stakeholders were told about how ORR is notified if a
child is separated. Sometimes.

"There's no agency-wide policy on what to do if it is found
out that a child has been separated from a parent. Cases are

worked on at the individual level," it was explained to her, she recalled.

None of that was much help in November, and again several months later, Podkul found herself equally frustrated.

"We didn't want any kids to fall through the cracks."

Others in the room, of course, had a strong indication of what was going on: internal ORR data about the increasing number of separations; overheard conversations by White House staffers; carelessly shared details by the Border Patrol. But White and other ORR officials present used the session to gather intelligence from those with boots on the ground, like Podkul, more than to answer questions that were raised.

"Even though it's in question format, it's a way for them to tell me: 'This is what we're seeing. X, Y and Z,'" an ORR official who was in the room later told me. "They probably know I haven't seen X, Y, and Z but that I'm going to go look for X, Y, Z."

While Commander White was hearing similar anecdotal reports, there was nothing he could officially confirm about a separation policy. It was continually denied by his superiors.

The conversations in this and other stakeholder meetings stayed secret, by design.

"It's not an official government meeting," the ORR official told me, "because otherwise I would have to broadcast it," allowing others to join who may not share the same goal, in this case, preventing family separations.

As Podkul walked out of the meeting, she was "very, very worried."

"They knew this would harm kids on a personal level," she told me, "and on a personal level I felt bad for the ORR employees there. But they would have to clean up the mess."

White remained distressed, too. Meanwhile, on the border migrants kept coming, oblivious to what was awaiting them.

January 17, 2018

An email landed in my inbox just after lunch. Subject: "The Wall." It was from Paul Ryan, a senior producer at *Dateline*, the legendary NBC newsmagazine. Though today it's most often associated with true crime stories, *Dateline* is also the network's venue for deep dives into newsy issues and investigative journalism. Copied on the email were Izhar Harpaz and Simon Doolittle, two *Dateline* producers.

> Hey guys—we want to do an hour on The Border for March. Jacob, we'd love it if you could be the correspondent. Izhar and Simon will co-produce.
>
> Simon and I wrote a pitch over a year ago for this. I'm attaching it here. The idea is to travel the length of the border, stopping in a few key places. Some of this pitch is probably out of date—Simon is figuring that out now. Given recent developments and the current situation, we'll have to have new elements, too. Plus—Jacob, you've no doubt shot a ton along the border the last year or two. It would be great to know what that is, maybe there are things you've already done that we can integrate.
>
> Jacob—I see you're in NY. Maybe we can all get together in person or over phone to discuss later today or tomorrow.

I couldn't contain my excitement—and wrote back right away.

I'd absolutely love this—and am currently working on
our next story on the wall to be pegged to SOTU so I'll bring
you up-to-date. And yes, I'm here. Any time after 2 I'm free.
What works for you? And for reference, here's our reporting
on the wall/immigration over the past year. I highlighted the
stuff that's most relevant. . . . I had pulled this together for
Janelle last week. . . .

I attached the list of stories, as promised, that I had as-sembled for my boss Janelle Rodriguez, NBC News' senior vice president of editorial, who had consistently pushed us to work from the border to show the realities on the ground.

That same day, we met and discussed the project and agreed to get to work in February. But first, as I told everyone by email, I had to head out on assignment for an immigration story pegged to President Trump's first true State of the Union.

"DID YOU SEE two that went south?"

A border patrol agent rolled up to me and two officials from Hidalgo County, Texas, as, on the twenty-fifth day of January, we were touring portions of twenty miles of exist-ing steel bollard border fencing high atop a levee constructed during the George W. Bush administration.

President Trump was days from the State of the Union, where he would be pushing for Congress to fund his "big, beautiful" border wall, including in this part of South Texas, where I was getting an up-close look at the border infrastructure already in place. Still up in the air: a federal budget deal to fund a Trump wall, and the fate of the hun-dreds of thousands of DACA recipients.

We were just out the back door of the Old Hidalgo Pump-house, today a museum and part of the World Birding Center, a global attraction for many bird watchers but a century ago the facility performed exactly what it sounds like: pump water from the Rio Grande to farms along its banks. I was finally visiting the Rio Grande Valley for the first time, now the place where more migrants were crossing into the United States illegally than anywhere else.

The previous month, newly-confirmed homeland security secretary Kirstjen Nielsen had visited the area, proclaiming it would be the first place the Trump administration would build his border wall. I wanted to check it out for myself.

In order to get a local view of what was happening here, our team had linked up with elected officials Judge Ramon Garcia and Commissioner David Fuentes. A generation apart, Garcia was on the precipice of retirement and Fuentes newly elected to the County Commission. Both were Democrats, the rule rather than the exception for local elected officials in the borderlands, despite the national conversation about their home being dominated by Republican talking points. What we were witnessing was familiar to both of them, lifelong residents of the Rio Grande Valley.

"No sir," one of them said to the agent, who was still sitting in the unmarked four-door gold pickup truck he had arrived in, responding to his query about missing migrants. The agent had parked at an electronic gate in front of the fifteen-or-so-foot-tall, rust-colored border barrier.

I ask Garcia, "They're out doing what they do, right?"

"They're out doing their job."

"And this is part of that, I guess," I quip, pointing to the border wall behind us.

As I do so, the agent, stocky and not quite as tall as his pickup, slides down from his seat, boots kicking up dust from the dirt road beneath us. He walks up to an electronic keypad that operates the gate in the fencing.

"Well, as you can see it's not holding them," Garcia points out to me.

"Right. It's not holding them," *them* being the migrants, of course, who were now on the run from the Border Patrol in the brush surrounding the Old Pumphouse.

"Riiight," the judge repeats, with a Texas drawl. "It's a very impractical thing, very expensive thing to construct, and it doesn't work."

The agent taps the code into the keypad, which starts the gate opening, and he jumps back into his truck to search for the "two who went south" as other agents arrive as backup.

"So what you're saying," I say, falling into a verbal tic I have when reporting on camera—repeating back to the subject what they've just told me, "is that even though the president wants to build new stuff, we're seeing in real time an example of people who are crossing right around this fence right here."

"That's correct," Garcia confirmed.

We walked several yards down the dirt road, where the border wall ended, but it became clear we weren't just at the base of a border wall, we were atop a levee here. I peeked over and made note that even without the fifteen-foot border wall on top, the levee itself was not easy to scale.

"There's no wall here but if you look over the edge—come check this out, Carlos," I say, motioning to Carlos "Cao" Huazano, the cameraman who made the trip with Aarne and me from Los Angeles. "We're talking about at least fifteen feet down. You don't have to have a fence in order for it to be a border wall."

"You build a fifteen-foot wall, they'll build eighteen-foot ladders," Commissioner Fuentes responds as my head dangles over the side of the levee, looking at the drop below.

I don't get it, I think to myself. What's the point? If you build it, they will get around it. Maybe the Trump administration knows something I don't.

"The secretary of homeland security came out here, stood right in front of a wall just like this, and said this is gonna be the first place we build new wall in the country. Is that true?"

Fuentes raised his eyebrows, shrugged his shoulders, and cracked a half smile. "You'd probably have to ask her," he said with a chuckle. "You know what I mean?"

I still didn't quite get it, exactly.

"If that's what they're thinking," Fuentes continued, "I think the most natural way would probably be that they'd have to start on federal property. Because I can't see anybody here locally that has already agreed to sell their property."

As we talked, the chase continued, with agents on both sides of the border wall, the Old Pumphouse side and a strange no-man's-land that was in between the wall and the Rio Grande, the real border with Mexico.

Fuentes's point was a good one: here, that no-man's-land was owned by the county, which is why during the Bush administration the federal government was able to make an agreement and build this portion of border fencing here. But it wouldn't be as easy to build elsewhere in the Lone Star State, home to more of the U.S.–Mexico border than anywhere else.

Ninety-five percent of land in the state is privately owned, including much of the border.

Fuentes explained to me that there were only a few miles of border that would be readily available to the Trump administration to build on, and they were owned by the federal government itself, including the Santa Ana Wildlife Refuge, eight and a half miles to the east by car. Off we went.

The refuge is more than two thousand acres and it, too, is a world-class birding destination. It's home to nearly three "river miles" of border—the actual distance of winding Rio Grande that passes through it. But a proposal uncovered by the Sierra Club to build a border wall through it would render most of the park itself a no-man's-land, with a wall built on the existing levee, designed to protect the area from a flood, miles away from the river itself.

I met Jackelin Treviño there, a yoga teacher and student who in her spare time is a volunteer activist for the Sierra Club. She was dressed, like I was, for weather from another part of the country. It was chilly in South Texas, meaning the temperature wouldn't break sixty. Her red pea coat and scarf punched through the gray of the sky, a fog that hung low over the Santa Ana refuge.

As we walked along the levee right out the back door of the visitors' center at the park, Treviño, another lifelong resident of the Rio Grande Valley, gave me a tutorial in how many residents bordering the river have lived there since before the end of the Mexican-American War in 1848, and retained property granted to them by the Spanish before that. It's for that reason, her colleagues at the Sierra Club uncovered, the Army Corps of Engineers ranked the Santa Ana refuge as the place it would be easiest to build new border wall in the area. Most people, as Commissioner Fuentes told me earlier that day, wouldn't sell.

"It is very low-hanging fruit for the administration because it's a federal wildlife refuge and they already own the land," she reminded me.

We entered the park, walking the winding paths and past groups of chachalacas, birds that looked like a cross between a quail and a turkey. They screeched at each other as they battled for territory in the tree branches around us, not able to fly for long distances. Breeding season was approaching. They scared the hell out of me—it felt like a rooster had been placed inside my ear canal.

Treviño brought us to a white lookout tower several stories tall. We climbed the stairs, and at the top, above the tree canopy, we could see smoke rising from Reynosa, Tamaulipas, just across the Rio Grande in Mexico.

"This is the highest elevation," she points out.

"The middle of the Rio Grande is the actual U.S. border, which is miles in that direction," I say, pointing to the smoke cloud over Reynosa. "So in between what they would build as the border wall over there, and the river over here, what would this become?"

"No-man's-land," she replies.

Back down on the levee, it's becoming clear to me that Trump's dream of an end-to-end border wall was destined to be a mirage, at best. Even if Congress gave Trump every penny of the wall funding he was going to lobby for during the State of the Union, it would not be nearly enough to overcome the obvious obstacles.

"The reason they want to build here is there's a chance they can't build anywhere else in Texas," I say to Treviño.

"Right. It will get tied up in courts. Eminent domain law-suits and such," she says, referring to the fact that a third of those cases that started during the George W. Bush adminis-tration are still not resolved. "They could extend another ten, twelve years before construction actually begins."

"So there's a chance that during Donald Trump's presi-dency he may not build any border wall unless he builds it where we're standing right now?"

"Absolutely."

WE RETURNED TO Los Angeles and spent most of the next five days on the back lot at Universal Studios Hollywood. Thanks to our corporate parents at Comcast, it's where the NBC News Los Angeles bureau has been based since 2014, the year before I arrived at the company.

After I wrote out a first draft in a shared Google Doc with producers Mitch and Aarne, we went through several rounds of notes with our bosses in New York on the report we filmed at the border, answering questions about the details of our story. Once we had approvals from Janelle Rodriguez and Betsy Korona, who were both supervising our tiny unit within NBC News from offices inside of 30 Rock back in New York, I carefully crafted an email pitching the story to the senior producers who run the daytime shows on MSNBC, and to the executive producer of *Morning Joe*. I said I envisioned going back down to the border, this time in San Diego, to present the report live on the day of the State of the Union.

The shows bought it and down we went, overnighting in San Diego. Early the following morning, around four, we hopped in the car and drove to the border again, this time nearly two thousand miles to the west. We got set up at a place known to the Border Patrol as Arnie's Point, an overlook where those same primary and secondary fences I had seen on previous trips here, were directly below us, illuminated along with the all-weather road between them by stadium-style lighting. Just beyond it was Colonia Libertad, one community in Mexico through which hundreds of migrants used to cross daily for work, though today they are not able to because of the shift in tactics, including the layers of fencing built by the Border Patrol during the Clinton and Bush administrations.

First up for the day was *Morning Joe*. Camera set, earpiece in, coffee starting to do its thing. It was around half past five local time.

"In tonight's State of the Union address, President Trump is again expected to call on Congress to again fund his border wall," said cohost Mika Brzezinski, on set back at 30 Rock in front of a video image of the White House on the giant digital screen behind her. "But if he does, will it ever be built? MSNBC correspondent Jacob Soboroff went to the U.S. southern border to investigate and he joins us now. Jacob, what did you find out?"

"Here near San Diego, they already have a border wall," I start to explain, doing my best to stick to the script I wrote on the back lot. I swept out my arm to draw attention to the fencing that divides two communities through which for decades people traveled freely.

"The same cannot be said across the country in Texas's Rio Grande Valley, and in fact, that's where, in her first week on the job, the secretary of homeland security said 'this is gonna be the first new place that we build the President Trump border wall.' But residents down there know, and they've known for a long time, that's a promise that's pretty hard to keep."

With that cue, the experiences we had less than a week earlier began broadcasting to the American people: the border patrol chase for the two men who went south around existing border fencing, my conversations with the local elected officials, and finally my tour of the wildlife refuge with Treviño, the Sierra Club activist.

Back live again, I wanted to put as fine a point as I could on our story. "Even if the administration got every penny they asked for to build the wall—twenty-five billion, thirty-five billion—whatever the number is, the reality down there is, it's going to be up to the private landowners of South Texas whether or not this wall ultimately gets built. And get this: from the Bush administration, when they tried to build a wall down there under President George W. Bush, there were around three hundred lawsuits about the wall. Still today, a third of those are tied up in litigation. This is something that might never, ever happen down there even during Donald Trump's presidency, guys."

"Wow, Jacob Soboroff, thank you *very* much for that report," Mika replied. Almost immediately, the on-air conversation shifted to the Russia investigation under way by special counsel Robert Mueller. That, to me, was an indication of how the day might go and another reminder of the vacillating level of interest in what was actually happening at the border.

I was right. I appeared on-air twice more that day, to little effect. "We're clear for the day," I told Aarne, after a phone call with headquarters, in which I learned our services were not going to be needed during our marquee prime-time coverage of the State of the Union. Not even to fact-check President Trump in real time. We packed up our cars and hopped on the freeway. It was only around noon local time, and on both the 805 and 5 there was something missing—an indication of why, it seemed, nobody back in New York was much interested in having us on-air.

For decades, yellow road signs framed both of those freeways as you drove away from the U.S.–Mexico border, with images of a silhouetted mother and father literally pulling their little girl by the arm, ostensibly running across the freeway and away from immigration enforcement. The iconic "immigrant crossing" signs were placed on these very roads by Caltrans, the state agency that oversees highways in California.

At first, according to the *Los Angeles Times,* the signs were text-only, reading "Caution watch for people crossing road." When motorists couldn't digest what they said in time, Caltrans hired John Hood, an artist, to create the image now so familiar to so many drivers in this part of the country.

"It doesn't just mean they are running across the freeway," the *Times* quoted Hood as telling the *San Diego Union-Tribune* in 2005. "It means they are running from something else as well. I think it's a struggle for a lot of things—for opportunities, for freedom."

Now, at a time when migrant crossings, particularly here in the San Diego sector, were near all-time lows, there wasn't a need for the signs. The last one was pulled down in September 2017.

WE MADE IT home in time to catch Trump's State of the Union speech live on television. The president, of course, hammered his immigration applause lines.

"For decades," he boomed, "open borders have allowed drugs and gangs to pour into our most vulnerable communities."

Nobody told him why they took the signs down, I thought to myself, or more likely, he just doesn't care about what's *actually* happening at the border.

President Trump introduced parents of children killed by undocumented immigrant gang members and used their stories as justification for calling on Congress to "close the deadly loopholes that have allowed MS-13, and other criminals, to break into our country. We have proposed new legislation that will fix our immigration laws, and support our ICE and Border Patrol agents, so that this cannot ever happen again."

He went on, at one point strongly implying that he wasn't going to need his border wall to deter migrants from coming into the country: "Crucially, our plan closes the terrible loopholes exploited by criminals and terrorists to enter our country—and it finally ends the dangerous practice of catch and release."

What he didn't say was that this "plan" to "close loopholes," a euphemism for how his administration would deter asylum-seeking families and unaccompanied children from coming to the United States, was already moving from theory to practice.

THE MORNING AFTER the State of the Union, Commander Jonathan White fired off an email to a health and human services colleague. He admitted he had gotten into an argument with Gloria Chavez, the commander of the Border

Patrol's Migration Crisis Action Team, or the MCAT, in Washington.

Chavez was the same Border Patrol official who, in December, had inadvertently admitted to an Office of Refugee Resettlement staffer the Border Patrol had been working on scaling up family separations. Now, she had written Commander White with a request. Chavez wished to better understand the release of unaccompanied minors in the custody of his department. Children who were separated would be rendered "unaccompanied," despite the fact they didn't arrive as such.

> Good afternoon. Can you assist with the below? I
> found the below statement on your HHS website and am
> wondering if one of you are available to discuss further.
> We are trying to get educated on the below process as it
> pertains to UACs and their sponsors.

White politely replied, "yes—we sure can." Still, Chavez's request annoyed White, who wrote to his colleague to suggest it might be better for someone else to help with her request.

> I alienated this group last week when I called BS
> on the DHS argument that the combination of the MOA
> [Memorandum of Understanding] and a new policy to
> separate children from family units and designate them
> UAC [Unaccompanied Alien Children] would only require
> 4,000 DHS ORR beds for the MOA and 9,000 for the
> MOA plus family unit separation. So we can start cutting

beds now! According to DHS' estimates. So I need to be
solicitous and kind to them today.

Bed space, technically speaking, is the number of children the agency can care for. Each bed comes with a cost,
and that money needs to be appropriated by Congress.
Chavez was arguing for a reduction in the number of beds
from current levels. Commander White found that ludi-
crous in the face of a potential separation policy and an
in-development memorandum of understanding signed between Health and Human Services and the Department of
Homeland Security.

The controversial document would require the fingerprinting of all members of a household in which a minor
discharged from ORR custody would live, including undocumented family members. Commander White feared both
would slow discharge rates, thereby creating a need for more
beds, not fewer, as Chavez was suggesting.

Commander White's team had calculated that those policies, if enacted, would require a threefold increase in the
number of children referred to ORR. His estimate was that
over thirty thousand beds would be necessary in a worst-case
scenario. Despite the fact that a DHS statistician had mod-
eled the same number as Commander White's team, Chavez
claimed the number was too high, as it did not account for the
broader deterrence effect of both policies.

That set off Commander White, who, in essence, called
bullshit on the argument directly to Chavez. That meant, at
least for today, he wanted someone else to speak with her.

"Got it!" his colleague wrote back.

February 20, 2018

"That's it?"

I was staring through a tiny hole in the sheet metal of "primary" border fence in Otay Mesa, California, six miles to the east of the San Ysidro crossing where I had, by now, visited many times.

"That. Is. It," replied Border Patrol agent Lance LeNoir, not lacking bravado. "That's the infamous lowering bathroom floor entry."

"What do you mean?"

"The bathroom floor literally lowered down to provide access to the tunnel."

"So, inside that warehouse," I said, while again peeking into Mexico to see the giant white industrial building with a turquoise stripe across the top, "the bathroom floor just goes down and you get into the tunnel?"

"Yeah," confirmed LeNoir, wearing tan fatigues and a hat with a black American flag on the side of it, a uniform different from the green of most Border Patrol agents.

I had been to Otay Mesa before, in 2016, when Agent Wendi Lee told me the Border Patrol can "manage with what we have" and didn't need candidate Trump's border wall. My return trip was the first day of a planned month of shooting for the *Dateline* documentary hour I had been asked to front the month before. The project would be led by *Dateline* producer Izhar Harpaz. The Israeli-American Harpaz, eccentric and quirky and insanely organized, would be supported by Simon Doolittle, a *Dateline* field producer out of Columbus, Ohio, and our unit.

Before we went down in the tunnel, I interviewed Chief

Rodney Scott, a Border Patrol agent for decades who worked his way up from patrol agent to chief of the San Diego sector, the largest in the nation. He brought us back to Arnie's Point, where we had broadcast from the previous month on the day of the State of the Union. Chief Scott knew how things used to be at this exact spot in the early nineties when migrants literally ran into the United States daily for work, often turning around and going home the same day.

"We were outnumbered back then," he told me, looking out at a valley where not a single migrant was in sight. "You've got a group of a couple of hundred coming at you. When I say coming at you, they're not coming at you, they're not coming at the whole shift, they're just coming at you and your partner in that canyon.

"I remember in 1994 when management came out and they said they have to figure out how to restore law and order and they came up with a deterrent strategy," Chief Scott said, using a word I would hear time and again along the border. Humanitarian groups believe the Clinton-era policy of "prevention through deterrence," while leading to a drop in border crossings, also made those crossings purposefully more dangerous and deadly.

It's an uncomfortable conversation for some in "the resistance" to have: in nearly three decades of deterrence-based bipartisan immigration policy, starting with Clinton, the United States border with Mexico has become increasingly militarized. Consequentially, fewer migrants have attempted to cross the southern border, but the most desperate among them haven't stopped trying. Moreover, the number of people who die trying to cross in more dangerous and deadly areas has remained constant.

Clinton built the first modern wave of "infrastructure," the euphemism for fences, levees, and walls to keep people out. Under George W. Bush, in post-9/11 America, border and immigration enforcement became a part of the Department of Homeland Security. The size of the departments exploded as additional border fencing and interior enforcement went up. Under Barack Obama, more people were deported than under any other administration, earning him the nickname "Deporter in Chief." Prisonlike facilities—including some with cages—were built to process an influx of unaccompanied Central American minors seeking asylum in 2014, during Obama's second term. Once it started, deterrence, as a government policy, never stopped. The idea is that scaring people would stop them from coming to the United States; instead migrants just kept going to different parts of the border to avoid the deterrents put into place.

Whatever you think of the policy, I pointed out to Scott, the numbers were nearly as low as they've ever been.

"You're welcome," he deadpanned.

THE GALVEZ SMUGGLING tunnel between Tijuana and Otay Mesa was a by-product of deterrence. I now stood at its mouth with Agent Lance LeNoir.

"Sometimes we'll see twelve in one year, sometimes we'll see four or five," LeNoir told me of his Confined Spaces Entry Team. They call themselves the Tunnel Rats.

He and his colleagues in this elite Border Patrol unit threw a ruby-red harness over my street clothes, tossed me a helmet and work gloves, and attached a safety cable with a carabiner to my harness.

"Here we go," I said, stepping into the void. It was a seventy-foot descent by ladder. The tunnel was so deep the ladder had several spots along the way to get off and rest before continuing down to the muddy floor below.

"Watch your head and buttonhook to the left!" shouted an agent once I got to the bottom.

I had never seen anything like it.

"Oh, wow!" I said. "Is this a pretty standard tunnel?"

"No, this is definitely not standard. This is like the Cadillac of tunnels."

"The Cadillac of tunnels," I marveled. "Who built this thing?"

"Mostly low-level guys told to dig in a straight line."

"Told by who? Cartels?"

"That's a safe assumption," LeNoir said.

Soil and water sloshed under our feet; cars and trucks hummed overhead, speeding into the Otay Mesa Port of Entry. At one point, I started to get dizzy, keeping that detail to myself as I leaned back against the wall and the crew watched LeNoir and I talk. He was unfazed, not even buckling the chin strap on his helmet when I had tightened mine within millimeters of suffocating myself, somehow thinking that would save my life if the roof collapsed in on us in an earthquake.

"Once you're deep enough," I asked LeNoir, "you can go as far as you want?"

"Mmhmm."

"You can get under just about anything?"

LeNoir nodded and allowed himself a single-word response. "Right."

"Including a border fencing or a border wall?"

"Yes. As long as they can get from point A to point B in secret, they're gonna do it."

"You anticipate finding more of these?"

"Oh yeah. Stick around. There'll be something," LeNoir said with certainty.

We all climbed back out of the tunnel. The fresh air and sun and dust kicking up from the all-weather road in the shadow of the flimsy border fencing never felt so good.

Our first *Dateline* shoot day in the books, we packed up and headed toward San Diego before making our way to the Arizona border. As we did, something about that tunnel nagged at me. I had already learned that most hard narcotics are coming through legal ports of entry, and that marijuana smuggling, the type of bulky load that tunnels were perfect for, was declining because of the same pot legalization in California I had been reporting on. Apprehensions of migrants looking to sneak across were near all-time lows, too. Further, after forcing a brief government shutdown following his State of the Union, Trump balked, signing a budget that did not fund his border wall (nor fix the problem he created for DACA recipients).

So what was the point of that tunnel tour? Part of me felt a little hoodwinked, like what we just saw was a cheesy public relations stunt—how a Hollywood producer would draw up a border scene if it was on the back lot at Universal by my office. I wasn't even the first reporter at my own organization to tour it—the Border Patrol had taken Steve Patterson, fellow NBC News correspondent, down for a look in 2016.

The truth was the San Diego border was by all accounts relatively quiet. If Otay Mesa, where the tunnel was dug years earlier, was of any great import to the plan President Trump had announced at the State of the Union to deter migration, it was the ICE detention center here, not the tunnel.

Indeed, locked up there was the Congolese asylum seeker who for the last four months had been separated from her daughter, now in an ORR shelter in Chicago. For all the border reporting I had done since I was here last, nothing about her crossed my radar. But others were on the case.

February 26, 2018

As the ACLU's lead attorney fighting the Trump administration's Muslim ban, Lee Gelernt knew well how the White House was attempting to use policy to stop migrants from entering the United States. For the first year of the Trump presidency, he battled multiple versions of the ban in court. By December 2017, the administration had narrowed the policy to pass muster at the Supreme Court, allowing the United States to block residents from mostly Muslim-majority countries and nominally making waivers available for residents of those nations.

"It discriminates on the basis of religion," Gelernt told NPR when the ACLU first challenged the executive order in 2017.

Gelernt has the air of an avuncular college professor. He's always slightly disheveled, his thick plastic-frame black glasses often perched where his hairline met his scalp. On TV, he sometimes looked exhausted, and rightly so.

Gelernt, as the deputy director and chief litigator for the ACLU's Immigrants' Rights Project, had been chasing his second massive case of the Trump era. After Lomi Kriel's article in the *Houston Chronicle* revealed the Border Patrol had been separating hundreds of children in the El Paso area, two national outlets followed her. Both the *New York Times* and *Washington Post*, on the same December day, confirmed the Trump administration was again considering a national family separation policy, the same story colleague Julia Ainsley broke back in March 2017.

The *Times* cited evidence from a consortium of groups, including KIND, the Women's Refugee Commission, and other organizations, many of which had submitted questions to ORR the previous month at their stakeholder meeting. Those organizations and others, including the Florence Immigrant & Refugee Rights Project in Arizona, were signatories to a letter in December sent to the Department of Homeland Security's Office of Civil Rights and Civil Liberties and the DHS acting inspector general, the two institutional checks on abuses of power or violation of policy within the department.

The letter documented 155 cases of family separation, including ninety in the last quarter of the year. The separated migrants had come from Honduras, El Salvador, Mexico, and Guatemala.

"Our organizations have for years and in great detail documented the immense trauma created by the separation of family members and the impact of separation on their ability to pursue legal immigration relief," they wrote. "The separation of parents from their children at the U.S.–Mexico border and within the United States, absent justifiable child protection grounds, is so fundamentally unconscionable it defies countless international and domestic laws on child welfare, human rights, and refugees."

Gelernt was keeping tabs on all of it, clueless of how many children in total were being taken away from their parents, but certain of one thing: "the administration wasn't *considering* the separation of children from their parents—it was already doing it," he later wrote.

He was convinced he needed to file a class action lawsuit as soon as he could to stop family separations. Gelernt viewed the policy as a clear violation of the due process rights of families. But he didn't have a separated parent to represent. That changed when Gelernt received a tip that led him to Otay Mesa and the Congolese woman whose six-year-old daughter had been sent to Chicago.

Gelernt flew out to San Diego from New York as quickly as he could, along with an asylum lawyer and a Lingala translator. The mother appeared "distraught" when the team met her.

"Dressed in a detention jumpsuit and gaunt from not eating or sleeping, she was wary at first, though she smiled when I attempted to say hello in Lingala," Gelernt recalled in an essay he penned for *The New York Review of Books*. "Through a translator, she explained to the asylum lawyer and me that she feared for her and her daughter's lives, and that the Catholic Church helped them flee. They traveled through ten countries over four months, and requested asylum when they legally presented themselves" at the San Ysidro Port of Entry.

When she was handcuffed and her daughter was taken from her, she heard the child scream, "Don't take me away from my mommy!" Gelernt explained, "That was the last time they would see each other for months, even though [she] had passed her asylum screening interview."

Neither Gelernt nor the ACLU had enough evidence to

file a class action lawsuit. But he felt the situation was so dire and urgent that he needed to sue immediately to help. They did, and the Congolese woman and her six-year-old daughter became *Ms. L.* and *S.S.* The defendants were a who's who of Trump administration officials and agencies, as underscored in the first paperwork associated with the case.

Ms. L.,
Petitioner-Plaintiff
v.

U.S. Immigration and Customs Enforcement ("ICE"); U.S. Department of Homeland Security ("DHS"); U.S. Customs and Border Protection ("CBP"); U.S. Citizenship and Immigration Services ("USCIS"); U.S. Department of Health and Human Services ("HHS"); Office of Refugee Resettlement ("ORR"); Thomas Homan, Acting Director of ICE; Greg Archambeault, San Diego Field Office Director, ICE; Joseph Greene, San Diego Assistant Field Office Director, ICE, Otay Detention Facility; Kirstjen Nielsen, Secretary of DHS; Jefferson Beauregard Sessions III, Attorney General of the United States; Kevin K. McAleenan, Acting Commissioner of CBP; L. Francis Cissna, Director of USCIS; Pete Flores, San Diego Field Director, CBP; Fred Figueroa, Warden, Otay Mesa Detention Center; Alex Azar, Secretary of the Department of Health and Human Services; Scott Lloyd, Director of the Office of Refugee Resettlement,

Respondents-Defendants.

"This is an immigration case involving the United States government's forcible separation of plaintiff from her seven (7) year-old-daughter, S.S.," the lawsuit began.

The message from the ACLU to the Trump administration about family separations was clear: we'll see you in court. While Gelernt and his colleagues were, for the time being, only representing one mother and daughter, they would soon have the evidence they needed to raise the stakes significantly.

THE SAME DAY Ms. L.'s suit was filed in court, the *Dateline* crew and I made our way to Mission, Texas. There, Border Patrol agent Robert Rodriguez took us beneath the Anzalduas Bridge to show us where most migrants entering the Rio Grande Valley sector of the border turned themselves in after illegally swimming or rafting across the river. An increasing number of them were using this tactic in order to seek asylum when legal ports of entry, like the one Ms. L. and her daughter used to enter in San Diego, were effectively closed by a process known as "metering," or limiting the number of people who would be let in on any given day.

After we had left the tunnels of Otay Mesa six days earlier, we crossed the border into Tijuana, Mexico, the nation's most violent city. At the time the city was experiencing six murders a day. We literally held our noses to go into the morgue where dozens of bodies were kept in refrigerators, most of them homicide victims. And we had met the leader of a human smuggling ring who crossed migrants into the United States for a living and who said nothing, including Trump's wall, would stop people from paying him to get into the United States. But the situation on the ground in Tijuana, and the way people crossed there, was nothing like the crossing under the Anzalduas.

The bridge itself is the longest international bridge between the United States and Mexico, and once a migrant makes it across the Rio Grande, there's still thousands of steps to go before they will find a Border Patrol agent, usually on the levee that we were standing on, that will take them into custody.

The Trump administration claimed migrants were entering the country in this way in order to exploit American laws, bringing their children because they had a better chance of gaining protections and avoiding deportation. The families told a different story. It was there I met Edwin and Edwin Jr., who arrived from Honduras with only the clothes on their backs—the father in a leather jacket and light blue polo shirt, his hair recently trimmed. His son, a full head and shoulders shorter than him, was wearing a gray hoodie under a puffy vest, hands tucked in his pockets while he tried to push his face down into it as well.

"Why did you come to the United States?" I asked him.

"Because we have a lot of problems in our country," he said in Spanish, which I could make out. Agent Rodriguez translated the rest.

"He has his business, but he can no longer work safely, is what he's saying."

"Were you scared to come to the United States?" I asked Edwin Jr.

"Sí," the little boy, maybe six years old, replied.

"Por qué?" I asked back. He shot his eyes over to Agent Rodriguez, then back to me.

"Porqué gente mala—muchas," I heard as he tucked his face back into his clothes.

"A lot of bad people, a lot of bad guys," I said back to him.

They intended to seek asylum, and Edwin Sr. brought with him a driver's license and birth certificate to give over to American authorities. I thanked them for talking, and they were loaded into the back of a white van operated by a contractor to be taken for processing, likely at a facility I was unaware existed but would, in a matter of months, see for myself.

Agent Rodriguez said nothing about separations, and I didn't know to ask.

THE NEXT DAY we flew from South Texas to Arizona, where we would again meet with the Border Patrol.

While we were in the air across the southwest, a calendar invite was sent to ORR for a call the following day. "FW: Separated family discussion ICE and CBP," the subject read. The call would take place on the "EROLD conference line," the Enforcement and Removal Operations Law Division inside Immigration and Customs Enforcement, or ICE. The Department of Homeland Security's Office of General Counsel and the Office of the Principal Legal Advisor at ICE, of which EROLD was a part, had organized the meeting.

It would be another major opportunity for those looking to expose family separations to hear what was being planned. If anybody knew what was going on with family separations, it would be ICE. Separations would be carried out on the front line by the Border Patrol, but in order to get separated parents and children to adult detention and ORR shelters, respectively, ICE would have to transport them.

Claire Trickler-McNulty came to government service from the nonprofit sector, hoping to help change ICE from the inside. After leaving an organization providing care for migrant adults, she worked her way up through the ranks at ICE, ultimately rising to become the deputy assistant director of the Office of Detention Policy and Planning, in charge of custody policy reform and managing ICE's detention networks.

"I focused my whole career on adult detention," she explained to me, and "stayed to hold down what I was working on" when President Trump took office. But her office, she said, was dismantled within the first weeks of the administration. Undaunted, McNulty decided to stay the course and keep her job. As the number of family separations along the border started increasing without warning, she was getting word it was presenting challenges to the agents in the field. McNulty was seeing lists of children saying they were separated—sent to ICE by ORR in an attempt to reconnect the families.

"We knew we should be able to track who was who. ICE's goal was to remove both," she later told me, meaning deport parents and children together. "It's in ICE's interest to know" they were separated. But nobody could seem to easily figure out if families were, in fact, separated. That was because the IT systems used by the different component agencies that had actively been separating kids, CBP, ICE, and the Border Patrol, all used different programs to keep track of people in their custody, and those systems did not talk to each other.

That made it, according to McNulty, "much harder, longer, and more complicated to trace back kids—and created a greater possibility for error."

She wasn't alone, and colleagues of hers within ICE were actively working to fix the back-end system that was making family reunifications difficult, if not impossible, in some cases.

"Problem, proposal, solution" is how she thought of it,

and she explained as much to the lawyers at ICE who would be on the phone call the following day. If children were going to be separated, McNulty was going to make sure a solution would be worked out.

WE ARRIVED IN Tucson that night and drove straight to the border.

It was pouring rain and pitch black when we arrived in the Organ Pipe Cactus National Monument, part of the Sonoran Desert in southern Arizona. The dirt road we are driving on is rapidly filling with water. My head is pounding. An intermittent flash of a bright blue light disrupts the void outside. It's a rescue beacon, affixed atop a tower, meant to signal safety for anyone out here in distress. We pulled up to it, and got out.

The United States–Mexico border is off in the distance, maybe over that mountain, or the other one, or along a horizon I can't even see because my eyes are filled with water. In that moment, it's not hard to understand why this has been the most deadly place for migrants to attempt to cross illegally into the United States.

Crippled by a migraine, I try puking. The only thing rising from my throat is a nasty, painful bunch of air as the muscles contract. Every attempt is making it worse, even though for the last hour I've been nursing a Gatorade I bought for the journey out here. Every drop of rainwater on my head feels like a sledgehammer. And anything and everything else going on around is amplifying my symptoms—including my anxiety.

This "hostile terrain" is exactly where the Clinton administration predicted, in a government document, they would "force" migrants to cross when they enacted their "prevention through deterrence" border enforcement strategy. They were right. Here alone, in the Border Patrol's Tucson sector, nearly three thousand have died since then. The local medical examiner's office in Pima County has more than nine hundred unidentified remains believed to be migrants. They find them in and around places just like where I am right now, and have since the first wave of fencing was put up here, along the border with Sonora, Mexico. Of those who die, some starve, many die of heat exhaustion, while others are killed by animals whose venom is too potent to overcome without medical attention.

I came here, fortunately, before reading Luís Alberto Urrea's book *The Devil's Highway,* the true story of twenty-six Mexican men who attempted to traverse this isolated and dangerous part of the border in 2001. Only twelve of them survived. Those who brutally perished in 115-degree heat are known as the "Yuma 14." Of one of the men's final moments, Urrea wrote, he "felt death catching up to him. It was a force that came from outside him. He tried to outwalk it, but it was faster, stronger than he. He stumbled. He thought it was no use to fight any longer—the battle was finished. Death caught his clothing, and he started to fall asleep as he walked, knowing he would fall and never awaken."

Now directly above me, that blue light keeps flashing. It's supposedly visible for miles in all directions, but the Yuma 14 never saw it, or any of the dozens operated by the Border Patrol. The beacons didn't exist when they died, but amid intense public scrutiny of the deterrence strategy and the rising death toll, the government set them up. The first thing you notice when you look closely at the base of one, if you're not delusional from dehydration or starvation or suffering from severe bodily injury, are panels that show, in English, Spanish, and pictographs, what to do if you need help.

I'm standing with the people who would rescue you if you pushed the button. Two Border Patrol agents, Chris and Dan, brought our crew out here to experience what crossing the Sonoran Desert in the dead of night is really like. The ordeal did me in. I couldn't move from the front seat of a white and green Border Patrol Suburban. Chris tells me he's provided intravenous fluids for migrants found out here countless times. But he's not offering me an IV—just an offer to turn around and head back to the Border Patrol station we set off from hours earlier. I take him up on it.

I feel like a chickenshit. I bet the agents are of the same opinion. Tens of thousands of migrants have traversed this desert before me, and I can't handle being bucked out here in a Border Patrol four-wheel-drive SUV to learn how it "really" is. As we head back toward the Border Patrol station, where we set out from, there's no way to avoid thinking about the thousands of lives lost and the desert crossers who made it— all far stronger than my weak constitution. Chances are, one of them is living or working near, with, or for you.

Who would ever choose to take this journey, or a risk like it? People like Juan, who, to provide for his family, had crossed into Arizona twice after the deaths of the Yuma 14. Some of the most desperate people on earth.

SUCH PEOPLE WERE the subject of the call on ICE's EROLD conference line the following day. A technical issue preventing the sharing of information between agencies was complicating reunifications of separated parents. ICE and ORR couldn't easily tell if the Border Patrol had separated a child.

Everyone knew what they were seeing on the ground—ICE, ORR, and of course the Border Patrol, whose agents were doing the separation. But reunifications were not happening expeditiously or easily.

The solution was an IT change: a simple box Border Patrol agents would check as they processed migrants, like the one Jennifer Podkul had suggested to ORR in January, to indicate if a parent and child were separated. In the meantime, they would use a workaround by looking at background data manually in each of the systems.

While ORR continued to find out more about the challenges ICE was facing, McNulty, who was not on the line, was feeling mounting pressure. She and others scrambled to find a solution, if not to stop separations, to at least make sure families could be put back together as quickly as possible.

"It was very stressful. This was awful and I felt like kids were being traumatized and abused."

FOUR DAYS LATER, on Saturday March 3, Tyler Houlton, the press secretary for the Department of Homeland Security, forwarded a request for information about Ms. L, the separated Congolese asylum seeker, from the Washington Post Editorial Board to top DHS staff.

> Here is the latest inquiry from WaPo. Every major
> outlet asked about specifics on Wednesday. Any updated
> language/guidance would be very helpful. I don't imagine
> this is going away any time soon. Thanks.

Chad Wolf, Secretary Nielsen's chief of staff who in December 2017 shared a draft of the family separation policy with Gene Hamilton, the aide to Attorney General Jeff Sessions, sent it along to Nielsen.

> Ma'am,
>
> [For your situational awareness]—we're receiving a number of press inquiries regarding an asylum seeking Congolese woman and her child who have been separated and are currently in detention facilities.

Wolf pasted a statement that was currently being distributed to the press. It began "DHS does not currently have a policy of separating women and children."

Nielsen wrote back, making sure that Wolf knew that news about Ms. L was "also one of the stories I asked about last week."

Two days later, Ms. L was abruptly released.

The statement Wolf sent to Nielsen directly contradicted what the ACLU, Ms. L's lawyer, was seeing on the ground. While the ACLU was able to win her release from detention in San Diego with the help of a DNA test, separations were continuing. Lee Gelernt returned to federal court, this time to expand Ms. L's case into a class-action suit against the federal government.

"Whether or not the Trump administration wants to call this a 'policy,' it certainly is engaged in a widespread practice of tearing children away from their parents," he said in a statement on March 9. "A national class-action lawsuit is appropriate because this is a national practice."

···

I am a citizen of Guatemala and am seeking asylum in the United States. When I came to the United States, I presented myself at the border at San Ysidro, California, asking for asylum.

I came to the United States on or around April 20, 2018, with my biological son, E-Z-G-A. My child is from Guatemala and seeking asylum.

When we came to the United States, we reported at San Ysidro, California, and said that I wanted to seek asylum.

Shortly after arriving, I was told that I was going to be separated from my son. There were no doubts expressed that I was my son's biological mother and I have a birth certificate to show our relationship. They did not say that I was a danger to my son or was abusive.

I was sent to the Eloy Detention Center in April 2018. My children were sent to an ORR facility in Phoenix, Arizona.

I have not seen my children for 1 month. I worry about E-Z-G-A constantly and I don't know when I will see them. We have talked on the phone only once. I was given a number to call, but no one answers the phone. I hope I can be with my child very soon. I miss him and am scared for him.

I declare under penalty of perjury under the laws of the United States of America that the foregoing is true and correct, based on my personal knowledge. Executed in April 24, 2018.

—DECLARATION OF MS. M.M.A.L.

MS. L V. ICE

CHAPTER FIVE

"Get Rid of the List"

April 3, 2018

Strapped into red webbed jump seats in the back of a hulking C-130 Hercules transport plane, Aarne and I lifted off from McGuire Air Force Base in New Jersey. Once at cruising altitude, we were invited to climb into the cockpit to say hello to the pilot. We discovered an airman who looked like he had just graduated from high school.

"What's it like to fly up here?" Aarne asked him nervously, trying to feel him out.

"I don't know," he said. "Never flown this route before."

Aarne looked at me like he was going to pass out.

A full year before the ACLU had accused the Trump administration of carrying out a "national practice" of separating parents and children at the border, then homeland security secretary John Kelly justified a potential separation policy by saying he wanted to deter people from traveling on what he called an "awful network," the dangerous journey from Central America, through Mexico, and to the United States. Then, and now, if you want to understand why a record number of Central Americans are migrating to the United States, the country of Greenland, of all places, is a great place to start.

Erin McGarry, the head of the NBC News weather unit, had lined up rare access with NASA to fly to Thule Air Base in Greenland, 750 miles north of the Arctic Circle. Once there, we'd hitch a ride on their P3 Orion, a former spy plane, now being used for Operation IceBridge, a mission designed to buy scientists time as they put an advanced satellite into orbit that would measure land and sea ice levels at climate change's ground zero.

Thule in the spring is lovely. The low temperature the day we landed was negative fifteen degrees Fahrenheit, and the mercury spiked at three above zero. After we deplaned we got a tour of the base, including the hangar that housed NASA's team, then drove down to the sea ice to go dogsledding with a local who has seen the climate changing in real time.

First thing the following morning, I left Aarne and Erin behind—there were only so many seats aboard IceBridge—and we took off for what was scheduled to be an all-day flight at the ridiculously low altitude of 1,500 feet. Our destination was Petermann Glacier.

John Sontag, mission scientist and navigator of the trip, was able to break away from keeping us on track and we talked about why Operation IceBridge and funding for it—at risk under President Trump—was so critical.

"What you guys see up here every year is what climate change actually looks like," I said to him.

"Yeah, this is kind of the front lines of climate change," Sontag replied.

"That sea level rise here is what we all feel down at home."

"Yeah, if you take away some of the sea ice, you make the whole planet darker and make it more able to absorb the sun's energy."

When we were talking, I was thinking about sea level rise I had seen covering Hurricane Irma while in Miami. Only now can I make the connection to the Dry Corridor in Central America. Cutting through Honduras, El Salvador, and Guatemala, it's a massive stretch of land in which its residents are suffering from severe malnutrition and poverty, exacerbated by a years-long drought due to the climate variability of El Niño. Rising temperatures are also fueling a rapidly spreading fungus affecting coffee leaves, the region's cash crop and livelihood for tens of thousands, at higher-than-ever altitudes, and in so doing, destroying lives.

People in Central America were starving to death, in part because of warming here in the Arctic, and it was driving hundreds of thousands to flee to the United States, the same people President Trump was trying to stop from coming. Bouncing around violently through the turbulence as we traversed Petermann Glacier, I had no idea I was on the front lines of a crisis playing out over 4,000 miles away in Guatemala. This, however, was not where Donald Trump was looking for a solution.

THREE DAYS LATER we flew home from Thule, this time on a military passenger jet carrying troops and their family members back to the States. The same day, President Trump issued a memorandum for a select group of his cabinet members: the secretary of defense, the attorney general, the secretary of health and human services, and the secretary of homeland security. The subject: "Ending 'Catch and Release' at the Border of the United States and Directing Other Enhancements to Immigration Enforcement."

President Trump was seeing the number of migrants illegally crossing the southern border steadily rise. After he was inaugurated, migrants were at first holding back because of Trump's tough talk, arriving in smaller numbers: under 400,000 were taken into custody in Trump's first full year in office—as low as that number had been in decades. Though the numbers were still below those of the final year of the Obama administration, a graph showing an increase was posted regularly on the website of Customs and Border Protection. The "Trump Effect," as agents on the front lines called it, was wearing off. In March 2018, more than 50,000 migrants were detained trying to enter the United States illegally. The year before, the number had been only 16,794.

Trump's memo had a deliverable: by mid-May, end the practice of releasing migrants apprehended at the border to the interior of the country while they wait for their immigration court case to be adjudicated.

> Within forty-five days of the date of this memorandum,
> the Secretary of Homeland Security, in coordination with
> the Secretary of Defense, the Attorney General, and the
> Secretary of Health and Human Services, shall submit a
> report to the President detailing all measures that their
> respective departments have pursued or are pursuing to
> expeditiously end "catch and release" practices.

Forty-five days. The clock was now ticking.

One of the agencies directed by President Trump to end "catch and release," the Department of Justice, got to work that same day. Attorney General Jeff Sessions, in a message to all U.S. attorneys' offices on the Southwest border, announced the implementation of a "zero tolerance" prosecution policy for those stopped crossing the border illegally—including asylum seekers. During the Obama and Bush administrations, most migrants apprehended were charged with a civil offense and allowed to proceed with their immigration cases in immigration court. But the Trump administration wanted to change that, sending every migrant caught into the federal court system to stand against criminal charges.

"The implementation of the Attorney General's zero-tolerance policy comes as the Department of Homeland Security reported a 203 percent increase in illegal border crossings from March 2017 to March 2018," a press release announcing the plan declared, ignoring the fact those were still near-record-low numbers, continuing "a 37 percent increase from February 2018 to March 2018—the largest month-to-month increase since 2011."

The practical impact of Sessions's direction, as members of the Obama administration had debated and discovered but never implemented, would be profound. If you were a parent traveling with your child and charged under the zero tolerance plan, that meant you would be separated from your child in order to be charged in criminal court. Your child would be referred to the Office of Refugee Resettlement having been rendered "unaccompanied."

"To those who wish to challenge the Trump administration's commitment to public safety, national security, and the rule of law, I warn you," Sessions said in a statement, "illegally entering this country will not be rewarded, but will instead be met with the full prosecutorial powers of the Department of

Justice. To the Department's prosecutors, I urge you: promoting and enforcing the rule of law is vital to protecting a nation, its borders, and its citizens. You play a critical part in fulfilling these goals, and I thank you for your continued efforts in seeing to it that our laws—and as a result, our nation—are respected."

KEVIN MCALEENAN, PRESIDENT Trump's commissioner of Customs and Border Protection, who had been confirmed by the Senate in March, also received Trump's memo. McAleenan, too, wanted to end "catch and release" and had been involved in some of the Trump administration's earliest conversations about family separations, but he also believed that one potential way to stop catch and release was to address the "push factors" fueling migration in the first place, including a changing climate.

As I flew home from Greenland, aid flowing from Washington to Central America to alleviate and mitigate the effects of the climate-caused drought and food insecurity was working. The United States Agency for International Development was funding a variety of programs that targeted communities in which extreme poverty and malnutrition were pushing residents to leave for the United States, the best option left to help their families.

Guatemalans were heading north by the tens of thousands, most from regions affected by drought or climate change from the country's western highlands to the arid center of the country. In the north of Guatemala, the Department of Petén, where Juan and José lived, was also feeling the effects of a changing climate.

"Four million hectares of sub-tropical forest are found in

Guatemala, 70% of which are located within natural protected areas like the Maya Biosphere Reserve in the department of Petén," USAID reported in an analysis of Guatemala's environment. "Guatemala is one of the most vulnerable countries to the impacts of climate change which disproportionately affect rural indigenous farmers and exacerbate poor land management practices."

That instability caused by climate change was creating an opening for drug cartels moving narcotics from South and Central America through Mexico and into the United States, with many farmers in the region finding the drug trade more lucrative than their work in unreliable fields.

President Trump, however, was no fan of foreign aid, even if it kept farmers afloat and potential migrants at home. He still felt the same way after evidence was presented to his administration later in 2018 by Custom and Border Protection, which showed climate change and variability were fueling the food insecurity driving migration. The administration ultimately ignored the consequences of climate change, which candidate Trump had called a Chinese hoax, when in 2019 it defunded programs to mitigate its effects, instead choosing to continue punishing migrants when they made it to the United States in lieu of helping them at home. But punishing migrants was a strategy that was already well underway by the time Juan and José were faced with a life-changing decision.

THE FIFTEENTH DAY of April in Petén, Guatemala, Juan's brother received a phone call. The farmworker picked up his cell and an unknown voice asked to speak with Juan urgently. He raced to his brother's home, the one up the hill from the soccer field. When he arrived, another call came through from the same man.

Juan took the phone.

"Something's wrong," Juan told his brother after hanging up. He was shaken by what he had heard.

Juan's nephew had sold a car that was still legally registered in Juan's name. The new owner, who Juan believed to be a member of a drug cartel, wanted him to sign paperwork turning over ownership of the car, something Juan did not think he had the right to do. If he didn't, the man threatened, he would be killed, and he feared, so would his son José.

Juan, a devout evangelical Christian, was terrified. He thought of his family, María and their two girls. He knew what could happen if he tried to push back. Any dispute with someone threatening his life was not one he wanted to have. In a place where narco-violence was commonplace and murders were not unusual, he felt as though he faced certain death.

Juan, who had twice before made the journey to the United States, believed doing it again, this time with his son, was his only way to survive. His wife and daughters, also in danger, would seek shelter outside of his home. And he told his brother that in the face of the threat he had just received, he felt he needed to leave the country as soon as possible. He would start planning the journey immediately.

April 18, 2018

"Threat" was how Commander Jonathan White, in drafting a memo for Scott Lloyd, the Trump-appointed head of the Office of Refugee Resettlement and the man with legal custody of thousands of migrant children, characterized the specter of wide-scale family separations in the fall of 2017.

Commander White had worked for Lloyd until March, when he sought out another role within HHS outside of ORR in protest of Lloyd's attempts to stop all female unaccompanied minors from having abortions. It was a blow for the department—Commander White and his years of institutional knowledge about caring for migrant children would take a post within the office of the assistant secretary for preparedness and response, the arm of Health and Human Services that responds to natural disasters and outbreaks.

The following month, Caitlin Dickerson, the award-winning *New York Times* immigration reporter, was digging into family separations. She had obtained data showing family separations were no longer an initiative isolated to certain parts of the border, but a widespread practice, just as the ACLU had alleged in federal court. Less than two weeks after President Trump issued his memorandum to end catch-and-release, Dickerson had in hand documents that showed far more migrant children were separated from their parents in government custody than had previously been reported. And, after presenting the Trump administration with what she knew, she was waiting for answers.

"Hi," wrote Dickerson on a Wednesday afternoon to officials at the Department of Health and Human Services, the federal entity ORR is a part of. "We've passed my deadline. Where are we on a response to these questions?"

Two days before Dickerson, on the verge of breaking her story, sent the email to HHS, I was on the Arizona border shooting our *Dateline* NBC special near the small town of Arivaca. It was there I had my second visit with rancher Tom Kay, a cowboy pushing eighty years old who this time, to stay comfortable, wore white sneakers with his white cowboy hat instead of boots. My last trip here, I picked up a pistol off his dashboard to ask him what it was for.

"It's just safety," he told me as we drove in his pickup truck not far from his ranch, where on his own personal stretch of border he claimed to have once seen a migrant crossing through it with an AK-47. "We don't know who's stopped on the road here."

The following day I met some of those who might soon be traveling through Tom Kay's land, and they didn't have an AK-47. After crossing the border into Nogales, Sonora, from Nogales, Arizona, the *Dateline* crew and I met a family from Nicaragua at the Juan Bosco Migrant Shelter, set on a hillside overlooking a train station and the city below. They explained to me they were getting ready to cross the border.

"Everyone wants to come to the U.S.?" I asked the mother of the family inside the church attached to the shelter, a small white building topped with a solitary cross.

"All of us," she told me. "We have problems in Nicaragua, and we cannot go back. We are afraid to go back to Nicaragua. They threatened him," she told me, referring to her husband, who was sitting with her children, including a curly-haired toddler who reminded me of my boy. "We work on a farm, and the owner of the farm was killed. And then they came to where we were."

"You came to Nogales because you want to cross into the United States. How are you going to cross? Are you going to ask for asylum? Are you going to go into the desert?"

"We are going to ask for asylum," she told me.

"What if they say no?" I asked.

"I don't know what we're going to do because it's our hope. Because we can't return to Nicaragua. And here, neither, because here they can kill us, too," she said of Nogales. She was right. Some on our team who knew the city well said that directly above the shelter they believed we were being watched by cartel members.

"If they say no to you at the checkpoint," I wondered, "do you think you would try to cross in the desert?"

The father chimed in. "If there isn't another option, maybe."

WHAT CAITLIN DICKERSON knew, but I didn't, was that where they crossed wouldn't matter—the threat they faced either at the Nogales Port of Entry or the desert around it was the same: they could be separated, just like the U.S. government was beginning to do to hundreds of other families. Dickerson was still pressing the federal government to confirm her reporting. The details she sent them would send the organization into crisis mode.

We are preparing to publish a story based on ORR data provided to us by Homeland Security officials on background that shows more than 700 children have been separated from their parents since last October. According to our sources, the data shows that about half of the children are under 10 years old and more than a quarter are under five years old. The story will also say that ORR-contracted shelters have struggled increasingly to track down the parents of children who show up at their facilities after being separated—so the children effectively become lost in the system until ORR contracts can track the parents down. We wanted to run this by you to ensure that HHS/ORR doesn't dispute any of our findings or care to add context or further comment.

Dickerson had a major scoop on her hands, but, curiously, not everyone inside HHS was so sure. In a sign of the extraordinary confusion surrounding family separations that would follow, not everyone could say if what the *New York Times* was poised to report was actually happening.

A public affairs specialist at the Administration for Children and Families, the part of HHS that encompasses ORR, finally emailed Dickerson back on Thursday, more than a full day past her deadline, to tell her that they "cannot verify the numbers because they do not come from the Office of Refugee Resettlement."

"The numbers do in fact come from HHS/ORR," Dickerson replied.

The specialist now wasn't positive, emailing three other ACF employees for guidance within twenty minutes.

"Can ORR provide any insight as to where she may have gotten the data or why she would be so insistent the data is from ORR?"

By this time, the work day was ending, but the flack realized there was a public relations crisis brewing. "I will be staying after hours until approx. 6:45 P.M. And look forward to hearing back from you on a proposed response, please ensure that Scott has approved any response we will provide," he wrote, referring to Scott Lloyd, ORR's director. "Please let me know if you have any questions; happy to discuss by phone or come upstairs in person—am here to assist in this as needed."

Twenty-three minutes later a reply came through from one of those colleagues, clarifying the source of the data Dickerson had in hand, and suggesting a proposed response.

> *Sounds like DHS shared some ORR data (that does not represent the full picture of DHS actions). It also sounds like a symptom of breakdown in interagency communications.*
>
> *You could develop something like this, although I don't know if it will clear:*
>
> The Department of Homeland Security does not inform the Office of Refugee Resettlement that a particular referred child was separated or the whereabouts of the parents. In pursuing the best interests of the child, ORR and it's [*sic*] service providers work diligently to identify if each child was separated and to locate the parents. While ORR does not receive information or data on DHS actions, ORR has worked to resolve several hundred of these types of cases in the past year.

Within three minutes, two other ACF officials were looped in on the email, and seven minutes after that, Trump appointee Lloyd was added, too. He had already been made aware of the *New York Times* request. The confusion among colleagues in the agency caring for allegedly separated children was evident in the questions posed by one employee.

> *What is unclear to me is: if DHS does not share family separation UAC data with ORR, then where would any such data come from?*

In other words, is ORR building its own data set based
on what we learn upon searching for a parent?

The answer was yes. The ORR "data set," or informal list of separated minors in the custody of the department, was being kept by Jim De La Cruz, the senior field specialist who had first noticed a similar practice during the Obama administration in 2016. At the time, case managers at government shelters throughout the country were reporting a small number of children saying they had been taken from their parents, despite senior members of the Obama administration opposing the practice, as had De La Cruz, in emails to colleagues. The numbers they were now seeing were far beyond anything during the Obama administration.

Ten minutes later the proposed response was sent back to the group based on input from the assistant secretary of public affairs. It added a line at the top about how ORR "cannot and will not corroborate a data report we have not seen or from an unknown source." If released, the statement would be an admission that family separations were increasing in the Trump era.

Ten more minutes passed, and at exactly six in the evening, a career ORR employee weighed in to confirm that, indeed, the data supported it was happening.

For your background:
I think that DHS shared with the press the number from
the working list that our field recently compiled and shared
with DHS field (a working field document to try to get a
handle on this problem—not an official count). It is likely not

*a complete or accurate list/number. It grew to over 700. So
the actual number of separations is probably larger.*

The *New York Times* was right. More than seven hundred
separated children. Within three minutes the ORR staffer's
boss, Scott Lloyd, wrote back with questions of his own.

*How do we know that they were separations, is it
through the reunification process?*
*Do we know whether these cases represent a rise in
the percentage of UAC in care? The numbers of referrals
generally have been rising.*

Lloyd was asking not only how his agency becomes aware
of separations, but if the percentage of separated children in
his custody was increasing relative to the overall population.
Nearly instantly, he received a reply.

*Yes. It may become known through the ordinary course
of work in ORR. Then ORR reaches out to DHS to try to find
the parents and establish communication.*
*As to your second question, It looks like the field found
around a hundred a month. Yes it is an increase. Before
2017, family separation happened, but not often.*

Within minutes, it became clear to a communications official on the email chain what was happening. ORR was denying something that was true. The more than seven hundred
separations was their number, and the practice was happening on an unprecedented scale—far beyond anything in the

previous administration, when Jim De La Cruz had started tracking the numbers.

> Okay, so we have a problem here when we told the New York Times today: "We cannot verify the numbers because they do not come from the Office of Refugee Resettlement at HHS' Administration for Children and Families."
>
> ORR field staff numbers are ORR numbers on UACs, even if they aren't in the form of an official report. Especially when they are shared with DHS.
>
> ORR, would you propose revised language, including numbers/data, based on what we now know? We need to amend our New York Times statement ASAP.

Less than two hours after Caitlin Dickerson showed her cards, sending ACF and ORR officials scrambling before the *Times* published, everyone finally seemed to be on the same page. The career ORR employee replied with a final suggestion at 6:31 in the evening, encouraging more specificity than the proposed statement circulated earlier.

> From a programmatic perspective, since DHS is now using ORR working data to describe their actions, I don't have a problem with using the last two paragraphs below, or even more specifically saying that the number exceeded 700 instead of "several hundred."

Fourteen minutes before the public affairs specialist who fielded Dickerson's request had hoped to head home for the night, there finally seemed to be agreement on the number of separated children in the custody of ORR. But inside the tiny department tasked with caring for thousands of migrant children crossing the border, its Trump-appointed leader still wanted more details.

"I'd be interested to know the story of this communication with DHS," Scott Lloyd wrote back only to the email's author at 6:45, who waited until late that night, after eleven in the evening, to reply. The explanation was that the DHS information technology infrastructure didn't share the key detail of whether a child had been separated between relevant agencies, including ORR, resulting in confusion about the number of family separations, making reunifications difficult if not impossible. This described the exact scenario that had been raised previously by officials including ICE's Claire Tricker McNulty, who was actively trying to fix it. But separations proceeded nevertheless.

> The Communication with DHS goes back a long while. ORR and DHS tried to figure out a solution to the lack of notice and coordination. DHS realized about two months ago that they had in [sic] internal glitch causing the problem of lack of notice. That was during an OGC/OPLA call.
>
> DHS and ORR are never supposed to communicate each other's data—each are supposed to refer to the respective comms team. So I am surprised that DHS shared ORR field info with the press as a representation of their own enforcement actions.
>
> Also, it almost looks like the reporter is talking to staff or grantees. Or maybe with DHS staff . . .
>
> Let me see what I can find out.

On Friday, April 20, the *Times* article went live. "Hundreds of Immigrant Children Have Been Taken from Parents at U.S. Border," the headline read. In the article, HHS confirmed Dickerson's numbers were correct.

Whether or not the journalist was aware of the internal debate that led to the admission HHS made, she detailed how difficult it was to receive confirmation.

Officials have repeatedly declined to provide data on how many families have been separated, but suggested that the number was relatively low.

But new data reviewed by the *New York Times* shows that more than 700 children have been taken from adults claiming to be their parents since October, including more than 100 children under the age of 4.

The data was prepared by the Office of Refugee Resettlement, a division of the Department of Health and Human Services that takes custody of children who have been removed from migrant parents. Senior officials at the Department of Homeland Security, which processes migrants at the border, initially denied that the numbers were so high. But after they were confirmed to the *Times* by three federal officials who work closely with these cases, a spokesman for the health and human services department on Friday acknowledged in a statement that there were "approximately 700."

This admission, that the federal government was systematically separating families, was the exact type of action Senator Kamala Harris had asked of Secretary of Homeland Security Kirstjen Nielsen about during Nielsen's confirmation process.

In response to a question specifically requesting Nielsen report back on whether DHS was drafting or considering separations, Nielsen replied, "I commit to sharing additional policy guidance and appropriate information with Congress."

But she never did. Harris and others, including myself, would get confirmation the policy was being carried out first in the *Houston Chronicle*, and now in the *New York Times*.

AS THE DIRECTOR of the office keeping the leaked list of seven-hundred separated children now publicly contradicting the Trump administration's denial of a family separation policy, Scott Lloyd was pissed off. He wasn't the only one.

Inside the White House's Eisenhower Executive Office Building on the Friday the article was published, the man with custody of those separated kids came face-to-face with Katie Waldman, the Department of Homeland Security spokeswoman, at an immigration Policy Coordinating Committee meeting. She wanted to know how the *New York Times* could have gotten a hold of the Office of Refugee Resettlement's list of separated kids.

"How is this possible?" Waldman, the pugnacious twenty-seven-year-old, asked Lloyd.

Leaking was the cardinal sin of the Trump administration, and the president himself would call leakers "traitors and cowards" the following month.

"I'm trying to get to the bottom of this," Lloyd told Waldman. "I didn't ask anybody to create a list. When I get to the bottom of this, I'll let you know."

Throughout his tenure, when Lloyd had been asked by staff about family separations, he had been using a version of the carefully crafted White House line that "there is no family separation policy," echoing Waldman and her colleagues at DHS. Now, with the *Times* article published based on Lloyd's own data, family separations were undeniable.

Caitlin Dickerson's exposé, and the resulting pressure from Waldman, made Lloyd irritated. He was left to stew about the leak over the weekend. If the existence of the list itself took Lloyd by surprise, it shouldn't have. It was the same dataset he had discussed with then-acting CBP and ICE heads McAleenan and Homan after Commander Jonathan White flagged an increase in separated children in November 2017.

"In the attached spreadsheet, details including specific names and A # s for separation referrals received in September and October may be found," read a November 17, 2017, email from White to McAleenan, which Lloyd also received.

Embarrassed, Lloyd knew the leak came from his department, on his watch, under an administration that appointed him to his position. When considering how to handle the fallout from the leak, Lloyd's first thought was a drastic one.

Let's get rid of the list.

If he followed the idea through, it would destroy the critical linkage between the seven hundred separated children in his custody and their parents despite the fact that the list itself was the best hope of reuniting them. Lloyd knew that in order to discard the list, he would have to instruct his staff to do so. Lloyd wanted to hear from them before deciding on a course of action. Once back in the office, he queried staff.

Why are we keeping the list? Can't we just email with DHS on a case-by-case basis? You see the problem this created, how can we prevent another leak?

The answer he would receive, of course, was that the list

was the only way separated children would be reunited with their parents. The document, Lloyd was reminded, was kept by ORR's senior federal field specialist Jim De La Cruz for explicitly that reason. The "problem" wasn't the existence of the list, but the separations themselves.

"We're the *only* ones tracking," one ORR official later told me about what was explained to Lloyd. "We can't rely on our colleagues at DHS to give us information after."

Lloyd listened. But his apparent bewilderment didn't sit well with some colleagues.

"It sounds like Scott had no idea what the fuck the [*Times*] article was talking about when he had been elevating [data about separations] through our leadership," one official told me. "Not only were we in the field seeing these kids—ORR stakeholders were saying it too."

That Tuesday, April 24, Lloyd would have the opportunity to act on his instinct to get rid of the list. On that day, key Health and Human Services officials would gather for a weekly ORR coordinating meeting in the office of Steve Wagner, the acting assistant secretary of HHS's Administration for Children and Families.

In the room, when the topic of the list was raised, an ACF public affairs official, who had the following week been a part of the hurried email exchange in advance of the Times publishing, had a suggestion. He believed the "half baked" and "casual" list would lead to both internal confusion and public affairs crises like the one the Times article caused. So he put forward an option he felt would help avoid the problem in the future.

"Can we not keep the numbers?" he asked.

Lloyd, who had already thought of the idea, and Wagner,

both indicated their support. They turned to Jallyn Sualog for her response. Sualog attended this weekly meeting having replaced Jonathan White, acting as the deputy director of ORR since he left in March. She was the person in the room closest to the list itself.

Sualog, who has a masters degree in clinical psychology and twenty years of child welfare experience, knew she never could or would let that happen because of the consequences, she later told colleagues. So she said as little as possible to her boss, Lloyd, and his boss, Wagner.

"OK, I'll see what I can do," she replied.

The meeting ended, without Lloyd acting on his earlier impulse to specifically and literally order the destruction of the list. But quickly, word spread throughout the office about what had happened and what those in the meeting understood their director's intention to be.

"It was insane [Lloyd] was even surprised this number would come out in the media and pretend he didn't know what the hell it was about," an ORR official told me.

Sualog conveyed her feelings about what had happened to De La Cruz, who had been keeping the list since the limited separations occurred at the end of the Obama administration. If Lloyd expected Sualog to instruct De La Cruz to stop keeping the list, she never did. Nor did De La Cruz do anything of the sort. On the contrary, he continued adding to it as the number of separated children rapidly grew.

Had the keeping of the list been stopped, any reunification of those seven hundred children would have been made needlessly more complicated, compounding the pain and trauma suffered as time apart from their parents grew longer. Neither Sualog, nor De La Cruz, would allow the destruction of the list to happen. But they were powerless to stop the policy itself.

April 23, 2018

After you leave Brownsville, Texas, and head east, the Rio Grande seems to inch closer and closer, until at times, you can see it out the window and you're almost driving next to it. In the final stretch before the river meets the Gulf of Mexico, Highway 4 splits northeast and the waterway bends south, hugging the Las Palomas Wildlife Management Area on both sides.

As the *Dateline* team and I approached the sand dunes at the end of the highway, I felt we were reaching the end of our story. This was our eighteenth day of filming. We had only a handful of locations left before we were scheduled to head into the edit booth to put our hour-long prime-time special together about realities of life along the border.

We carried on, driving, as is allowed, out and onto the sand. Seagulls flew overhead as wind-pushed waves washed up along the shore out my driver's-side window, water coming to within three or four yards of the car. We drove in silence until we hit the spot where the Rio Grande empties into the extra-salty water of the gulf. We were on the border, but there was no wall, and not a single Border Patrol agent.

Standing on a sand bar in the middle of the river, halfway between the United States and Mexico, or maybe standing in both countries, were Mexican fishermen with nets attached to the end of their poles. At least five of them were there, fully clothed, in waist-high water, as the confluence of the two bodies of water churned around them.

On the U.S. side, we were so close I could shout across to

people enjoying their Monday afternoon out around the back of a pickup truck.

"Hi! Hola!" I projected.

"Hola!" a man screamed back. He was selling something, and he decided we were a potential customer. So he grabbed his blue cooler, and without taking off his T-shirt started swimming through the murky water of the Rio Grande from Mexico into the United States, maybe a fifteen-yard journey. When he made it, he braced himself on the muddy bank, only his head and shoulders above the waterline.

I crouched down as he was opening his cooler, which had also acted something like a flotation device on his swim across. Inside were dried shrimp, along with a giant bottle of hot sauce and limes. When he realized we were filming, the man—a heavyset guy with a closely cropped haircut—hid his face behind the cooler.

"How much?" I asked.

Five bucks, he told me. I gave him twenty and told him to keep the change. He gave us extra bags of shrimp. We shook hands and I thanked him in English. He had clearly done this before.

"All right, nice to meet you. Be safe!" I shouted as he swam away.

"All right!" he said back.

I wished him well.

"See you later, buddy!" he said back to me, turning to swim back toward Mexico, diagonally against the current as it pushed out into the gulf.

I looked back at our crew and couldn't help but laugh as the camera kept rolling. It was hard to believe that with everything we had seen—dead bodies in the morgue in Tijuana, families getting ready to cross and getting caught after doing so, migrants lost in the mountains in the black of night—this peaceful setting was the terminus of a two-thousand-mile-long, politically charged dividing line.

AS I WAS buying dried shrimp from a guy who swam across the Rio Grande, Secretary of Homeland Security Kirstjen Nielsen received a pair of contradictory memos. One urged her to put in place a family separation policy. The other warned it was on legally shaky ground and may well be unconstitutional.

The Department of Homeland Security agency heads who would be responsible for carrying out family separations— Kevin McAleenan, the commissioner of U.S. Customs and Border Protection; L. Francis Cissna, the director of U.S. Citizenship and Immigration Services; and Thomas Homan, the acting director of Immigration and Customs Enforcement—initialed their names on a "secretarial decision memo" that provided three policy options aimed at slowing or stopping migrants—even asylum-seeking families—from crossing the southern border in between ports of entry.

The first option was titled "Scalable Approach." It called for gradually increasing prosecutions over time, yielding a "modest initial impact" until asylum officers could increase their capacity.

The second, "Refer All Amenable Single Adults," would be "quickly scalable" but limited to adults traveling alone, not families.

The third and final option was the one that had been considered and rejected during the Obama administration, one flagged by Claire Trickler-McNulty at ICE as a scenario that could result in children "traumatized and abused" in a system that wasn't ready to reunite them: separate all families crossing the border.

> **Option 3—Refer All Amenable Adults, including those presenting as part of a FMUA:** Work with DOJ, the Department of Health and Human Services, and other interagency partners to develop a quickly scalable approach to achieve 100% immigration violation prosecution referral for all amenable adults, including those initially arriving or apprehended with minors.

McAleenan, Homan, and Cissna justified the potential separation of "family units," or FMUAs, arguing that Nielsen's powers would withstand scrutiny of the U.S. judicial system. "The Secretary of Homeland Security has broad legal authorities to carry out her responsibility to enforce the immigration laws," they wrote. "DHS could also permissibly direct the separation of parents or legal guardians and minors held in immigration detention so that the parent or legal guardian can be prosecuted pursuant to these authorities." An accompanying footnote read: "For full legal analysis of this initiative, please see attachment."

That attachment was a secret legal memo, authored by John Mitnick, the general counsel of the Department of Homeland Security whose job it was to vet proposed policies for potential legal challenges. Family separations, by his analysis, were anything but legally sound.

Mitnick was a twice-failed Republican candidate for office, U.S. Congress then the Georgia State Senate, who later went on to serve in various roles for President George W. Bush before entering the private sector as a vice president at the weapons manufacturer Raytheon. He was tapped by President Trump to come back to DHS while still acting in a leadership capacity for the conservative Heritage Foundation. Mitnick assessed Nielsen's options:

> We understand that you are presently considering three propos-
> als that, in coordination with the Department of Justice ("DOJ"),
> would increase prosecution against aliens who cross the border
> illegally. One proposal would establish a scalable approach for
> increased prosecutions consistent with DHS and DOJ opera-
> tions. A second proposal would seek to refer all single adults
> who commit criminal immigration violations for prosecution.

Those two options, Mitnick believed, were safe choices. But they were not the option endorsed by Nielsen's deputies: family separations.

> The third proposal would seek to refer all adults who commit
> immigration violations for prosecution, including adults who are
> apprehended as part of a family unit. In referring all adults for
> such criminal prosecutions, it would be legally permissible to
> separate minors from adult family members or other unrelated
> accompanying adults.

But there was a catch. While separations might be "legally permissible," Mitnick made very clear he believed systematic family separations would likely end up in court.

> The third option, which prioritizes prosecution referrals for *all*
> adults who commit criminal immigration violations, could lead to
> a significant increase in the prosecutions of adults who are part

of family units. Although it would be legally permissible to separate adults and minors as outlined above, any such decisions will
face legal challenges.

The court challenge Mitnick warned of wasn't one that
would have to be hastily assembled as the policy unfolded.
In fact, it was already in the federal court system, brought by
Lee Gelernt and his colleagues at the American Civil Liberties
Union two months earlier on behalf of Ms. L., the Congolese
mother separated from her daughter in the basement of the San
Ysidro Port of Entry. What Mitnick wrote might have stopped
any other secretary of homeland security in her tracks.

Whether this issue is addressed in the Ms. L. litigation or in
another case, a court could conclude that the separations are
violative of the INA, Administrative Procedure Act, or the Fifth
Amendment Due Process clause.

In other words, Secretary Nielsen's lawyer was making clear that family separations could be deemed illegal—
including on the grounds it would violate the constitutional
right of fair treatment in the judicial system for families. And
yet, despite Mitnick's legal guidance that family separations
were potentially unconstitutional, McAleenan, Cissna, and
Homan pressed ahead, pushing their boss to implement the
policy in their memo.

Recommendation: We recommend Option 3 as the most effective method to achieve operational objectives and the Administration's goal to end "catch and release." This initiative would
pursue prosecution of all amenable adults who cross our border

illegally, including those presenting with a family unit, between ports of entry in coordination with DOJ.

Secretary Nielsen's lieutenants were endorsing family separations. Now it was up to their boss, who with the stroke of a pen could change the face of immigration enforcement. At stake, according to the projection of Commander White at Health and Human Services, was the fate of around 30,000 children.

Nielsen read their memo, but decided not to sign it right away.

THE FOLLOWING MORNING, April 23, in McAllen, Texas, I stepped aboard a Customs and Border Protection Black Hawk helicopter piloted by crew wearing tan jumpsuits and bullet-proof vests reading "POLICE Air & Marine Federal Agent." CBP's Air and Marine unit is tasked with watching the border from the sky and on the water, and today, early, I was getting a tour of how border enforcement happens from above.

My seat was almost exactly underneath the gold seal of the Department of Homeland Security, the same color as the rest of the lettering and numbers on the outside of the other-wise black chopper. The hulking piece of military machinery felt huge, and far more imposing than the white and blue CBP A-Star choppers I had seen fly overhead while on the border near San Diego. Sure enough, they were often used for special occasions and shows of force, their size and maneuverability not ideal for the run-and-gun operations along the border.

Our *Dateline* team got on board, and we prepared to go wheels up. We were warned that once the rotors got going it would be impossible to hear anything; our only communication would be through the intercom system. The crew pulled away the blocks holding the wheels in place and watched us lift off.

We headed east, following the Rio Grande toward Brownsville and Boca Chica State Park, where we spent the previous day marveling at the relative peace and serenity of the Rio Grande's terminus. This vantage felt exactly the opposite, winding along each twist and turn of the more than 270 "river miles" of border. I could hear on the comms system the pilots communicating with Border Patrol agents on the ground. It wasn't long before we were above what was reported to be migrants making a run for it.

I repeated for Dana Roecker's camera what I could hear in my headset, and see out the window. "We've just seen four migrants apprehended who were trying to run from the Border Patrol." Far below us I noticed a CBP chopper, the blue and white kind I had remembered seeing in San Diego, chasing the migrants, getting so close to them the trees were billowing as the chopper hovered above. We made several circles as we watched and listened to agents work to apprehend what they suspected to be men. I paused, hearing more activity on the radio, the pilots signaling we were going to move again.

We flew back toward the Anzalduas Bridge, where I had met the father-and-son duo of Edwin and Edwin Jr. in February. For the first time I realized how far the walk was, from the river itself to where migrants try to turn themselves in. I could see a long, winding dirt path.

A family appeared on the trail.

I started talking to Dana's camera again, narrating the

action below. "A call has come through that there's a family unit," repeating the words I had heard used on the radio, "crossing as well. Most likely looking to turn themselves in right in this area."

We could see them clearly from the Black Hawk, half of the family sitting and the others standing beneath a tree. I could make out five people, what looked like kids sitting on the ground, three adults standing. They were wearing pink, green, and black shirts. The rotor wash was blasting them with dust, dirt, and debris.

Looking down, the horror of the scene became clear. What must it feel like to enter the United States with the goal of turning yourself in on humanitarian grounds, only to have a military chopper circle you, welcoming you as if you were an enemy combatant with its deafening fury?

We circled for a few moments before heading out, tracing the Rio Grande again, oftentimes unclear which side was Mexico and which was the United States because of how windy the river was.

As we headed for the McAllen airport, the family we left behind could not have known they picked the worst possible moment to arrive on the banks of the United States southwest border.

While the children sat cross-legged beneath the tree, waiting to be picked up by Border Patrol agents they likely hoped would help them start a new life, on Secretary Kirstjen Nielsen's desk sat a memo that, should she sign it, would likely result in separation of those kids from their parents. Sometimes, everything looks clearer from above. But even with two countries, the river that divides them, and those who on this day moved from one side to the other all in my field of view, I could not see what was just ahead.

May 4, 2018

The decision homeland security secretary Kirstjen Nielsen had to make was crystal clear, and she was feeling overwhelmed. She weighed signing a decision memo that would put a potentially illegal policy of separating parents and children in place. She appealed for help to her top aides in a Friday morning email.

"Could I have topics/goals today so I can think about it over weekend? With hearing next week may be tough to focus prior."

Nielsen was planning ahead, knowing she would have to appear before the Senate Committee on Appropriations Subcommittee on Homeland Security the following Tuesday, in four days. She wrote to her deputies, Jonathan Hoffman, Miles Taylor, and Chad Wolf, requesting details on interviews scheduled three days away, on Monday. Subject: "Dateline and NPR."

Nielsen was scheduled to be the final shoot of our *Dateline* special. We had planned to bring to her our findings from our months of reporting along the border—findings that often differed starkly from the reality her boss, President Trump, presented from the White House. Since we started filming the project nearly three months earlier, much had changed along the border and at the Department of Homeland Security.

Chad Wolf, chief of staff to Nielsen, replied with the

background information requested by Nielsen, put together by the Department of Homeland Security about the two reporters who would interview her the following week: NPR's John Burnett and myself. Burnett's background was short and to the point.

NPR INTERVIEW

- *John Burnett of NPR will interview you on Border Security and the National Guard.*
- *This interview was scheduled at the request of WH COS. Immediately following Mr. Burnett's interview with you he will conduct an interview with General Kelly.*

The veteran border correspondent had better access than I had lined up—he was going to talk with the man who first publicly acknowledged the existence of family separations, and one of the driving forces behind the implementation of Trump's immigration policy.

And then there was the briefing about me—far more information, in disturbing detail.

DATELINE INTERVIEW

Jacob Soboroff from NBC will be interviewing you for the one hour Dateline special entitled "The Border." The special is set to air June 6.

AGENDA:

- *The interview will be no longer than 20 minutes and will stick to key topics on what life is like at the border.*

- *He is not expected to ask about news of the day or any topic that he did not personally see at the border.*

HISTORY:
- *Jacob's First visit was February 20 at the San Ysidro port of entry—interview with Port Director Sidney Aki.*
- *2/20/2018—San Diego—Interview with Operations Officer Robert "Lance" LeNoir for the Galvez Tunnel visit and the tunnels threat in the area.*
- *2/20/2018—San Diego Interview with SDC Chief Rodney Scott took place at the Prototypes and the Landing Mat wall nearby. Also went to an area called Arnie's Point that overlooks historic areas called Soccer Field and Colonia Libertad where a multitude of immigrants once staged on the north side of the border before there was infrastructure in the area. This area highlights the BIS for San Diego—two fences, stadium lighting, all-weather roads, camera towers. Also went to the Surf Fence in Imperial Beach to show the maritime threat. (Dateline stayed for the sunset.)*
- *2/21/2018—San Diego—Dateline video team came back without Jacob for B-roll that was not able to get to the previous day.*
- *2/26/2018—RGV Sector—Sit down interview with CPA Padilla (TPs attached) MCS Ride Along, Riverine operational ride along.*
- *3/22/2018—San Diego—Dateline video team came back without Jacob for B-roll with the Chief for office shots and other shots along the border.*
- *4/12/2018—Second visit was overnight (midnight until about 4 a.m.) April 12 at the Otay Mesa port of entry—Jacob saw two narcotics seizures (please note, the footage related to*

these seizures is still under embargo; there's a good chance
we won't be able to release it in time for the special as DOJ
is involved.)

- *4/22: NBC Dateline producer Jacob Soboroff will be at*
  planned meeting with RGV sector chief Padilla Tuesday and
  visited El Paso POE for filming B-roll of people/students
  crossing border.

They missed one. Whoever had been compiling all the time I spent in the field with the Border Patrol and CBP's Office of Field Operations forgot I was puking in the Arizona desert on the night of February 28. Nevertheless, the Trump administration had been watching me closely.

LATER THAT SAME day, in San Diego, the ACLU and the Department of Justice were in court, making oral arguments in the *Ms. L.* case, which Nielsen's lawyer had warned could torpedo any border-wide family separation policy she signed into existence. The lawsuit had now been expanded to class action to include other separations, like the one suffered by Ms. C. and her child, Brazilians who crossed in between ports of entry. After the *New York Times* article posted revealing more than seven hundred separations, and sending ORR chief Scott Loyd into a clumsy attempt to obscure the list documenting them, Judge Dana Sabraw wanted to know what was going on.

"There is also in the briefing argument," he said, referring to documents submitted by both the ACLU and the DOJ, "that the government has a practice, or perhaps even a policy, of separation of families as a deterrence mechanism. And the plaintiffs have cited a number of articles which have attributions to spokespersons within DHS and HHS.

"What is the government's position; is there a policy or is there not such a policy or practice?"

Of course, the policy itself was literally waiting for Secretary Nielsen's signature, but the practice had been going on since the summer as part of the Border Patrol's pilot program.

"I would say, your honor," said Sarah Fabian, the government's lawyer, "there is no—there is not such a policy. I think the statements that are referred to in the pleadings, that has been the consistent position of the agency. Whether there is a practice of separation, there is not."

The next day, May 5, the eighteenth Saturday of the year, Secretary Nielsen decided she had made up her mind. She put pen to paper in the section titled "Option 3." Despite intense public interest and dogged reporting of journalists who, unlike me, had uncovered the policy taking shape in real time, it wasn't broadcast, announced, or publicized. It happened without fanfare or a press conference, not even a presidential tweet.

But the consequences were seismic: with the stroke of Nielsen's pen, family separation was now the official policy of the United States government.

May 7, 2018

Attorney General Jeff Sessions's Alabama accent couldn't have sounded more out of place near a Southern California beach much like the one Aarne and I decided to surf in January, the night our report on Trump's immigration policy got little notice in the hours before the State of the Union.

Sessions was in California to announce what Nielsen had not: that family separations was now an official policy. He had chosen perhaps the most in-your-face location possible, Friendship Park, a public safe zone where people from both sides of the border could visit through the fencing, though access was limited under President Trump. After signing the decision memo, Nielsen had lain low, and was not aware Sessions would be speaking to the press.

Though the head of a wholly different cabinet department, Sessions stood behind a wood podium affixed with the seal of the Department of Homeland Security. He was wearing a light gray suit, crisp white shirt, blue and pink striped tie, and the type of reading glasses most associated with Santa Claus.

Sessions was flanked on his right by Customs and Border Protection's San Ysidro port director Sidney Aki and San Diego Sector Border Patrol chief Rodney Scott, two men I had spent time with for our *Dateline* documentary. On the attorney general's left was Thomas Homan, the acting director of Immigration and Customs Enforcement, one of the three men who recommended Nielsen institute "Option 3," to prosecute "all amenable adults, including those initially arriving or apprehended with minors."

"The Department of Homeland Security is now referring one hundred percent of illegal southwest border crossings to the Department of Justice for prosecutions," Sessions said. "And the Department of Justice will take up these cases."

"I have put in place a zero tolerance policy for illegal entry on our southwest border. If you cross the border unlawfully, then we will prosecute you—it's that simple. If you smuggle illegal aliens across our border, then we will prosecute you."

A protestor interrupted with a bullhorn. "Jeeeefffff Sessions!"

"If you are smuggling a child, then we will prosecute you, and that child may be separated from you as required by law," said Sessions.

"Get out of here!" the protestor roared. "Are you going to be separating families? Is that why you're here? Why are you doing this? Do you have a heart?"

Sessions continued, but couldn't keep talking long enough to speak over the protestor and his megaphone nonstop.

"Why do you work for this administration?"

Sessions looked up to his left and paused, clearly hearing the protestor.

"Do you want to enforce these policies?" the protestor continued.

Sessions looked to his right, over his reading glasses, and smiled.

The protestor, wearing a backpack and T-shirt that read NAZI-FASCISTAS NO! was pushed away gently by a female aide in aviator sunglasses and a floral print shirt.

Sessions continued his remarks, attempting to paint a picture of a United States under siege by migrants, while standing at a border crossing that Chief Scott himself had told me was as safe as it had ever been.

"We will finally secure this border so that we can give the American people the safety and peace of mind that they deserve," Sessions said.

Later that day, Sessions addressed family separations again, this time at a press conference in Arizona.

"If you don't want your child to be separated," Sessions declared, "then don't bring them across the border illegally."

That evening, Sessions's press conference and the protestor's reaction to it popped into my social media feed. A policy of family separations, which I had noticed only in passing when John Kelly first mentioned it more than a year earlier, now seemed to be the official policy of the Trump administration. So many questions ran through my mind.

What would happen to the family from Nicaragua I met waiting in the Nogales shelter to cross with the little boy who looked like my son?

To the family below the Black Hawk chopper who had wanted to turn themselves in?

To the Edwins from Honduras at the Anzalduas Bridge, especially the son who said he was scared of a lot of bad guys on his journey?

I could see in the video of Sessions's San Diego press conference that behind him were Border Patrol agents on horseback, the type that had apprehended a Nepalese family I saw jump over the primary fence as I toured President Trump's border wall prototypes in late 2017.

I wondered what ever happened to them, too.

Was this really happening?

I was finally about to find out.

May 9, 2018

At twenty-three minutes to noon, President Trump walked in and took his seat at the center of the massive oval mahogany table in the Cabinet Room to convene his thirteenth meeting of top advisors, flanked to his right by Deputy Secretary of

State John Sullivan and on his left by Deputy Secretary of Defense Patrick Shanahan. His eyes looked puffy, and the president sat with folded arms until he was ready to begin, leaning on the table in from of him and immediately looking down at his notes.

"Okay, thank you very much. We have a lot of things happening, as you know," began Trump, in a dark suit with an American flag pin on his left lapel, white shirt, and blue and white striped tie, before a bank of cameras assembled for the latest of his reliably unpredictable gatherings of the leaders of federal agencies.

Across from President Trump and under a cluster of outstretched boom microphones was Vice President Mike Pence. Directly to his left, Attorney General Sessions, fresh off his San Diego press conference announcing the family separation policy. Secretary Nielsen, dressed in a white blazer, sat four seats to the president's left. Chief of Staff John Kelly stood by the door to her left.

After opening remarks about North Korea, Trump glanced downward at his notes again, then turned to domestic politics. "We have a lot of things going on within our country. We've very much toughened up the border, but the laws are horrible. The laws in this country for immigration and illegal immigration are absolutely horrible. And we have to do something about it," the president said, not recognizing either of two cabinet members in the room who were responsible for just that—Nielsen and Sessions.

If President Trump was acknowledging family separations, he didn't say so explicitly. But Sessions knew they were now happening, and so did Nielsen, because she personally authorized them just more than two weeks earlier. So did

John Kelly, who first revealed the administration was considering separating families only one month into the Trump administration.

Then Trump repeated a familiar, but untruthful refrain, that his big, beautiful border wall was being built. "Not only the wall, which we're building sections of wall right now. We have $1.6 billion," the president continued, in a more honest vein, admitting what he was doing was replacing existing wall.

"We're fixing a lot of wall that basically is nonexistent because it's been ripped to pieces. It was poorly built and it wasn't—it was really only temporary, in some cases."

In previous cabinet meetings Trump had turned to different secretaries and asked them to make remarks on newsworthy issues of the day. Instead, on this day, he froze them out.

"Okay? Thank you very much," the president said, wrapping up the part of his meeting that was open to the media. "Thank you. Thank you."

"Okay, let's go!" an aide to Trump screamed.

As the press left the room the secretaries sat silent. The president bringing up immigration without recognizing Nielsen or Sessions was a bad omen.

Once the doors again closed and the press had been ushered out, the conversation about immigration continued. Attorney General Sessions, the target of Trump's ire because of his recusal in the Justice Department's Russia investigation, asserted that Nielsen could stop anyone from crossing the border. Nielsen felt panicked, believing not only that Sessions was throwing her under the bus to look tough in front of the president, but that was not legal nor possible. The president lit into her in front of the rest of the cabinet, so much so she immediately considered resigning.

Ironically what Trump failed to understand was that Secretary Nielsen and Attorney General Sessions were already working on how to "do something about that," as President Trump put it about migration: family separations. Despite the fact separations were likely taking place as they sat in the Cabinet Room, nobody brought the topic up, and Nielsen couldn't avoid the president's wrath.

"There is a huge culture of fear around the White House and the president," a former senior administration official later told me about Trump's outburst that day. "There are huge parts of the inter-agency process in fear for their jobs including General Sessions. They had to bluster and look tough to protect themselves."

On that front, and on that day, Nielsen failed to do so, to her own detriment.

"Every day on the phone it was F-bomb ridden conversation," the former official recalled, reeling off a list of outrageous ideas floated to Nielsen by President Trump to harm migrants in order to deter migration—ideas that were first publicly reported in *Border Wars*, the book from *New York Times* reporters Julie Hirschfeld Davis and Michael Shear.

"Painting the wall black. Shooting people. Snakes."

Despite the "crazy," Nielsen decided not to resign.

WHILE NIELSEN WAS getting an earful from the president, I was getting ready to head to the food court in the Ronald Reagan Building and International Trade Center, to prepare for my interview with her, scheduled at half past two. Having read Caitlin Dickerson's *New York Times* article, I planned to include a question about family separations, which I had written down in my notes:

Many who are apprehended today by Border Patrol are asylum seekers. Some put the number at almost half? Why would you separate them?

When I arrived, I sat at a two-top table with Izhar Harpaz, our lead *Dateline* producer, and drilled through questions with him as I sipped on a sparkling water to soothe my nerves. I felt good, and we made our way from the food court to a room adjacent to where we'd conduct the interview.

Moments later the secretary arrived, flanked by staff and a security detail. I ducked under the lights to stand up and shake her hand.

"Nice to meet you, Madame Secretary."

I also introduced myself to her two aides, Jonathan Hoffman, her assistant secretary for public affairs, and Katie Waldman, the agency spokesperson whose portfolio included immigration. It was Waldman who, unbeknownst to me, had the previous month demanded answers from Scott Lloyd as to why data from the Office of Refugee Resettlement tracking hundreds of children separated by the Trump administration before there was an official policy announced had leaked to the media.

They took their seats at the back of the room, up against the wall and visible in my peripheral vision. Nielsen sat down across from me.

"Madame Secretary," I began, "I've gotten to spend the last three months going back and forth across the border. But one thing that I hear over and over again from people along the border is people here in Washington have no idea what it is like to live along the border. Do you think you know what it's like to live along the border?"

"I have been doing my best to find out," she replied. "I think it's very dangerous to make policy and law in a vacuum. So I spend a lotta time working with the governors, working with sheriffs—going down again to meet with ranchers. I've had half a dozen trips myself down to the border."

Two questions in, a light panel fell, startling both Nielsen and myself and stopping the interview. While the crew adjusted the gear, Nielsen and I made small talk until we were ready to go again. She didn't mention, thanks to the briefing materials she had requested, that she already knew every detail of everywhere I had been in the past several months along the border.

After picking up where we left off, talking about whether or not border residents want Trump's wall, why one is or isn't necessary, and how dangerous the border is, Nielsen let out the first major lie of our conversation.

Citing statistics I knew by heart about how apprehensions along the border were nearly as low as they had ever been, I asked if it was "fair to say that it's really a surge in people coming across the southern border?"

"I think it's fair to say," she said. "I think the smugglers and the traffickers know our loopholes better virtually, than most of our lawmakers. But I would also just say, you know, extrapolated into the domestic environment, if I were to tell a family in a community, 'Oh, don't worry about it. You know, it's a two hundred percent increase in rapists and criminals in your community, but don't worry about it . . .' " repeating the line made famous by President Trump after he came down the gold escalators of Trump Tower to announce his candidacy. She didn't mention what had happened that morning, but perhaps she was trying to talk tough in the wake of a Cabinet-level scolding by the president.

I jumped in.

"But is that fair to say, there's a two hundred percent increase in rapists and criminals, or is it a two hundred percent increase in migrants crossing the southern border illegally?"

"What my point is, is that any amount . . ."

"But just to be clear," I persisted. "Is it a two hundred percent increase in rapists and criminals?"

"It's a two hundred percent increase in illegal aliens," she admitted. "What I am saying is any number is not acceptable."

We continued to go back and forth about whether violence was spilling across the border, to which Nielsen said "Absolutely." I presented her with facts from the Drug Enforcement Administration and what we were told along the border. "That's not what the DEA says," I told her. We had several more exchanges just like this. Facts were getting us nowhere. Eventually, I made my way to my question about family separations.

"While we were out there, the attorney general announced this new policy," I told her, not knowing she herself secretly signed it into place. "I think it was just last week, that anybody who crosses into the United States illegally is gonna be prosecuted. And children will be separated from their family members when they do that. With so many people coming into the United States looking to seek asylum, is that the right strategy?"

"Let's be clear about that," she said, not being clear at all about the fact she had, herself, signed the policy into place days earlier. "What the strategy is, is just like we do every day in the United States, we prosecute adults who commit crimes, whether they're single, whether they're part of a family, or whether in some cases they're pregnant. That's what we're doing. We will enforce the law. We're not exempting any class. So if you're part of a family and you break the law, you will be incarcerated, just as adults are every day in this country and every community when they break the law and they're separated from their family. It's not different."

In fact, it *was* different. Crossing the border is a civil crime, adjudicated in immigration court, and only if prosecutors decide to press charges do families get placed into criminal proceedings. Nielsen was hiding the truth, and in so doing, steamrolled through my attempt to understand what was going on. That was, embarrassingly, the beginning and end of our conversation about family separations. A better reporter would have been more prepared to keep pressing.

In fact, NPR's John Burnett did, engaging in a much more substantial back and forth with Nielsen about the policy and eliciting a glib answer about it from John Kelly. "The name of the game to a large degree," he said of separating families to deter migration.

Despite their confrontation earlier that day, Nielsen only mentioned President Trump's name once during the interview—when I pressed her on and she defended the pace of wall building, and whether or not the type of construction taking place was due to the work of the president.

"I think it's inaccurate to say anything other than it's Trump's wall."

After the agreed-upon twenty minutes of back-and-forth, her aide Katie Waldman chimed in to cut the interview off.

"All right, thank you, Madame Secretary."

We got up and walked out to the hallway together, the camera crews in tow, again making small talk about her family in California, my home state. After she left, Waldman and Hoffman returned, to have a conversation about one detail I pointed out to Nielsen: that more than 130,000 migrants were deemed "inadmissible" by Customs and Border Protection the previous year. I had characterized those migrants as being "turned away," but they wanted me to know inadmissible only meant they had been taken into custody at ports of entry (like Ms. L. and her separated daughter), not sent back into Mexico. They also wanted to be sure I wouldn't use the part of our exchange where Nielsen mistakenly said there was a 200 percent increase in rapists and criminals. We couldn't guarantee them that, I told them.

After pleasantries, we shook hands and exchanged phone numbers, everyone going their own way. As we spoke, separations were starting to affect operations along the border, crowding shelters run by the Office of Refugee Resettlement. Only five days into the policy's implementation, shelters were at nearly 90 percent capacity. And now they were regularly receiving children who had been taken from their parents. It wouldn't be long before I heard from Waldman again, and got another chance at learning the truth about family separations.

May 15, 2018

Nearly three thousand miles from Washington, D.C., Juan and his fourteen-year-old son, José, hadn't heard anything about the separation of migrant families at the border of the United States and Mexico. Juan had previously and successfully crossed undetected twice over the last decade, each time returning to his family in Petén, Guatemala, after years working to provide for them.

Since he received threats to himself and his son a month earlier, he had planned how they would leave home and, with the help of smugglers, make their way to the U.S.–Mexico border. Now the time had come.

The father and son had only slightly less information about the policy than I did, despite the fact I had asked the secretary of homeland security about it to her face six days earlier.

On this day, Juan readied to leave his now-pregnant wife and two daughters behind. Juan packed up José, closed their store, and left their home for the final time, en route to the only place they believed they would be safe and be able to send relief for their family.

Juan's birthday would be the fifth day of their journey, but any celebration would have to wait until they reached Arizona, a farther and less direct route to the United States than attempting to enter in South Texas. Arizona is where Juan had crossed before, and there he believed they would have the best chance of crossing together.

The day after they left, a warning was sent from the place Juan and José were headed, but they had no way of receiving it. Debra Thomas, a field specialist in the Office of Refugee Resettlement's Western Region of Arizona, alerted other field specialists across the country: be on the lookout for separated children that end up in the care and custody of ORR.

Hello,

I need to clarify a few additional items that have once again changed in a short time as well as address how we will work on these cases. Please review, and ask any questions you have, and please notify your staff who needs this information.

Finding separated parents:

- It is very important to locate the separated parent for all UAC in your program.

- For parents in ICE custody, you should be able to locate them and have a phone call with that parent as soon as possible.

Parents and UACs—"unaccompanied alien children," the government lingo referring to kids who arrived in the United States by themselves, or now were alone because they were taken from their parents and rendered unaccompanied—were not able to find each other once being separated. The people responsible for the care of these children were scrambling to figure out how to simply put them in touch with one another.

Border Patrol stations were beginning to fill up, the average length in custody quickly rising across the southwest border. The average time crept above the seventy-two-hour legal limit for holding children in the jails along the border.

Just starting their trip, Juan and José were clueless about America's new border policy. Nine days after Juan's birthday, he and José were still en route, guided by smugglers who had taken thousands of dollars from them in order to ensure safe passage through cartel-held territory, among the most dangerous regions in the world.

They could not wait for the joy and relief that would surely wash over them when they passed through this gauntlet and reached the United States.

PART TWO

Significant Incident Report

AGE: 5

CHILD'S COUNTRY OF BIRTH: Guatemala

ADMITTED DATE: 6/15/2018

ORR PLACEMENT DATE: 6/13/2018

CURRENT LOCATION: Bronx, NY

SYNOPSIS OF EVENT: During risk assessment, minor reported that due to separation from his aunt and cousin at the border, he has developed suicidal ideations.

DESCRIPTION OF INCIDENT: Minor reported that he was separated from his aunt and his 6 year old cousin. Minor reports that he developed suicidal ideations while detained after the separation. Ideations are active with no plan, no intent, and no Hx.

FOLLOW-UP AND/OR RESOLUTION: Clinician will complete PTSD Assessment to assess for possible trauma. Minor and clinician will review safety plan with minor. Family sessions with sponsor to strengthen relationship prior to and after discharge.

CHAPTER SIX

"These Kids Are Incarcerated"

June 4, 2018

Under the cover of darkness, Juan and José boarded a bus near the Hotel Internacional in San Luis Río Colorado, the Mexican border city directly across from San Luis, Arizona. They were a stone's throw from the United States. Travelers with the appropriate documents pass through the legal port of entry there by the thousands daily, but the father and son did not have that option.

To reach the border, Juan, carrying nothing but a backpack, had spent everything he had earned at his store back home in Petén, Guatemala.

He knew the two-week-plus journey would be a risky one, and that the price they would pay in money would likely change along the way, which it did.

He knew that on every bus, and in every hotel, they had to be extra aware of their surroundings.

He understood they would be targets for Los Zetas, the notorious and dangerous cartel operating where they came from in Guatemala and throughout Mexico, moving drugs and guns and trafficking humans—while killing civilians who crossed them.

For all the dangers that Juan and José faced since leaving Petén, there was no predicting what would happen on the final leg of this journey.

It was late at night, though temperatures were still in the eighties. Joining them on the bus for the short ride—less than six miles east—were by Juan's count thirty-five others, parents and children united by a desire to cross safely, if illegally, into the United States.

The bus pulled up to what appeared to be a small farm on the outskirts of the Mexican city. Just off the street were white metal cattle corrals, but there were no cows in sight. Beyond them, stadium-style lights that belonged to U.S. Customs and Border Protection were visible, part of the three-pronged and decades-old Border Patrol strategy of "technology, infrastructure, and manpower" designed to keep migrants like Juan and José out.

If the bus that brought them here had kept traveling east, it would soon be just south of the Barry M. Goldwater Air Force Range, where U.S. armed forces practice air-to-ground bombing. The range, just west of where I vomited uncontrollably in the harsh terrain of the Sonoran Desert, is where bodies of a dozen migrants were discovered by a humanitarian group. The number was only a tiny fraction of the thousands who have died attempting a similar crossing.

Juan and José would not meet that fate. With the others, they stepped off the bus and walked past the corrals toward the lights. In the distance they could see a short wall painted dark, the international border between the United States and Mexico. They quickly approached it and, helping each other, hopped over.

Plunk.

As their shoes hit the ground, the sand and dust around them absorbed footprints.

They made it safely into the United States of America.

They took everything in.

The fences, the desert, the bright lights, and behind that, a waning gibbous moon.

But no Border Patrol. Not yet.

It became clear they were standing in a no-man's-land, between two walls.

BY THE TIME Juan and José crossed into Arizona, family separations were happening at a rate nobody had ever seen.

At 11:43 P.M. EST, Jim De La Cruz, the supervisor of federal field specialists who was keeping tabs on care providers throughout the country, had an urgent message for them. De La Cruz was the career federal employee who had been told that his Trump-appointed boss, Scott Lloyd, wanted him to get rid of the list he had kept of separated kids after the New York Times uncovered the practice.

Now De La Cruz was doing the exact opposite—issuing instructions that would determine if the flood of separated children entering the custody of the Office of Refugee Resettlement would ever see their parents again.

De La Cruz had advocated for ending any type of family separation as far back as 2016. Now, as the practice was expanded systematically to the entire border under the Trump administration, at the direction of the attorney general and secretary of homeland security, De La Cruz knew, having informally tracked separations for years, that there was no way to automatically link separated parents and children once they were apart.

> Care provider staff, as many of you are aware, we are currently receiving an increased volume of UAC minors separated from a parent. Please find guidance to address two specific areas of SIRs [significant incident reports] for these cases.
>
> 1. If you become aware of a UAC separated from his or her parent and the separation was not previously reported by DHS to ORR, the care provider should write an SIR and route this according to ORR Procedures.
>
> 2. When you discover that a UAC separated from a parent IS NOT actually separated from a parent, after having stated this to DHS, an SIR stating the facts and circumstances should be written and elevated.

De La Cruz understood how important tracking parents and children would be to any potential reunification, and if separations were carried out on a scale projected by his former colleague Commander Jonathan White, ORR would be flooded with thousands more children than under normal circumstances.

Within hours of sending that email, it would apply to Juan and José.

At 11:10 P.M. local time Monday night, within a minute after they entered the no-man's-land in between the international border wall and the American fence, and two hours after Jim De La Cruz told colleagues across the country how to account for a flood of separated children that case managers said they were receiving, a white vehicle pulled up. It was the Border Patrol.

Standing under the high-powered lights that had been visible from the street in Mexico, agents began speaking with the migrants individually, taking notes. Juan and José were taken into custody after an agent conducted what is known as a field interview with them, concluding Juan was "a citizen and national of Guatemala illegally in the United States," as he wrote in his report.

In Border Patrol lingo, they had been "apprehended," or arrested. It was their last moment of freedom for what would be months.

Juan and José weren't sure what to expect, but this is in some way how they had hoped it would play out, in order to declare asylum and, once and for all, find safety from the dangers they had fled in Petén.

They could not have anticipated the danger that was coming next.

After the large group they were traveling with was apprehended, now a familiar sight to operators working along this part of the border, Juan and José were transported together to the Yuma Border Patrol Station for what should have been a routine booking: they'd have biographical information obtained, get fingerprinted, and snap a photo taken in order to be "submitted into all available databases."

In Juan's words, this is where they were "kidnapped." By agents of the United States. It was worse than anything he experienced in Petén or on their journey to Arizona.

As if it were routine, the father and son were led in different directions to two of the Border Patrol's notoriously cold jail cells, known to Juan as "hieleras," or ice boxes. They could see each other across a hallway, through the windows in the metal doors of the concrete rooms they were now locked in. Juan's cell was filled with other parents, José's with other children.

"We weren't told anything," he recalled.

José out of sight, Juan attempted to rest in the cell, where if you're lucky mats are provided to sleep on the floors, and where a single toilet, attached to the cell's water fountain, is shielded by only a waist-high cinder-block wall.

But all he could do was pray, seeing agents and staff come and go at night, but no sign of his boy. By ten in the morning on Tuesday, when another agent came to interview him, Juan had already been officially separated from his son for hours.

According to his arrest narrative written by the Border Patrol, Juan had been charged Monday night with three crimes: 8 U.S.C. § 1325, "entry of alien at improper time or place misrep/concealment of facts"; 8 U.S.C. § 1182, "alien inadmissibility under section 212"; and 212a7Ail, "immigrant without an immigrant visa." That meant, under zero tolerance, he would soon be remanded to the custody of the U.S. marshals in order to face a type of justice—a criminal charge instead of a civil one—that was different from the norm. It was a charge that would legaly necessitate the separation of him and José. He had no idea.

That first night, a Border Patrol agent told him, "Only your child can stay in the United States." Juan wanted to declare asylum for them both and explain why they had made the journey, but a Border Patrol agent told him to sign documents admitting he entered the country illegally, with no mention of asylum. So he did.

For two more nights Juan was locked up, with no sign of José, only the comings and goings of others who, like him, had no idea what they were getting into when they crossed the border. He felt like he was losing his mind.

"We knew nothing about what was happening," he later recalled.

In the middle of his third night in custody, a guard came to take Juan out of his cell. He asked to see José.

"Even for thirty seconds," Juan begged of the Border Patrol agent, who ignored his plea.

Inconsolable, Juan was crying as he was led out of Yuma station and into a transport vehicle. Tears wet his eyes on the three-hour drive, his anguish heightened by uncertainty, about where he was going or what would happen to his son. At five thirty in the morning the sun began to rise over the Arizona desert, near the same stretch I found myself with the Border Patrol in February when I was incapacitated by a migraine.

At seven fifteen in the morning Juan was booked into the staging facility operated by Immigration and Customs Enforcement in Florence, Arizona. At the Florence Detention Center, a seven-hundred-plus-bed facility owned and operated by the federal government, he was put under the supervision of the ICE Health Service Corps.

This fact came as news to him when I told him a year later, after reviewing his documents. "Which doctor if there is no phone? There was no communication."

Three days later, he was again moved without warning. This time, Juan was shackled. He was cuffed by his hands and feet and locked in place as if he were a violent criminal. For almost seven hours he was driven by bus, destination unknown.

Reconstructing his odyssey, his probable route took him past Phoenix to Palm Springs, California, then through the Cajon Pass between the San Gabriel Mountains to the west, which stretch into Los Angeles, and the San Bernardino Mountains to the east. He arrived in what Southern California natives refer to as the high desert, technically the Mojave, the driest region of North America. He was now more than four hundred miles away from his son. There was no good-bye.

Juan was headed to a federal prison in Victorville. The shackles that restrained him were meant for violent criminals, not asylum seekers. Victorville is home to convicted murderers, rapists, and gang leaders—and, since the start of the Trump administration's zero tolerance policy, migrants who have been convicted of nothing. They were here because they crossed the border in search of safety, security, and a better life. The prison complex is huge, home to more than 3,500 inmates, and under a plan hatched between ICE and the Bureau of Prisons, it would be filled with an additional one thousand migrants, including Juan.

Immediately after arriving, he started asking questions, as he and other immigrants, segregated from the rest of the inmate population, found themselves each with a single prison uniform, often on cell confinement or lockdown, and without access to legal counsel.

Where is my son?

Can I make a phone call?

Can I eat anything other than this bread and ham?

The answer from the guards, he said, was always the same. No.

JOSÉ, FOURTEEN YEARS old, had questions of his own while locked in a different jail cell from his dad along the Arizona border in Yuma. He remained there for days, even after his father was transferred out, unbeknownst to him, three days after they arrived. Still in the same dirty clothes he jumped over the border fence in, José wondered about what would happen to his father, who had begged to see him from within the same building, to no avail. His mother and sisters, thousands of miles away, wondered why they had not called. Finally, after what seemed like days without answers, the door to José's cell opened, and he was told it was time to leave. His father wasn't coming with him, nor did he know where he was.

He was taken to an airport, where José boarded an airplane for the first time in his life. Joining him were other children who had also been detained at the Yuma Border Patrol Station. They, too, had been separated from their parents. Like José, none knew where they were.

Where were they going? There were few answers. The adult traveling with them was clearly not a member of the Border Patrol. No green uniform. No handcuffs.

Inside an airplane for the first time, he wasn't sure what to do. The seat belts looked different from any he had seen before. Instructions were coming through the loudspeaker in English. He was exhausted. The stranger traveling with him, who likely told him to hold on to his belongings and ticket and not to lose them, was a social worker. He explained to José that he was going to be taken care of at the place where they were going. But the adult should have been trained not to make José any promises about where his dad was or whether he was going to see him again.

José was able to find out the answer to one question—what

their destination was. "Harlingen," the social worker told him. South Texas.

Seat belts buckled, the plane taxied onto the runway, and as his heart pounded, the plane took off. They were heading southeast, the opposite direction from where his father, Juan, had been taken. Once in the sky, exhausted, José fell asleep.

June 13, 2018

I quickly thumbed out a tweet before I was made to drop my cell phone in a Tupperware container to prevent any unwanted photographs, filming, or live-streaming inside the nation's largest shelter for child migrants.

It was two minutes to five in the evening, local time. The lobby of Casa Padre shelter, in Brownsville, Texas, could have passed for a spa or doctor's office—front desk with a sign-in sheet, tile floors, chairs in a waiting area. I was nervous and knew that whatever I and the assembled group of ten or so reporters would see beyond this lobby would be the first glimpse any journalist had been given of detained children separated by President Trump.

Next to the Tupperware phone box, I noticed a piece of paper meant for staff members at the facility—instructions on exactly what to do if you encounter a member of the media: 1) "immediately notify PD," or the program director, and 2) call the shelter communications director, whose name and number were also attached to the form. Employees at the 250,000-square-foot former Walmart were on edge.

Ten days before we showed up, U.S. senator Jeff Merkley, a Democrat from Oregon, had pulled into the parking lot unannounced while live-streaming on Facebook to attempt to get inside the facility. Merkley heard that the center, run by a giant nonprofit organization called Southwest Key, "may currently be housing hundreds of refugee children who have been separated from their parents," as he wrote on Facebook. He was right, and his surprise visit spooked staff, causing them to call local law enforcement and be on guard for others who wanted a glimpse inside the secretive world of detaining migrant children.

Now some of the same officials from both Southwest Key and the Department of Health and Human Services' Office of Refugee Resettlement, Southwest Key's client, were standing with us in the lobby, waiting for me to drop my phone in the plastic box so our pad-and-paper-only briefing could begin. I slid my phone on top of the others in the box, pressing down on the top to seal it shut. With the pen and a tiny blue notebook I had grabbed at Walgreens on the way here in hand, nobody outside of Casa Padre would hear from me again until I came back out after what was scheduled to be a short tour.

I was last in Brownsville in April, when I drove to see where the Rio Grande meets the Gulf of Mexico. I ended up back in the South Texas city after a bizarre and urgent phone call on a Tuesday night.

I HAD ONLY met Katie Waldman once previously. The twenty-six-year-old press aide to homeland security secretary Kirstjen Nielsen had played the part of wallflower perfectly as she sat in my line of sight as I interviewed her boss for *Dateline*. Our documentary was now delayed months past its original March air date. Ten days into June we missed the second scheduled air date after our "first cut" got sent back to us by the executives in charge. Waldman had kept in touch over phone and email, keen to know when the interview would air.

"You better get down there," Waldman told me about visiting the shelter in Brownsville. "I had HHS put you on the list."

She was offering me what Senator Merkley couldn't get—a firsthand look at separated kids in the custody of Health and Human Services. I was confused why she wanted me and other reporters to see where separated children were being taken when her boss had given me a lengthy explanation, as Waldman looked on, about how separating families at the border is "not different" than an American citizen parent getting arrested. Waldman candidly told me she would rather journalists characterize for the public what is happening inside than a group of Democratic politicians, who would soon be touring as part of a congressional delegation.

"Will there be another opportunity to go?" I asked her, knowing I had another unrelated shoot scheduled at the end of the week.

"You should go now," she said.

Something about the way Waldman was presenting the opportunity made it clear we should drop everything and scramble to get there. So I went through the checklist of phone calls I normally make when I have to mobilize and cover a story on short notice: I got approval from my boss, Janelle Rodriguez, who after I explained we would be part of the first group of journalists to see separated kids, put me into motion without asking another question. Then I sent a DM on Twitter to Chris Hayes, the host of the eight o'clock hour on MSNBC, who had been closely following President Trump's immigration policy since day one.

> *Hey there. Going to be touring an HHS facility for kids*
> *tomorrow at 5PM in Brownsville, Texas. Can go live from*
> *outside afterwards for you if interested. Going to drop a*
> *note to your team.*

As promised, I told Chris's producers, who told me he would take me live after I finished my tour since it would be during his hour Wednesday evening. I also reached out to our colleague Betsy Korona, who would be managing our live shots Thursday during the day, and Aarne, who booked travel and arranged for a crew and satellite truck to meet us on the ground.

The next morning, Aarne and I would take off for Brownsville, connecting through Houston, knowing that any delay could put our tour and access to a massive story in jeopardy.

"WE'RE NOT USED to so many people," the receptionist behind the front desk told me as I pushed down on the top of the Tupperware box holding the phones of the assembled journalists at Casa Padre. "It's an awesome place, it really is."

Phones tucked away, we huddled in between the electronic sliding glass door to the parking lot outside and the door behind the front desk. We were roughly where a Walmart greeter would have welcomed us to the supercenter, if it hadn't been bought and taken over by the largest nonprofit responsible for the care and custody of unaccompanied migrant children.

Southwest Key's leader, Dr. Juan Sanchez, a thin handsome man who referred to himself as El Presidente, wanted to go over ground rules and background information before we entered the facility.

I scribbled down most everything I could as he and his colleagues spoke. A press representative from the Administration for Children and Families, Brian Marriott, watched as I learned in real time about the Office of Refugee Resettlement, its mission, and its rapid growth under the Obama and now Trump administrations.

This place, Sanchez explained to us, was completely permitted and legal. It had a commercial certificate of occupancy, a child care administration license, a public health license, and permission to operate from the Texas Department of Health and Human Services. He talked so fast, it was hard to keep up.

"We've never had so much attention," he said, echoing the receptionist. For that he had the Trump administration to thank. He also explained to us they had the Trump administration to thank—or blame, depending on how you wanted to look at it—for the surge in unaccompanied migrant kids in his custody.

"We're happy to have you here," Sanchez said, explaining that Casa Padre was currently over capacity. Some 1,497 kids were inside a building meant for thirty-nine less than that—that day accounting for 13 percent of all children in the custody of the Office of Refugee Resettlement nationwide. As he explained it, the increase in referrals was a direct result of children being taken from their parents, children who would otherwise not require the services of his organization.

As he spoke, Sanchez was surrounded by supportive staff: Alexia Rodriguez, the chief programs officer and legal counsel; Elizabeth Schepel, the managing director of immigrant children's services; Martin Hinojosa, the director of compliance; Jaime Garcia, the program director; and Olga Garcia, the executive program director. Everyone, it seemed to me, was slightly uneasy.

We were warned not to speak with any of the children.

And with that, the door opened into the cavernous facility. All I could see were young boys everywhere I looked. I jotted down what I saw and what I was thinking in my spiral notebook while my head was on a swivel. I didn't look down at the notebook as I wrote, and my handwriting suffered for it.

If the boys weren't sitting in chairs along walls waiting together in a room, or sitting at cafeteria-style tables, they were in line to eat. In their hands were trays holding Oreo cookies, applesauce, Jell-O, chicken, and mashed potatoes.

I was walking side by side with Alexia Rodriguez, the lawyer for the facility. When I expressed amazement at what I was seeing, without skipping a beat she told me and another reporter standing near her to smile at the kids because "they feel like animals in a cage being looked at." I think she realized how truthful she had just been, because she immediately said she didn't want that comment to be on the record, which, of course, is not how that works.

In fairness to Rodriguez, "cages" was perhaps the wrong word. There were none here I could see, which I found important to note after Senator Merkley used the phrase about a Border Patrol facility in McAllen, Texas, not far from here, which led to confusion online.

Rodriguez was right, though. The kids were looking at us with a deer-in-the-headlights gaze, a group of ten reporters with notepads chronicling any detail we could vacuum up as we were herded like animals through the facility. As we continued walking, she explained all of the approximately 1,500 kids would eat in a two-hour window, rotating. Disobeying orders, I couldn't help saying hello, asking the children how they were doing the best I could with my limited Spanish. I soon was asked to stop.

As we were shepherded to an area where boys lined up to take a shower and to the rooms where they slept, I noticed the first of many quotes on the wall there: "Observe good faith and justice towards all nations."

With craned heads, we looked inside one of the 313 bedrooms. Five twin beds were arranged like puzzle pieces to fit in the small room. We were told five beds per room was unusual. Olga Garcia, the executive program director, told me these extra cots were part of a variance the facility had received starting in May, around the time zero tolerance was announced by Attorney General Sessions.

At this point I looked over at Brian Marriott, the stalky former Trump campaign aide and now senior director of communications and media relations for the Administration for Children and Families, and asked him if he had ever been to Casa Padre before. He hadn't, he admitted.

"Pretty nice," he quipped.

Not what I was thinking.

As we continued walking, we again passed by the cafeteria, where we started. For the first time I noticed there was a mural of President Trump that stretched the length of the entire wall. Incredulous, I read the quote that accompanied the mural: "Sometimes losing a battle you find a new way to win the war."

I walked away.

We wound our way through narrow hallways. Along one wall, I saw a phone, which signage made clear was for the young boys detained here to use if they wanted to raise a complaint outside of the building.

Next to the phone was a piece of paper with names of local service organizations children could call for help: the Cameron County Child Advocacy Center, a child abuse prevention advocacy organization; the Valley Baptists Medical Center, a hospital; and ProBAR Children's Project, a legal services agency for children and adults in immigration detention.

Almost as fast as I could register what kinds of horrors might compel a child to pick up that phone to call one of those service providers, we came upon another room, a barbershop where kids were getting a trim. Where am I? What is this? The thoughts that ran through my head were dizzying, but I tried to stay focused. I couldn't shake the phone booth. I went back to see it a second time.

At one point, I asked a staffer how separated families would ultimately reunite. After families are apprehended at the border and children are taken from parents, I was told, the Department of Homeland Security sends intake emails noting the child is going to be transferred. The Office of Refugee Resettlement, when receiving a child, completes the intake process within twenty-four hours after first immediately providing a shower and food.

It was during the intake process, I learned, that case managers would generally find out about separations, and they would then notify other relevant agencies that they were caring for a separated child. This is also how the list that Jim De La Cruz was keeping—and Scott Lloyd wanted gone—was created.

There wasn't enough time for me to think about how backward that was—that the agency doing the separating wasn't keeping track of the separations and transmitting that information over with the children it was referring.

And yet, that is exactly the nightmare scenario that Commander Jonathan White, Jennifer Podkul, Claire Trickler-McNulty, and others had been beating the drum about for months if not years. After children here completed the intake process, I was told, they'd be given the opportunity to make two calls a week to sponsors or family members in their home countries. These boys were ages ten to seventeen. What about smaller kids, for whom remembering a phone number, street address, or even last name wasn't possible? We had to keep walking.

Now making our way through what felt like the back of the facility, passing by more murals and song lyrics and patriotic phrases like "America the Beautiful," "Liberty and Justice for All," and "I Have a Dream," I had to do a double take. Not because of the American jingoistic display for children from around the world who ended up here, but because there was a tai chi class taking place.

At this moment, as our Southwest Key tour guides attempted to show off the extracurricular activities the children detained here received, all I could think about was that we felt like we were in a jail or prison. I had been in both, on stories for MSNBC—county jails in Southern California and Ohio, and a state prison in Northern California. No amount of recreation would make me feel otherwise.

In what was once the loading dock in this former Walmart, children sat in theater-style seats below the platform watching *Moana,* the Disney film, on a makeshift movie screen. Not far away, the former auto body shop was now a basketball court. Outside, we were shown what was in name a recreation area—but really a dirt field—where children were allowed only two hours a day—three on the weekend. That meant they were inside twenty-two to twenty-three hours a day. When I heard that, I asked right away—have kids tried to leave?

Yes, someone told me. Though not many, they quickly added. I had no way to confirm this was true.

Our tour was meant to be quick, but now stretched on toward an hour. I asked when or if the lights were turned out inside. Nine sharp.

We made it to our final stop, the clinical office, a small medical facility inside Casa Padre. We were greeted by staff wearing scrubs, in a room that was clean, orderly, and felt like it could be an urgent care center or ER. One of the men in scrubs told us the other services the children would receive: screenings for diabetes, tuberculosis, and sexually transmitted diseases, vaccines, a chest x-ray, blood labs, a blood pressure check.

Kids had the ability to see a mental health clinician or psychiatrist, who could prescribe children psychotropic medicines without the consent of their separated parents because while in their "care and custody," as they like to put it, the Office of Refugee Resettlement and its director Scott Lloyd are technically their custodians. If a child mentioned he was separated from a parent to the medical staff, one of the three physicians on call or forty-eight total staffers in the department would note it in the client file.

At this point, Dr. Sanchez, "El Presidente" of Southwest Key, was feeling chatty. He and I walked together as he told me he was a fan of MSNBC and his values aligned with what he felt he saw on our air. He said that separations had undoubtedly led to the overcrowded situation we were both walking through. But he went on to note that another Trump administration policy—fingerprinting potential sponsors of children and other members of their household—was scaring away people from picking up unaccompanied children, and was contributing to the situation. That meant a lack of bed space. Sanchez said there were more than five thousand kids in his custody alone at the twenty-six Southwest Key shelters across the country, representing nearly half of the total overall population in the care of the government. Sanchez wanted me to know that meant one critically important thing: unlicensed temporary shelters would be opening soon on federal property, and they would come with their own set of problems.

In the meantime, the hundreds of separated children in Casa Padre had to figure out where their parents were and how to reunite with them—or if that would even be possible.

THE SAME SCENARIO was playing out in shelters across the country, including ones not far from Casa Padre. Thirty-two minutes away by car was another large shelter, this one operated by BCFS Health and Human Services, a nonprofit with a portfolio far smaller than Southwest Key but still one of the larger players in the Office of Refugee Resettlement's network of care providers.

As I toured Casa Padre, fourteen-year-old José was there at the Harlingen shelter, having been flown to South Texas from Arizona. He had been there just long enough to settle into a routine—sleep, eat, and attempt to stay busy with the activities the shelter provided.

During his intake process, he told his case manager that after he and his father, Juan, crossed the border from San Luis Rio Colorado into the Arizona desert, he hadn't seen or heard from him since they were locked in separate freezing-cold jail cells at the Yuma Border Patrol station. He explained how he was taken from the facility, flown from Arizona to Texas. He made clear that all he wanted was to see his father again.

José, like the boys in Casa Padre, also had access to a telephone to make calls. The phone was his only lifeline. Not only had he never been to Texas, but he had no idea what the outside of the building even looked like. Less than two weeks had passed since he was taken from his dad, and he hadn't heard a peep from him since then.

José wasn't able to reach his mother, María, either. While he had her contact information and tried to reach her every time he was allowed to make a phone call, he couldn't get her on the line when he would try to call. Again and again he tried, with no luck. Even if he did reach her, he couldn't even describe where to find him, what it looked like, how to get him out, or where to go.

All José knew was that he was inside "Beh-Ceh-Eff-Ess," and that he was alone.

AN HOUR AND fourteen minutes after I tucked my cell phone into the plastic box designed to keep what was happening behind the doors of Casa Padre just that—behind its doors—I walked back into the lobby and pulled it out. I opened the Twitter app and started typing as I walked back across the parking lot toward where our satellite truck was located, dish pointed at the sky. I knew there was less than an hour before I was supposed to go live with Chris Hayes in prime time on MSNBC, but I was shell-shocked.

"Just finished the tour, don't even know where to start," I wrote. "One of the first things you notice when you walk into the shelter—no joke—a mural of Trump with the quote 'sometimes losing a battle you find a new way to win the war.' Presidential murals everywhere. But that one is 1st."

By the time I made it to the rented minivan where Aarne and our local crew were waiting, I decided I needed a minute to decompress. I sat in the front passenger seat of the car, with my blue notebook on my lap, as I plugged in my phone to make sure I'd have enough battery for what I expected would be a long night. While Aarne confirmed details about what time I would go on-air with Hayes, around 8:45, for the next hour and twenty-seven minutes I kept tweeting, adding to a thread about what I saw inside.

This shelter, Casa Padre, is the largest licensed childcare facility of its kind in the country. Nearly 1,500 boys 10-17 in here now. They're supposed to sleep four to room. Nearly every room has 5. They've received a variance from the state because of overcrowding.

7:23 PM ET

Officials here said they've never had an MS-13 member here, ever.

7:24 PM ET

Moments after we walked in a shelter employee asked us to smile at hundreds of detained migrant kids in line for a meal because "they feel like animals in a cage being looked at."

7:50 PM ET

Kids here get only two hours a day to be outside in fresh air.
One hour of structured time.
One hour of free time.
The rest of the day is spent inside a former Wal Mart.
7:53PM ET

At eight o'clock sharp on the east coast, Hayes began his show as he always does, with his "cold open"—the pretaped introduction telling viewers what they were about to see. "Tonight, on *All In!*" he bellowed as he started reading the headlines, including this one: "NBC News gets inside the detention facility that locked out Senator Merkley."

I didn't know it, but Hayes had also lined up an interview with Representative Mark Meadows, the Republican congressman who was the leader of the so-called Freedom Caucus, the right wing of the GOP, which he teased as well. I was focused on processing everything I had just learned. Writing was helpful in organizing the details, so I continued tweeting as Hayes launched into his show.

Instructions to employees in the lobby of the shelter if you encounter media:

1) "Immediately notify PD," or the police department.

2) Call the shelter communications director.

In that order.

For the record, nobody called cops on us. We were invited by HHS and the shelter.
8:04 PM ET

That tweet contained an error, one that was pointed out to me later by an employee of the shelter. PD referred, not to the police department, but the policy director. The point, though, was the same—media wasn't welcome without an invitation, which, in this case, we had. I kept sending messages out to the Internet.

> This mega-shelter is run by trained staff—a nonprofit.
>
> I believe the worker looking after these kids who said she'd like to see a day when they don't have to do this.
>
> But things are moving in the wrong direction—capacity is 1497 and tonight 1469 boys will sleep here.
>
> **8:09 PM ET**

> I have been inside a federal prison and county jails. This place is called a shelter but these kids are incarcerated. No cells and no cages, and they get to go to classes about American history and watch Moana, but they're in custody. Coming up on @allinwithchris next.
>
> **8:39 PM ET**

After sending that tweet I got out of the minivan, stretched my legs, and walked about fifteen feet to our live shot position. I hooked up my microphone, put the IFB into my ear, and made sure the control room back in New York could hear me.

Behind me was the guard shack I had walked past to first enter the facility, with a sign reading "Welcome to Casa Padre," though it was out of focus in the shot behind me. As the evening breeze started to pick up and employees were leaving for the night, still half an hour from the sun setting, I could hear Chris begin to introduce me.

"Two weeks ago Senator Jeff Merkley tried to get a tour of an immigrant detention center at an abandoned Walmart building in Brownsville, Texas, that houses children. Senator

Merkley was not allowed inside. No one would grant him an interview," Hayes reminded his viewers. "But today, for the first time since Senator Merkley was asked to leave the premises, our own Jacob Soboroff finally did get a tour. He joins me now just outside that facility in Brownsville, Texas. Jacob, you were with a few other journalists at that facility. What did you see?"

"You know, Chris," I began, "I have been inside a federal prison before. I have been inside several county jails. This place is called a shelter but effectively, these kids are incarcerated." I was so wrapped up in the gravity of what I saw, I goofed again. It was a state prison I had been inside, not a federal one—California State Prison Solano—but I repeated the error for Hayes I had made moments earlier on social media. The point I was trying to make again was the same: whether you wanted to call this place a mega-shelter, detention center, or former Walmart, there were nearly fifteen hundred kids inside, more than four hundred of whom were there only because they were taken from their parents when they arrived.

I continued, explaining to Chris and his audience of millions of people that while children were not locked in cages, I was told they felt as if they were. I told him about the cafeteria, the bedrooms, and the fact they were inside for twenty-two hours a day. I told him that 30 percent of the kids inside were separated, that the building behind me was the largest of its kind in the country, and that "it's organized chaos in there. It's hectic, but it's organized."

Hayes asked me about the ages of the kids inside. "They're all boys and from age ten to seventeen. The thing that strikes me as a parent of a two-and-a-half-year-old boy, what about from zero to ten? This is one of a hundred facilities like this across seventeen states." It was a question we would continue to ask in the days ahead.

Hayes inquired about the ratio of shelter workers to kids, and I remembered what I was told inside. "One to eight is the ratio. There's one staff member for every incarcerated shelter resident, is what they call them." We talked about the tai chi, the loading dock, *Moana,* classes where kids learn American history, and the mural with President Trump. I kept waiting for the segment to end, as they so often do too quickly in cable news, but Chris wanted to keep talking.

"What is the level of training of these grown-ups who, you know, watching eight boys per grown-up for twenty-two hours a day? That's very serious work that requires very serious training," Hayes pointed out.

I told him what I had tweeted moments earlier: "This is a licensed facility and it brings up the much larger issue—you have licensed teachers, clinicians, three on-call doctors around this facility at any time, a forty-eight-person medical staff that's inside here. But what's being talked about with the administration is moving or bringing children away from facilities, like this, licensed facilities, and on to tent cities on federal property. And what I was told tonight is that those tent cities that are being looked at here in Texas and throughout the state of California are unlicensed facilities. It won't require necessarily, on federal property because it's an emergency situation, the level of training, the types of professionals, that are taking care of the kids that are in this facility tonight when the lights go out at nine P.M."

I heard Hayes, in my ear, say, "Wow," when he learned

that information, and as he did again it hit me about how consequential what was playing out behind me truly was. Instead of ending the segment, Hayes, who had been covering family separations on his show and was clearly affected by what he was hearing, had a final question.

"Unaccompanied minors are one thing," he noted. "But the ones who traveled with a parent or guardian or grandparent and were taken away from them, are there regular contacts they get to have with that person?"

Hayes was asking about exactly what José was going through at that moment, as were thousands of other children across the country.

"They wouldn't say regular, but they said it's basically up to the penal institution where they are," I explained. "It happens, but it's not happening on a regular basis."

After Chris thanked me and before he moved on to talk with Congressman Meadows and Democratic congressman John Garamendi, who joined him, I expressed my gratitude for his focus on what was happening.

"Thanks for staying on this, man," I said to him, pursing my lips and shaking my head, bringing an end to our nearly ten-minute-long unscripted live back-and-forth, almost unheard-of real estate to be given up by a cable news host on a prime-time show.

"Thanks, Jacob, you're clear," I was told in my ear by the control room, as they always do. I pulled out the earpiece, looked at Aarne, and got back in the car, knowing we would again be live on the air later that night, and again likely all day the following day.

In between Hayes and appearing live with Lawrence

O'Donnell during his ten o'clock show, alongside Senator Merkley, who was appearing via satellite from Washington, I wrote an article for NBCNews.com explaining what I had seen. After the O'Donnell broadcast, Aarne and I headed back to our hotel, the Hampton Inn and Suites, where I recorded the voice-over for a report I would be filing for the *Today* show the following morning. In a matter of hours I'd have to be back outside Casa Padre, and I needed sleep. Before I closed my eyes the first of countless direct messages started streaming in via Twitter, including from James Corden, the host of *The Late Late Show* on CBS.

"Jacob, your account about the center for children has made my heart sink. What can we do? Is there anything?"

I replied, careful not to share how I was feeling—drained and discouraged—instead telling him that what I learned brought us to this point.

"The policy is the problem," I replied. And then I went to bed.

I SET MY alarm for before five in the morning local time, six in the morning in New York, where in less than an hour I would be leading the *Today* show. Before I got out of bed, I grabbed my cell phone and looked through my emails, then opened Twitter, where I was shocked to see my follower count grew by tens of thousands overnight. People were paying attention.

Sometime just before six in the morning local time, Aarne and I arrived back at Casa Padre, where we got set for the top of the broadcast.

In my earpiece, the NBC News chimes rang—the musical notes G, E, and C—then the headlines began.

"Border Battle!" I heard coanchor Hoda Kotb say in the top-of-the-show tease of the stories of the day. "An exclusive look inside the place where families are being split amid the growing fight over immigration," a somewhat accurate description of what I had reported the night before, though the separations were happening at the Border Patrol stations, not at the shelters. In fairness, this was complicated, and the Trump administration's response was making it even more confusing.

The show opened with a report on wild weather overnight, followed by the latest from the White House. At seven minutes after the hour, Hoda tossed to me.

While reporters in network television are generally asked to keep their opinions and emotions to themselves, I decided what I had seen was worth a slight breach of protocol. With the sun on the verge of rising at Casa Padre, and a large, noisy flock of great-tailed grackles calling out from the trees around me, I started my report.

"This was shocking to see, quite frankly," I began, calling to mind the kids I was reporting on. As groups including the American Academy of Pediatrics had warned for years precisely to prevent unnecessary family separations, they were likely already experiencing the irreversible trauma that was a direct result of forcibly taking children from parents.

"This morning there are fifteen hundred young boys waking up inside this former Walmart, and with so many families crossing right here in South Texas and now being split up, this overcrowding crisis doesn't seem like it's going to be letting up anytime soon."

I spent the rest of the morning giving live reports about what I had seen inside Casa Padre. Over and over, I shared what I had seen—and why the Trump administration's insistence that there was no family separation policy was plainly untrue, something I could prove myself.

By midday, I had spoken with a source in Washington, D.C., who gave me a tip: Dr. Juan Sanchez's warning was a prescient one. The Trump administration and the Department of Health and Human Services were about to erect a temporary influx shelter on federal land to alleviate overcrowding at places like Casa Padre, this one in Tornillo, Texas. Working with my colleagues, Julia Ainsley probing her sources at the Department of Justice and Courtney Kube hers at the Pentagon, we were able to break news that the Tornillo Land Port of Entry, in a remote desert area outside of El Paso, was selected.

"Jacob, you're getting a lot of attention for this report," anchor Katy Tur said during an appearance on her show, "because when you toured this, and we should note that cameras were not allowed inside, only reporters with pens and pads. But after you toured this, you went on television and you said 'these are basically prisons.' "

"That's exactly right. Let me do the breaking news first, Katy," I said to my fellow Southern Californian, a friend since high school. "The kids that would otherwise be going to facilities like this or this specific facility, Casa Padre in Brownsville, Texas, may now be diverted because of that Trump administration zero tolerance policy that separates migrant children from their parents when they cross the border in what the administration says is an illegal act. The first location will be at the Tornillo Land Port of Entry, that's not far from El Paso."

Tornillo was one of the places I drove right by on that November night in 2017 when Lomi Kriel's bombshell story broke, exposing the early stages of President Trump's family separation pilot program.

I told Katy what my colleagues and I had learned from working the phones, "that four hundred and fifty beds will be at that location, and that it will be, effectively, a tent camp, a tent city, however you want to characterize it." Once I got off the air with Katy, I learned that the high temperature earlier in the week at Tornillo was 103 degrees.

The rest of the day we continued our live reports, wrapping up twenty-four hours after I first went into Casa Padre by talking with Chris Matthews on *Hardball*.

I'm used to being on the road and apart from my family for extended stretches of time. It's part of the job as a TV news correspondent. Covering the 2016 presidential race, when for the first time I heard Trump advisor Stephen Miller's vitriol for undocumented immigrants in person, I was on the road for what felt like three quarters of the year.

But being at the center of the contest that would determine the future of the United States was fun and, I'm embarrassed to say, at times distracted me from was going on at home. That wasn't the case now. I had never wanted to see my wife and son more. Though nothing compared to what the families I was reporting on were going through, I found myself spent, emotionally shaken, and feeling out of it. Being with my family was all I could think about.

Once cleared by New York, Aarne and I raced to the airport and could see our small commuter plane on the tarmac as we parked our rental car. We ran inside, tossing the keys to the agent on our way to catch the flight, making it just moments before it pulled away from the jet bridge en route to Dallas, where we would catch our connection home to our families. Home. Family. Two things the separated children inside Casa Padre might never see again.

COMMANDER JONATHAN WHITE, the career civil servant who in March had left the Office of Refugee Resettlement over disagreements with his boss, Scott Lloyd, had been sounding the alarm on family separations since the early days of the Trump administration. Now, sitting home while watching family separations become an international news story on television, White was agonizing, experiencing the type of sorrow he for years worked to prevent in the children who were now separated from their parents.

White shared with others his personal feelings of despair about what he was seeing play out on television—that he failed to prevent widespread separations from happening and that despite his trying every trick he knew to keep this from happening, tens of thousands of children would now be ripped from their parents and irreparably traumatized. He would be watching it from the sidelines, unable to help in an official capacity after leaving the Office of Refugee Resettlement in March.

As this nightmare played out on national television, he sent a lengthy but informal email to a colleague in the Health and Human Services Department division that oversees public health initiatives. He included a list of suggestions, based on his extensive knowledge of issues relating to migrant children, of how best to prepare for potential family reunifications. The U.S. Public Health Service Commissioned Corps, the agency over which the surgeon general presides, had been activated to provide Border Patrol medical help (just as it would be, almost two years later, in response to the COVID-19 pandemic). White was offering his insight on how they best could be put to work.

The list included a recommendation to establish a close connection with Jim De La Cruz and members of ORR's Federal Field Specialist team. "That is the most important ground contact I can think of in terms of understanding the population and the context."

De La Cruz had earlier held strong, refusing Lloyd's suggestion to destroy the informal list he had kept on separated families. White wanted to make sure that participating staff would take a tour, like I did, "of a nearby ORR permanent shelter facility so they can see and understand" that "conditions for children are always better in ORR custody than in CBP custody," the type of jail cells that Juan and José had sat in separately on the border in Yuma. "It will help them make moral sense of their mission to expedite kids moving into and through that system."

White also warned that, like the emotions he was experiencing at the time, "officers may benefit from having a thirty-minute end-of-shift meeting of their own offsite, to debrief about what they have heard and seen that day." He concluded, "no one should stay longer than 2 weeks" to mitigate behavioral health issues.

White's colleague thanked him profusely for the input. White replied that he would let another colleague, "who is up to his eyeballs in the Tornillo stand-up," know they had been in touch "so there are no surprises later."

Now was the scramble to make sure children who were undergoing trauma in real time, including José, could get back to their parents as soon as possible. But the Trump administration had other ideas.

⬛ ⬛ ⬛

Significant Incident Report

AGE: 9

CHILD'S COUNTRY OF BIRTH: El Salvador

ADMITTED DATE: 6/17/2018

CURRENT PROGRAM: Bethany Christian Services TFC

SYNOPSIS OF EVENT: UAC was separated from parent at the border.

DESCRIPTION OF INCIDENT: According to the minor's Placement Confirmation e-mail, the minor was separated from her mother . . . due to "Zero Tolerance." According to the Online Detainee Locator System, minor's mother is being detained at the Port Isabel Service Detention Center. During intake, the minor confirmed that she was separated from her mother. However, the minor was unable to provide further details due to exhaustion from late night intake.

Why did you decide to travel to the U.S. at this time?

The minor reported that her paternal uncle did "exchanges" with a local gang for money. She went on to state that when he refused to do a trade deal (although she was unsure why he refused), the gang killed him, and began to insist that minor's father complete the "exchange." Minor stated that her father also refused, and the local gang began threatening her mother. Minor reported that she and her mother decided to travel to the U.S. following being advised by minor's father . . . to flee to safety in the U.S.

Did the arrangements change during the journey? If yes, how?

The minor reported that it was not part of the plan for her to be separated from her mother upon apprehension.

CHAPTER SEVEN

"They're Cages"

June 16, 2018

Juan was locked up in a federal prison in Victorville.

By common consensus, it was a hellhole. No sign of attorneys. No access to phones. Horrendous food. Dirty conditions. And, worst of all, not a word from his son, José, who by now was in Texas, thousands of miles from where they had been separated in Arizona.

There was no information about José in Juan's case file, meaning they couldn't be connected even if he wanted to be.

The same day, I traveled home from South Texas with Aarne, looking out the window at Brownsville as we flew away, landing in Dallas for our connection home to Los Angeles as the sun was setting.

Meanwhile, Lindsay Toczylowski was trying to get into Victorville to see the new migrant detainees. I didn't know her, but Toczylowski lived in the same neighborhood I did in Los Angeles, with children slightly older than my son. The executive director of Immigrant Defenders Law Center, a nonprofit law firm offering legal defense for migrants and refugees, she had spent her career defending people like Juan and his son, José, against deportation.

Every time I looked down at my phone, news reports from around the world highlighted what I and the other journalists had seen firsthand: what the reality of family separations looked like for young boys. It only compounded how anxious I was to get home to see my wife and son.

For her part, Toczylowski was desperate to get inside the federal prison she had heard was now home to an increasing population of migrants, including separated parents.

She called three times on June 11 in order to figure out what the guidelines were for entering the facility, but the phone kept ringing and ringing. Nobody picked up. The following morning, after dropping her kids at day care, she made the drive from Los Angeles to the prison, and asked to meet with detainees to offer free legal services, including Juan, whose name was on a leaked list of incarcerated migrants she had obtained.

She was turned away twice, first by an officer who told her he didn't know how those types of visits would work, since most of the men locked up were convicts, not facing civil immigration charges. Then she was told by another prison official that there was an across-the-board visitation ban because there wasn't space available and Immigration and Customs Enforcement hadn't given the go-ahead for them to take place. After handing over her list of detainees, Toczylowski was told she would hear from ICE. Dejected and physically intimidated, she got back in her car and returned to Los Angeles, not knowing what to believe.

What she did grasp was that the rights of those detained inside were being violated. Two nights later, Thursday evening, she went to sleep hoping that the formal visitation request submitted that day would gain her access. Friday passed, and she received no response.

ON THE SAME day I spent hours broadcasting from outside Casa Padre, breaking the news that the federal government was standing up the Tornillo tent camp for migrant children, Attorney General Jeff Sessions used the Bible to justify separating children.

He aimed to push back on one of many critical statements leveled at him and the administration, this one by the U.S. Conference of Catholic Bishops, which correctly observed that "our government has the discretion in our laws to ensure that young children are not separated from their parents and exposed to irreparable harm and trauma." The Conference of Bishops added, "Families are the foundational element of our society and they must be able to stay together."

Standing behind the seal of the United States Department of Justice, Sessions had the temerity to tell an audience made up of Rotary Club members in Fort Wayne, Indiana, that "many of the criticisms raised in recent days are not fair or logical and some are contrary to the law."

The audience sat silently.

He continued, evoking "the Apostle Paul and his clear and wise command in Romans thirteen, to obey the laws of government because God has ordained them for the purpose of order. Orderly and lawful processes are good in themselves and protect the weak and lawful. Our policies that can result in short-term separation of families is not unusual or unjustified."

The Fort Wayne Rotarians, for their part, regretted participation in Sessions's speech, posting online "we have instituted policies to never allow it to happen again."

Also on that Thursday, White House Press Secretary Sarah Huckabee Sanders, from the briefing room in the West Wing, played verbal gymnastics with the assembled press corps, who pressed her on separations. She insisted "it's not a policy change to enforce the law," when, indeed, in early May Secretary of Homeland Security Kirstjen Nielsen had signed the still-secret secretarial memo putting the nationwide separation policy into place.

That night I finally arrived home late after connecting through Dallas. Our plane landed at Los Angeles International Airport just before midnight and by the time I got home my son was already in his crib sleeping, and my wife was long passed out. As I joined my wife in bed, I thought about the boys who, as of 9:00 P.M. Brownsville time, were sitting in their bedrooms inside the former Walmart known as Casa Padre.

"Night," I said to my wife, planting a kiss on her head.

Before the sun came up the following morning, I was at my desk in the small office we kept off our kitchen. With the TV on next to my desk tuned to MSNBC, anchor Stephanie Ruhle started her broadcast with some tape playback of President Trump, who had just done an interview on *Fox & Friends,* his favorite (and friendly) morning program. She interrupted the playback as the three familiar notes of the NBC jingle played and the "Breaking News" banner whooshed across the screen.

"President Trump's taking questions right now on the lawn," Ruhle said. "Let's listen in."

At three minutes after nine in the morning, he started chatting up the White House press corps en route back to the

West Wing. With jockeying journalists surrounding him, he was peppered with questions about the Mueller investigation, Kim Jong Un, and pardons for his former campaign associates. Finally, President Trump stretched out his left hand, pointing at a journalist behind the frontline scrum of cameras, who asked him about the story that had dominated our airwaves for twenty-four hours.

"Mr. President, do you agree with children being taken away from—"

"No, I hate it, I hate the children being taken away. The Democrats have to change their law. That's their law. They will force—" the president stopped short, interrupted by a follow-up question.

"Sir, that's your own policy. That's your own policy. Why do you keep lying about it, sir?"

"Quiet. Quiet. That's the Democrats' law," President Trump said, indeed lying.

President Trump, the White House, and cabinet members were all parroting some version of the same line Nielsen herself served me when we sat down in the basement of the Reagan Building just over a month earlier: "It's not different," she told me then.

After I heard the president, something in me snapped, born from the frustration of hearing the commander in chief say something I knew personally not to be true.

For a moment I thought about holding my fire, thinking about what executives back at 30 Rock might say or do, but what I saw had left an indelible mark. Moreover I had borne witness to facts that were contrary to what the Trump administration, including the president himself, was insisting.

Eleven minutes after Stephanie Ruhle signed off the air,

and just a little bit longer after the president walked off the White House lawn, I opened Twitter on my phone and decided to tweet.

> Since we toured the Brownsville border shelter Trump, Sessions and Sanders have all lied about what's happening there.
> Overcrowding is a crisis manufactured by Trump, a direct result of new policy to prosecute 100% of people who enter the US illegally, which separates families.

That night my wife and I went to dinner for our sixth anniversary, delayed a day because of the reporting trip. Lindsay Toczylowski was still waiting for any word from the Bureau of Prisons about when she would be able to see the migrants locked inside Victorville.

The following morning, I joined Joy Reid on her Saturday program.

"It's complete BS," I said, "to hear the president, the attorney general, Sarah Huckabee Sanders saying there's nothing new about this, there's nothing unusual, or that it's the Democrats' policy. This has never, ever been done before as a systematic policy to take kids away from their parents at the rate of a hundred percent—is the goal of the Trump administration—as a matter of immigration policy."

Again, in my head I briefly paused thinking about the consequences of giving my opinion instead of directly sharing by reporting, but what I had seen was too important to make it about some kind of neutral take.

"It's just never been done before. It's reminiscent of Native American children being taken away from their parents

or children separated from their families at Japanese intern-
ment camps. This is not an immigration policy that we have
seen before from the federal government."

LATER THAT DAY, my wife and I took our son to a birthday
party at a local elementary school around the corner from our
house. It was walking distance, and along the way my phone
buzzed. Katie Waldman, the press aide to homeland security
secretary Nielsen, was calling again. Enjoying the afternoon
with my family, I hesitated in picking up the call, but I ultimately did.

"Where are you?" Waldman asked me.

"Home, walking with my wife and son to a birthday
party," I told her. "What's up?"

"Can you get to McAllen tomorrow?"

"Tomorrow? But tomorrow is Father's Day. Why?"

"We're letting journalists into the CPC," Border Patrol
lingo for the Central Processing Center. "This is the epicenter," she said.

"The epicenter?"

"Of separations."

I let out a deep exhale. The congressional delegation
would be visiting tomorrow afternoon, she explained. The
tour she was offering me would happen before—first thing
in the morning.

"I'm not even sure I can get there," I said, looking at the
time. I told Waldman I would call her back.

I quickly explained to my wife what was going on, and
shot a text to Janelle Rodriguez, my boss. It was nearly

Saturday evening in New York, and I had no idea if she'd even be available to talk. Just in case, I called Aarne, too, and told him about the access we had just been offered.

"Hey, man, what's up?" he asked when he picked up the call.

"If we can get to McAllen by tomorrow morning, we can get inside the place they're separating most of the kids on the border. Just messaged Janelle. No word back."

"Okay, I'll start looking at flights and for a local crew," he said without skipping a beat.

We hung up, and I, too, started checking out travel options. It wasn't looking good.

There are no direct flights from Los Angeles to McAllen. It takes at least one connection to make it to the tiny airport. It's the same one from which Customs and Border Protection launches its aircraft in the area, including the Black Hawk chopper we rode in that April. The family we saw surrendering to the Border Patrol from our sky-high vantage point back then could very well be among the ranks of the separated now.

Time running out, the only flight that seemed like it might work was an American Airlines red-eye that left early on Sunday morning, connecting through Dallas.

By that time I was sitting in the parking lot of the local elementary school, where the parents throwing the birthday party had hired a miniature train to drive in circles in the parking lot and take kids for a whirl. My son loved trains, so we didn't even make it all the way into the party before jumping on. After one loop around the parking lot, my phone rang again. I told my wife and son I had to jump off, and walked out of the parking lot and onto the street in front of the school.

It was Janelle calling back, and she was unequivocal. "Let's do it."

I had to go back in and break it to my wife. She was completely understanding, and I told her I would have to leave the party, too, to go pack. I kissed her and my little man goodbye. As I walked home, I let Katie Waldman know I would be there first thing tomorrow and to ask for details.

Just days after I left, I was heading back to South Texas.

June 17, 2018

Father's Day in the United States is always observed on the third Sunday in June. In Guatemala, it's always observed on the seventeenth day of June. This year the holiday happened to coincide in the United States.

Juan spent the day locked up in federal prison in Victorville, while his fourteen-year-old son was thousands of miles apart in a shelter for migrant children in Harlingen, Texas.

María, Juan's wife and José's mother, hadn't heard from either of them for thirteen days, since the day they were planning on crossing the border into the United States.

At 12:59 A.M. on that Sunday, my wife and son were asleep as Aarne and I took off to Dallas. We touched down before sunrise. Aarne and I transferred to a small commuter plane, launched into the Texas sky, and around ten thirty, landed in McAllen. Within an hour I would be inside, in the words of Katie Waldman, the "epicenter" of family separations.

JUST BEFORE 11:30 A.M. in McAllen, I appeared on-air, still in the same pants and red socks I had on when I left Los Angeles.

Watching the TV on Father's Day morning, my son slapped himself on the mouth while staring up at me on the screen.

I was reporting from a conference room inside the Border Patrol processing center, awaiting a press conference from Manuel "Manny" Padilla, the chief of the Border Patrol's Rio Grande Valley sector.

"Dada!" little Noah screamed. He turned around and looked at my wife, who had pulled out her phone to film him, his bushy dirty blond mop of hair swinging as he did.

He was, I'm ashamed to admit, used to talking to me through a screen, FaceTime becoming a constant while I was away on one reporting trip or another.

"Dada? Aah?" he asked with the sounds he could muster. Then he walked closer to the TV, stretching up on his tiptoes to reach his hand up behind it, as if I were hiding on the other side, his diaper popping out of his striped purple pajamas.

Children my son's age had been taken from their parents and kept inside the building I was about to tour. Chief Padilla, the Border Patrol official we were about to hear from, had told the *Washington Post* they stopped separating children under five years old by now. Customs and Border Protection commissioner Kevin McAleenan had reportedly given the order to stop the separation of such young children, amid what he told others became his own crisis of conscience about the policy. A policy he urged Secretary of Homeland Security Kirstjen Nielsen to adopt. The same policy that was discussed at a meeting convened in his conference room at a Valentine's Day meeting less than a month after President Trump was inaugurated.

In my hand was the little blue spiral notebook I had bought four days earlier on my way to see the hundreds of separated boys in Brownsville. Those boys may very well have passed through and been separated from their families in the facility I was now standing in, before being sent on to Casa Padre. Or Harlingen, where José was in custody. Or any of the dozens of other shelters throughout the country.

"It is not something that needs to be happening right now," I told anchor Alex Witt back in New York about family separations. "It is something that the Trump administration decided they wanted to be happening. Contrary to what the president and Jeff Sessions and Sarah Huckabee Sanders have said: they have said it is a Democratic law, that is not true. The attorney general said this is not unusual to separate children like this. . . ."

I stopped as Chief Padilla walked into the room. "Here is Chief Padilla," I told Witt. The start of the press conference was carried live. After a lengthy introduction, Padilla got to the topic the dozens of assembled journalists were there to see themselves, backing up the point I had just made on TV.

"I think everybody is aware that the attorney general signed the executive order, or the order," Padilla corrected himself saying, "on April sixth. DHS secretary signed the implementation guidance May fifth of two thousand and eighteen. So Border Patrol," he said, turning to his agency's role in the policy, "we implement that guidance. We are the implementers of that guidance."

What that meant in practice, he told us, was that 1,174 kids had been taken from their parents since separations began under zero tolerance; 711 of those children were transferred to shelters like Casa Padre, where I was days earlier.

Padilla was peppered with questions. I asked whether any

children under five had been separated in his custody (he said no); CBS's David Begnaud inquired where girls were being held (he explained that all separated children went to ORR custody); and another reporter pressed him on whether he would stop separations if a court halted the policy (he said he'd have to talk with his lawyers).

"All right, folks," interrupted Robert Rodriguez, the public information officer detailed to the Rio Grande Valley sector and whom I had gotten to know while working on our *Dateline* documentary.

"From this side of the room, this way," he said, pointing to the area I was standing, "y'all are going to be taken out to the CPC," the Central Processing Center, where migrants were detained.

"As a reminder, folks, visitors shall not bring any electronic or recording devices, cameras, laptops, or wireless communication devices, such as smartphones or mobile phones. We shall not have any physical or verbal contact with the detainees without the consent of CBP."

That refrain was becoming a familiar one to me.

After Rodriguez finished, I approached Padilla, who was still at the podium getting ready to deliver the same press conference in Spanish, to ask him how long he thought it might take to get to 100 percent prosecutions, since he had just mentioned only 40 percent of the families were being separated at this point, approximately the same figure I had heard from Dr. Sanchez at Casa Padre.

"It changes because if the strength starts going down, we'll get there quicker," he said of the flow of migrants crossing the border.

"So basically," I replied, "it depends on if the deterrence is working."

Padilla nodded, and flashed me a thumbs-up.

Following orders, I took off the lavalier microphone I was wearing and gave it back to our crew, and headed out of the conference room and down a hallway where we would meet our guides, Carmen Qualia, assistant chief patrol agent in the Rio Grande Valley Sector, and John Lopez, the acting deputy patrol agent in charge, both, like Padilla and Rodriguez, dressed in their green Border Patrol uniforms.

I was shocked to discover that only steps from where we just sat during Padilla's press conference was the door to the processing center. We were told the facility was just over 75,000 square feet; the first portion we would walk through, around 22,000 square feet, was for single adults. Padilla had warned us the area would be busy—it is where intake is occurring, property is being confiscated, and medical screenings take place—and he was right.

When we walked through the door, men were crowded inside cells, some flashing thumbs-up while others clung silently to silver Mylar blankets meant to keep them warm. Several shouted to get the attention of the reporters, reminding me again of other jail tours I had been on. Cell eighteen was labeled "do not use." There was a woman inside. Another migrant spit as we walked past. The occupant of cell seventeen muttered, "mucho frío." Very cold. We were moved quickly through this side of the facility.

When we entered the other portion of the processing center, a former warehouse converted into a holding pen for, at that very moment, 1,129 humans, it was much, much quieter.

This, we were told, was where we would see children separated from their parents in two of four "pods," in Border Patrol lingo. To anyone else, they'd be called cages.

As we approached the enclosures, chain link fences on all sides twice as tall as I was, my first thought was dog kennels. The big kind you might see in a boarding facility or in back at a veterinarian's office. But inside were children.

In front of us were boys seventeen and under, the same age group as I saw the week before at Casa Padre. We asked how the children—currently lying on green mats atop concrete floors and under Mylar blankets, as they were supervised by a security contractor in a watchtower—made it from here to there.

"ICE is the conduit for ORR to get them to the facilities," Agent Lopez told us in front of another cage filled with humans. "These are family units, male head of household," he continued, responding to another question as he pointed to the fathers and children who were kept together.

Not far away were cages with young girls, alone, and another with children and their mothers. Four "pods" total, holding 525 members of families together, and another one with 179 children who either had arrived alone or were separated from their parents.

Other than the occasional high-pitched voice of a child or the crinkling of the Mylar blankets, it continued to strike me how the volume differed in this area of the processing center. It was as if the people here knew that talking, at this point, wouldn't help.

I kept scribbling notes in my little blue spiral book, as Agent Lopez stood in between us and the migrants locked inside.

I asked Agent Lopez if there were social workers here, and he admitted there were only four for the hundreds of children. We requested to speak with them. The answer was, again, no.

Another reporter, in Spanish, snuck a question to a caged woman, who told us she wasn't aware of separations happening, likely meaning she had not yet had her case processed by agents, or had arrived with a child younger than five.

Migrants were being told of the policy only if they were involved in a separation. Then they were given an informational "tear sheet," which explained in English and Spanish that they were about to be charged with a crime and their child would be moved to the custody of the Office of Refugee Resettlement, where they could find them by dialing a phone number.

The tear sheet only recently had been added to the process on the orders of CBP commissioner McAleenan, meaning hundreds if not thousands previously went through the process without that information.

Another mother told us that even if a parent was charged and sentenced to "time served," meaning they were free to come back to pick up their children, there was the possibility that children would have already been moved out to an ORR shelter and were now in the custody of the federal government for the foreseeable future. This, and separations, were happening more in the facility we were standing in than anywhere else along the entire border.

We asked how long children would be here, after their parents were taken away. The answer was that facilities like Casa Padre, and the Office of Refugee Resettlement, needed to be notified within twenty-four hours if a child is separated and left alone—rendered unaccompanied. With only ten

permanent processing agents, that was making things difficult.

Our tour was now stretching multiples longer than the
scheduled seven minutes. Finally, the agents began escorting
us out.

"We're strained and struggling," Agent Lopez admitted
to me around that time. As we passed back through the processing area, he showed me what he meant. They did not have
enough agents to deal with the practice of separations, something they had never done on this scale before. To account for
the unprecedented workload, virtual processing was being
employed. Seated at computer screens, some separated parents were being processed by agents in another Border Patrol
facility—El Paso, El Centro, or Corpus Christie—over video-
conference. An impersonal touch to an inhumane process.

As we were escorted back out to the lockers where we
left our electronic devices, we were told we would receive
approved footage shot by Customs and Border Protection—
images and video—while we were inside. But waiting for
the media to come through wasn't an option. As soon as I
walked out of the red-roofed Border Patrol building that was
attached to the warehouse, I crossed Ursula Street and stood
on the street corner where Aarne and the crew had set up our
live shot location while I was inside.

David Gura was in the middle of anchoring the two
o'clock afternoon hour on MSNBC; at forty-six minutes after
the hour, he broke back from commercial announcing I was
about to present breaking news, describing what I saw inside.

"Jacob," Gura began, "I remember your vivid descriptions
of the children's center you visited a couple days ago. What
did you see today?"

"Whereas at the other detention center—which is actually a shelter run by the Office of Refugee Resettlement—there were fourteen hundred young boys between the ages of ten and seventeen; there were no cages, there were no fences. That's what there is inside of here. Everybody is inside effectively very large cells with multiple people."

I continued with Gura until we ran into technical difficulties, but rejoined him the next hour, this time with Dr. Colleen Kraft, the head of the American Academy of Pediatrics, who in May when the zero tolerance policy was announced wrote an op-ed in the *Los Angeles Times*. Kraft had eviscerated the policy on the grounds that the damage it would inflict on children would never be reversed.

Studies overwhelmingly demonstrate the irreparable harm caused by breaking up families. Prolonged exposure to highly stressful situations—known as toxic stress—can disrupt a child's brain architecture and affect his or her short- and long-term health. A parent or a known caregiver's role is to mitigate these dangers. When robbed of that buffer, children are susceptible to learning deficits and chronic conditions such as depression, post-traumatic stress disorder, and even heart disease. The government's practice of separating children from their parents at the border counteracts every science-based recommendation I have ever made to families who seek to build, and not harm, their children's intellectual and emotional development.

The same day I had gone inside Casa Padre, Dr. Kraft had given an interview to CNN in which she had called the zero tolerance policy "government-sanctioned child abuse." Her words caught the attention of one of the world's most famous people, though she had missed the call and only received a surprising voice mail.

"Hello, Dr. Kraft," the message ran. "Oprah Winfrey calling. I am calling regarding the article I saw on CNN regarding the children in immigration. I wanted to talk to you. And I was struck by something that you said about it being government-sanctioned child abuse. So I want to have a conversation with you about what we can do. I feel so, you know, I don't want to be hopeless about it. But it is so disturbing to me. So I am going to be traveling for the next few hours. I do have your cell number, this is your cell number, so I will try to reach you tomorrow. Thank you. Thank you very much."

Now, on-air in a double box with me, Dr. Kraft continued to sound the alarm from my hometown of Los Angeles, her blue suit jacket a slightly darker shade than the fake skyline behind her, her red hair framed by two hanging pearl earrings. "We have to speak out about it, talk about the right policy, which is keeping kids and families together. Our children have a limited amount of time to grow and develop. We have to give them the best start we can."

I appeared on our air several more times that afternoon and evening, ending the day with Kasie Hunt, who was anchoring her program from Washington.

"This is the first time ever that children have been separated on a systematic basis. Look at those photos right there," I said to Kasie, pointing to the monitor in front of me where the handout images I had been waiting for were now on-screen, children lying on the green mats under Mylar blankets I had walked by earlier, mothers lined up single file, some with children, some without. The wind started to pick up, blowing not just the palm trees that framed the Border Patrol station behind me but my hair and microphone.

"From their parents! And that is because of the Trump administration. People in here are locked up in cages, essentially what look like animal kennels. I don't know any other way to describe it. And strangely, the *Washington Post* gave Senator Jeff Merkley what they call 'three pinnochios' for saying kids are locked up in cages and that's exactly what I saw today."

An hour and forty-five minutes later, the *Post* published an op-ed by former First Lady Laura Bush. In a tweet, she shared the piece with her followers, writing, "I live in a border state. I appreciate the need to enforce and protect our international boundaries, but this zero-tolerance policy is cruel. It is immoral. And it breaks my heart."

Bush, too, pointed to the words of Dr. Kraft to rally the nation against the separation policy.

Recently, Colleen Kraft, who heads the American Academy of Pediatrics, visited a shelter run by the U.S. Office of Refugee Resettlement. She reported that while there were beds, toys, crayons, a playground and diaper changes, the people working at the shelter had been instructed not to pick up or touch the children to comfort them. Imagine not being able to pick up a child who is not yet out of diapers.

Bush concluded there had to be another way and the policy must be ended.

In 2018, can we not as a nation find a kinder, more compassionate, and more moral answer to this current crisis? I, for one, believe we can.

She was not alone. The following morning, her successor as First Lady, Michelle Obama, retweeted Bush's article despite the fact that, to address an unprecedented flow of families crossing the border during his second term, her husband's administration built the facility in which separated children were caged. "Sometimes truth transcends party," she tweeted.

The numbers were staggering: between May 5 and June 9 more than 2,300 children had been taken from their parents—more separated in a month than in the entire previous year. As Commander Jonathan White and statisticians at the Department of Homeland Security projected, there was not enough bed space for all the children coming to ORR.

Father's Day over and the workweek beginning, the challenge was to keep the pressure on the administration to end the policy with so many separations happening so quickly. With President Trump specializing in the art of the deflection and gaslighting, this promised to be a difficult task.

He was backed up by a cadre of officials who had carefully considered family separations since the first days of his administration. Officials from the Departments of Homeland Security, Health and Human Services, and inside his own White House had been made aware of the likely disastrous aftermath those separated would have to endure. Trauma. Difficulty reuniting. Potential permanent separations. But none of that stopped the woman in charge of the Border Patrol agents doing the separating from denying what I, and now the entire nation, was seeing happening.

Earlier that day, President Trump's homeland security secretary, Kirstjen Nielsen, often the subject of the president's scorn and abusive behavior, tweeted a doozie she must have figured would please the tweeter in chief.

"We do not have a policy of separating families at the border. Period."

My eyes widened when I saw it. You've got to be kidding, I thought. Come on.

Not far from where more family separations were happening than anywhere else along the border, I decided to reply to her tweet with one of my own: three "face-palm" emojis of a guy slapping his visage in disbelief.

What on the one hand felt like a childish response also felt somewhat perfect given the circumstances. And if Nielsen's tweet seemed like peak lying, it was only the start of the deflection, deceit, and dishonesty to come.

■ ■ ■

From: Lloyd, Scott (ACF)

Sent: Friday, June 22, 2018 11:43AM

To: Wagner, Steven (ACF); Wynne, Maggie (HHS/IOS); Harrison, Brian (HHS/IOS); Urbanowicz, Peter (HHS/IOS); Kadlec, Robert (OS/ASPR/IO)

Subject: Update

Importance: High

- *We have two categories of separated kids: one from the beginning of the fiscal year, the other from May 6, the beginning of zero tolerance.*

- *CBP chiefs started separations before the announcement of the zero policy and we noticed it and started tracking.*

- *As of June 18, we have received 1911 UACs from zero tolerance (May 6).*

- *Of them, 114 were discharged.*

CHAPTER EIGHT

"No Way to Link"

June 18, 2018

Lights had just come on in the overcrowded sleeping quarters of the children who had been separated from their parents in the Rio Grande Valley, but the man responsible for their suffering was awake in the White House residence and lashing out at his opponents. It's been a lifelong strategy of his to, in the words of his wife Melania, "punch back ten times harder" if he's under attack. The president, boxed in by relentless media attention for days, had started swinging wildly on Twitter. Monday morning, before Michelle Obama retweeted Laura Bush, Trump lashed out at the outrage his separation policy was generating on television and social media.

> Children are being used by some of the worst criminals on earth as a means to enter our country. Has anyone been looking at the Crime taking place south of the border. It is historic, with some countries the most dangerous places in the world. Not going to happen in the U.S.
>
> **9:50AM ET**

As a matter of fact, I had. Realizing the social media conversation around what was happening was capturing Trump's attention, I replied, again, sharing what I learned during my border reporting.

> His own DEA says the violence in Mexico is *not* spilling over the border in alarming levels. And has said the same thing for years.
>
> **11:02AM ET**

I was growing frustrated, and I wanted to use any platform I could to share what I knew. Social media was becoming an effective complement to the work I was doing on-air. Meanwhile, our border special still had not been broadcast. In calls to *Dateline* producer Izhar Harpaz, a Peabody and DuPont award–winning veteran of television news, I kept saying that if our hour had aired as scheduled earlier in the year, this information would be out there already, and maybe we could have made a difference in fact-checking the justifications around the policy that had resulted in the caged children I had just seen. He urged me to be patient.

For me, and those watching from across the world, there were more questions than answers. I had been able to see where separated boys ages ten to seventeen were taken once they were split from their parents. But that was it. Where are the girls? Where are the toddlers? The world wanted to know. At the same time, I was getting inundated with messages of support for the children and for the reporting we were doing.

> Would you be able to get me some access to the folks being held in or near Laredo, Texas? . . . I'm gonna be heading down there for work next month for almost three months and would like to use my "new car" fund (about $500) to deliver the immigrants some pizza. I

want to let 'em know our president's actions don't define us. Most of us still give a shit about the well-being of others (even strangers).

I received dozens of messages like this.

Anger and grief only intensified when, that afternoon, ProPublica published the wailing sounds of separated children crying in a Border Patrol facility. The audio was nearly impossible to listen to, but it spread like wildfire. The cries of "Mami" and "Papá" were so visceral and real, whatever language you spoke. Even Washington, D.C., was listening.

Later, in the early evening, homeland security secretary Nielsen kicked off a combative and disastrous press conference by insisting, "this administration did not create a policy of separating families at the border." The problem with that argument was that she herself had signed the policy into existence. It was as if she was oblivious to the news coverage of the policy. Nielsen "never knew what the fuck was going on," a person familiar with her planning for the press conference told me, blaming her communications team.

That morning, across the country, the president's eldest daughter and advisor was in California's Central Valley, where she had landed earlier in the day by private jet in nearly ninety-degree heat at Fresno Yosemite International Airport. She and House Majority Leader Kevin McCarthy had flown there from Los Angeles, and on the flight the first daughter spoke with the congressional leader about her desire to do something about family separtions. McCarthy agreed that family separations, leading the news everywhere, was a building political crisis. After deplaning from the sleek Embraer Legacy 600, Ivanka Trump, dressed in a white sleeveless dress and sunglasses, joined a suit-and-tie-clad McCarthy to headline a "Protect the House" fundraiser.

She arrived there after motorcading through Fresno, not in but near McCarthy's own district, home to some of the most fertile agricultural land in the world, much of it tended to by undocumented immigrants. That day, as family separations spiraled from a poorly planned immigration policy to a full-fledged political crisis for the president, Ivanka Trump sought to exert her influence over her father.

"We have to do something. This is totally unacceptable," she said in frustration having been monitoring the news.

Following the fundraiser luncheon, hosted at a local construction company, things were only getting worse. Trump spoke to her father from inside one of the white SUVs in the motorcade as they rolled back to the airport protected by the Secret Service, the Fresno Sheriff's Department, and the California Highway Patrol. With the president, she was clear: something had to change as soon as possible. But thousands of miles away and cut out of meetings about the policy by senior White House officials, including Chief of Staff John Kelly, one phone call was not enough to convince her dad.

President Trump had faced widespread protest before. The Women's March and his Muslim ban in the early days of his administration drew tens of thousands to the streets and airports. But what was happening in South Texas sparked a new and intense energy. The live shot position from which I broadcast on Sunday next to a handful of crews was packed by the time I had showed up in the dark to appear on *Morning Joe* and the *Today* show. Gayle King, the coanchor of *CBS This Morning,* was directly next to us, shepherding her program from outside the Ursula processing station. Her friend Oprah Winfrey encouraged her followers to tune in via Twitter. Republicans and Democrats both were speaking out against Trump's practice of separating families. It felt as if all eyes were on that tiny parking lot corner across from the epicenter of the policy.

I received word that we were going to flood the zone. In a call from Phil Griffin, the president of MSNBC, I got moral support and encouragement to keep going, along with news that anchors Chris Hayes, Lawrence O'Donnell, and Stephanie Ruhle were heading to South Texas on Tuesday. So, too, were Lester Holt, the anchor of *NBC Nightly News*, our flagship broadcast, and Craig Melvin, the *Today* show's primary national correspondent. Gabe Gutierrez would join Mariana Atencio, who had been on the border all weekend as well, reporting from Mexican cities on the other side of the dividing line. Cal Perry, another correspondent, headed to Tornillo to see the tents Health and Human Services had erected to house the overflow of children, as would anchor Joy Reid that weekend. All the while, children were continuing to be separated in the building in front of me.

At the same time, career officials inside HHS's Office of Refugee Resettlement had felt like the Department of Homeland Security and the White House had been engaged in grade-A gaslighting. Now that their plan was out in the open, the lies were only amplifying.

Commander Jonathan White, who had resigned his position as the head of the Office of Refugee Resettlement in March over a disagreement with his Trump-appointed boss, Scott Lloyd, was watching from the sidelines. In conversations with friends and associates, White expressed what it felt like to be on the outside looking in, having attempted for a year to stop systematic family separations and failing. He used a clinical term: he was suffering from "moral distress."

Inside ORR and Immigration and Customs Enforcement, the "glitch" that was identified and raised in a February phone call—the inability for each agency's systems to communicate with one another in order to identify and reunite separated parents and children smoothly—still existed. ORR was sending ICE lists of kids and their parents in an attempt to make contact, a manual process that required countless hours of work, often without positive results.

Claire Trickler-McNulty, the deputy assistant director in ICE's custody management division had, with her colleagues, been tasked with organizing reunification handoffs between parents and children. But with the policy still ongoing and the government saying it would only expand, it was crushing chaos.

"Many, many mistakes" were being made, she told me.

On the border, we continued to press for answers from both HHS and Homeland Security. We weren't getting very far because the agencies themselves were struggling to stay ahead of what was happening on the ground. If there was a plan, or knowledge of what was happening, officials in Washington didn't seem to have a handle on it. Katie Waldman, the spokeswoman for the Department of Homeland Security handling inquiries about separations, admitted to me that neither she nor DHS secretary Nielsen had been to the border to inspect the facts on the ground inside what she herself told me was the "epicenter" of the separation policy.

That evening, Ivanka Trump made her way back to Washington on an overnight flight after another fundraising stop with McCarthy in Los Angeles.

Back in Washington on Tuesday morning, she headed to

the White House. Having been iced out of meetings with her father about the separation policy, and excluded from emails, including a set of principles that would define the administration's response, Trump used her privilege as First Daughter and walked into the Oval Office, where she spent much of the day.

She told her father she had decided the best course of action was to end the policy by executive order, sharing her visceral response to the images and sounds flooding the airwaves and internet.

"You have to do an executive order to stop this," she told the president.

Trump, moved by his daughter's passion, agreed. He was scheduled to go to Capitol Hill that evening for a meeting with House Republicans and asked her to join him. She declined, and the president went without her, but her advice stayed top of mind.

At the Capitol Hill meeting, President Trump admitted to the assembled members of Congress that his daughter was pressing him to bring an end to the policy.

"Daddy, what are we doing about this?" he told the group she asked him, in remarks reported by Maggie Haberman of the *New York Times*. Not letting on that she had pushed him to sign an executive order, the president demurred.

"Tough issue," Haberman tweeted he said of separations, before he changed the subject.

That night, President Trump called Kirstjen Nielsen to talk about the policy, and she had come to her own realization about the gravity of the situation.

"Sir, I'm going to have to change this decision I had made with respect to implementing zero tolerance."

It was unclear Trump understood what she meant.

"What are you talking about?" the president asked.

"Oh, this is that thing those people are upset about," she told him.

"The thing is," Trump responded, "I'm trying to unravel what is going wrong. But it is clearly going wrong."

"As you saw in that White House briefing, there is a lot of concern" Nielsen said, referring to her embarrassing performance. "We need to rectify that."

"Alright, we need to stop it. We need to stop it. Come to the White House this morning, and we're going to write an EO and we're going to end it," the president told her.

THE DAY PRESIDENT Trump wrestled with how to contain the public outrage over the administration's family separation policy, NBC executives decided our *Dateline* hour would finally air that weekend. We'd need to reframe everything we had shot in the context of the president's systematic separation of thousands of children: San Diego's Border Patrol chief and Tijuana's rampant violence, Arivaca's ranchers and Nogales's migrants, cross-border students walking freely between El Paso and Ciudad Juárez daily, and in the Rio Grande Valley, where I would be for the foreseeable future, the militarized border and the man on the other side selling shrimp. A broken immigration system imploding under the weight of a president and advisors who were slammed for weakly responding to public displays of white nationalism. It all had led to the separation tragedy.

We decided we needed an update. While I had been inside the facilities in which the separated children were being detained, the interview I had done with Secretary Nielsen the day President Trump nearly made her resign was outdated. We called Robert Rodriguez, the public affairs officer for the sector I had seen on Father's Day, and asked to set up another interview with Chief Padilla. They told us to get up to sector headquarters. We left as soon as we finished our morning live shots on MSNBC from under the Anzalduas Bridge, where we were kicked out by the local constable for filming without permission. Everybody was on edge.

"Is this a deterrent?" I asked Chief Padilla inside his executive office at the Border Patrol's Rio Grande Valley sector headquarters in Edinburg, a fourteen-mile drive from Mexico. "Is that the point? Are you trying to deter people from coming by separating children and their parents and prosecuting one hundred percent of the people who come here?"

"Yes. The point is that we have an upward trend, right? So if we do not do anything we are going to be in a crisis mode."

"Separating parents and kids is to put consequences on them coming here together?" I asked, attempting to clarify.

"Yes. Yes."

He cited as justification an increasing danger from "very, very, very violent criminals," the same talking point I had taken issue with the president using the day before. "You're talking about murderers," he said, referring to the MS-13 street gang, which started in Los Angeles and was exported to Central America during the Clinton administration.

"Do you know how many MS-13 members you caught here?"

"That have made it through?" he asked.

I shrugged my shoulders, as if to say, "Yeah."

"I can tell you right now we're looking at a three hundred percent increase over last year," Padilla claimed.

"And how many people is that?" I asked, my thumb and finger wrapping my chin.

Looking up and to the left, as if to search for the numbers, Padilla said, "It comes out to about a hundred and—I think it's a hundred and eighty."

"And how many total people did you catch last year?"

"Last year we had one hundred and eighty-seven thousand people."

The chief Border Patrol operator on the ground in the sector separating more children from their parents than anywhere else had just told me that catching MS-13 members along the border was like finding a needle in a haystack. Further, he had admitted that family separations were meant to punish families looking to enter the country, even those seeking asylum. Both messages directly contradicted the nonsense coming out of the White House.

That night, my colleague Rachel Maddow broke down, crying live on the air as she read a late-breaking Associated Press story.

"This has just come out from the Associated Press." She paused for three seconds while reading the copy on the page in front of her. "This is incredible."

She began reading the article aloud. "Trump administration officials have been sending babies and other young children," her voice breaking, she stopped, waved her pen with her right hand, pointed to her mouth, pursed her lips, and let out an audible sigh.

"Hold on," she said, still not looking up from the page

and laughing a nervous laughter I had never seen her do before. Her right index finger stretched under her nose as if to hold in what she could not, she kept reading through intense emotion.

"To at least three . . ." She stopped again, finger back under her nose. She wagged her finger at the camera and shook her head, I think trying to make what she was feeling go away. For five seconds, she said nothing, breathing heavily, and then out loud, a message to her control room.

"Put up the graphic of this. Thank you. Do we have it? No." She had nowhere to hide.

"Three tender-aged shelters in South Texas. Lawyers and medical providers . . ." She started crying.

"I think I'm going to have to hand this off," she said through tears, right at ten o'clock exactly, the moment that Lawrence O'Donnell was set to take over MSNBC's airwaves live from the border in Texas.

"Sorry. That does it for us tonight. We'll see you again tomorrow."

I was speechless. About the story itself, but also about Rachel's reaction to it. Seeing someone you know absorb this information in real time was so profoundly affecting.

Rachel soon tweeted out an apology, which I felt wasn't necessary.

"It's how we feel out here, too," I replied.

June 20, 2018

As hundreds of separations continued to take place daily, and the mystery deepened about what would happen to the babies taken from their parents, those who had already been taken from each other awoke on Wednesday morning still locked up and confused. Incarcerated for the last ten days inside a federal prison in Victorville, California, Juan was told he was being moved yet again, for the third time.

Leaving Victorville seemed like it might be a positive step. After having arrived in the United States expecting humanitarian relief, he felt as though he was being treated worse than an animal. Victorville was eating him alive. Strip searched and made to wear a double-extra-large prison uniform that made him look like a clown, he hadn't spoken to his son for ten days.

Lindsay Toczylowski, the executive director of Immigrant Defenders Law Center, had been trying to reach the immigrant detainees inside Victorville for nearly a week with no luck. On the day Juan was told he would be moved to Adelanto, an eight-mile drive away from Victorville, she still hadn't heard anything about access to Victorville. She began to think of it as a "black site" immigration detention center on American soil, referring to the CIA's notorious covert prison facilities.

Meanwhile, fourteen-year-old José was sitting in a shelter in Harlingen, Texas. Flying to Texas, his feelings alternated between exhaustion and joy, believing he was headed to see his dad. Once he arrived he was given a shower and new clothes. While he never did get the jacket back that the Border Patrol took from him, he was finally out of what he had jumped the border wall in.

In Harlingen, José had been trying to reach his mom for days to explain what had happened, but his calls went unanswered. He kept trying her at night, not knowing she would sleep elsewhere, scared of the men who threatened her husband and son. Where she was hiding did not have cell service.

José and his dad had escaped the narcos' death threats in their hometown, avoided kidnapping or abuse by the Mexican cartels that control the smuggling routes through the country, and had safely set foot in Arizona to declare asylum, only to be split up by the U.S. Border Patrol. Now, in an unfamiliar building without access to the outside world, or his dad, it was too much to bear.

Inside the Harlingen shelter where José was in custody, it took days to finally reach his father by phone. When a social worker was able to finally track down Juan—once he had been transferred from the Victorville prison to the Adelanto immigration detention center—they were finally able to connect. Instead of catching up after so many days apart, the phone call was a conduit for raw emotion. Father and son spent most of the time on the line only crying. Both finally realized that neither of them was going anywhere anytime soon, and that they were not alone in their forced separation.

"That's the end of my life," fourteen-year-old José thought to himself.

In South Texas, rain was dumping violently. I was on-air by eight in the morning local time, talking about the news that broke the night before, regarding the separation of "tender aged" children.

"I really hope you get inside more of these centers," Stephanie Ruhle said.

"Working on it," I replied.

"Especially the tender-aged center. I want to see inside. I want to see these girls."

Ruhle continued her broadcast as I stepped out of frame, explaining that President Trump and House Republicans, besieged by outrage over the policy, had met about the separation issue for forty-five minutes the night before. Trump, Ruhle reported, "wants it taken care of through legislation, rather than reversing it unilaterally." That, of course, was the exact opposite advice President Trump's daughter had given him in confidence before he headed to the meeting of which Ruhle spoke.

Around the time we were on the air, homeland security secretary Nielsen arrived at the White House to meet with President Trump in the Oval Office. He was ready to sign an executive order, and Nielsen was on board.

The prospect of family separations ending sent the West Wing into chaos.

White House Counsel Don McGahn walked into the Oval Office, having received conflicting direction from various factions within the White House.

"Stephen Miller is freaking out losing his mind. Kevin McAleenan is losing his mind. Homan. Because they did think in their minds that we were close to this having a huge deterrent effect," said an official with knowledge of the deliberations.

McGahn exited the Oval Office to prepare the document. The resulting Executive Order ended the Department of Homeland Security's family separations, but not the Department of Justice's zero tolerance policy.

Less than three hours later, the rain still falling in South

Texas, the president reversed course, heeding Ivanka Trump's advice.

I was sitting off set when the news came through. I immediately got up and ran over, threw a microphone on, and joined Ruhle on the air.

"We have breaking news from the White House specifically on President Trump's zero tolerance immigration policy," Ruhle said. As White House correspondent Kristen Welker, who had been tenaciously going at the administration, including the president himself, for answers about family separations, got ready to join Stephanie on-air, I slid on set. "Jacob, you've been here for the last week. So many people on both sides of the aisle and faith leaders urging the president, and I know you have some news."

"We're just hearing," I said, reading off the lower third red breaking-news banner on the monitor in front of both of us, "the president has just said 'I'm going to be signing something in a little while to keep families together,' and he said that it will be followed up later by a legislative fix."

I was processing what this meant as I stood there live on-air. "Essentially, if that's what it sounds like, he may be stopping this family separation from happening right now. The question that comes to mind for me: Is he is undermining a policy that was put into place by his own attorney general? What's going on inside the White House right now?"

"Maybe he changed his mind!" Ruhle said.

"Maybe he changed his mind," I replied. "The big question," I continued, "is what does that mean for the twenty-five hundred children that have already been separated from their parents? The ones that could become permanent orphans according to a former ICE official that we talked to yesterday. If the president has just decided now, a couple months later, that he just doesn't like this policy anymore, what happens to the kids he's already ripped away from their parents?"

As the rain around us started to slow, I caught my breath. Reflecting, it occurred to me that the pressure building along the border—both from news media reporting and activists who were on the ground with us—may very well have pushed the president to sign an executive order to stop the separation policy.

"The ability to tell the story of these children," I said to Ruhle, "[and] the work of the activists who have been speaking out, has brought this to the attention of the United States, all the way to the White House, far away from here in McAllen, Texas, where they clearly had no idea what was going on, on the ground."

Sure enough, the president soon confirmed as much in the Cabinet Room, where he was meeting with members of Congress about the situation at the border.

"Mr. President," a reporter asked, "did the images of those young children at the border change your mind on this?"

"Yes," President Trump replied. "Those images affect everybody." He went on to point a finger again at Democrats and the previous border policy. But the message was clear: he was going to back down.

He reiterated his position hours later in an Oval Office signing ceremony, flanked by DHS secretary Nielsen and Vice President Pence.

"I didn't like the sight or the feeling of families being separated," the president said.

And then, with the stroke of his Sharpie, Trump ended family separations. It was a few minutes after three in the afternoon, seven days after we first stepped foot into Casa Padre to tell the world about the former Walmart holding hundreds of separated boys.

In truth, the president and his aides hoped the executive order would put pressure on Congress to change immigration law to allow them to indefinitely detain migrant families and send back unaccompanied migrants from Central America without having to shelter them.

Meanwhile, there was a much larger problem at hand— the one I had identified on the air. What would happen to the thousands of children separated by the Trump administration over the last six weeks, including José, a short drive from me in Harlingen?

Nobody seemed to know.

June 21, 2018

First Lady Melania Trump determined it would be a good idea to show up at the border the day after her husband ended his policy of systematically separating migrant children from their parents. I would leave South Texas that same day, en route to NBC News headquarters in New York to finish our *Dateline* documentary, which was scheduled to air Sunday night. By the time I touched down with Aarne at Newark airport in New Jersey, the First Lady's visit was making news. She and HHS secretary Alex Azar, who had been confirmed to the post in early 2018 after the ouster of Tom Price, Trump's first HHS secretary, in late 2017 amidst a scandal about private and military jet use, were touring a shelter that was housing separated children.

I called into Andrea Mitchell's midday program to point

out that the First Lady, on the ground as we spoke on the air, wouldn't be touring the Central Processing Center in McAllen, where a large number of the separations were occurring, nor Casa Padre, the former Walmart I had been inside exactly a week earlier. Administration officials still hadn't seen the facility where most of the crisis was being created.

That day, Secretary Azar, who according to both career and political staff within HHS was not aware of the separation policy in the planning stages, removed Scott Lloyd, the director of the Office of Refugee Resettlement, from operational control of efforts to reunify separated children with their parents.

Now in charge would be Dr. Robert Kadlec, the Assistant Secretary for Preparedness and Response at HHS, who, along with his chief of staff, Chris Meekins, was more used to responding to natural disasters and public health emergencies. Those were far different than the man-made crisis he now faced: caring for thousands of migrant children who were apart from their parents and perhaps thousands of miles from their extended family. It was Kadlec and Meekins who, less than a year earlier, had been huddled in the Secretary's Operations Center in Washington making sure that all citizens, including the children in the care and custody of ORR, would be safe if Hurricane Irma landed a direct hit on South Florida.

As the details of the crisis recovery program were being sorted out, the First Lady departed McAllen. She wore a puzzling jacket as she walked up the stairs to board her flight back to Washington, D.C., having completed her tour of a shelter. In white letters seemingly painted on the back of her green coat, were the words, "I REALLY DON'T CARE. DO U?"

By then, I was inside NBC News headquarters in New York. I walked the stairs that connect the MSNBC studios and newsrooms with the edit suites used by *Dateline* on another floor. As I shut the door behind me, the air was sucked out of the room. Sitting in an edit bay was Izhar Harpaz, listening to every word I spoke as I read a script detailing how decades of failed border policy had led us to this point: what experts were calling government-sanctioned child abuse that, despite President Trump's executive order, wasn't anywhere near ending.

June 22, 2018

At half past eight on Friday morning, Commander Jonathan White, who had been sitting on the sidelines of the family separation crisis after warning of its imminent arrival, received an email asking him to come to the office of Dr. Robert Kadlec, his boss since March. Kadlec had been only just placed in charge of family reunifications by HHS secretary Alex Azar. Kadlec's chief of staff, Chris Meekins, advised him to call White in based on his extensive experience working at ORR. When he arrived, Kadlec peppered White with questions about how reunifications would take place now that President Trump had ended the separation policy. Their direction from the White House was to find a way to get parents and children back together. In the course of that conversation, Dr. Kadlec told Meekins to join him for his senior staff meeting at noon where they would continue to talk.

There, Dr. Kadlec announced to his senior staff in the room that the Secretary's Operations Center would be activated and that a new incident-response model, tested but never put into practice, would be used to reunite the children. That incident-response model called for a federal health coordinating official to take the lead; Dr. Kadlec told his staff Commander White would be that person. This was news to Commander White, who learned about his new role at that moment.

White, shocked to be given an opportunity to fix the crisis he had tried to stop, retreated with Dr. Kadlec, Don Boyce, his deputy assistant secretary, and Meekins to his private office. Once there, he clearly expressed what he needed in order for this operation to, against long odds, succeed. On the whiteboard in his boss's office, he wrote his goals plainly and clearly, numbering them one through seven. He wanted the support of a list of personnel he selected by name, as well as the help of his colleagues from the U.S. Public Health Service's Commissioned Corps and the full support of the emergency managers in the Secretary's Operations Center. Most important, he wrote the names of those to whom he would report: Kadlec, Meekins, Secretary Azar. Next he listed the colleagues he wanted nowhere near the reunification effort: Maggie Wynne, Steve Wagner, and Scott Lloyd, the man nominally in charge of the care and custody of the thousands of separated children.

Scott Lloyd, White told them, "couldn't put out a small grease fire, and this is a global cataclysm."

Kadlec agreed to White's terms. Lloyd, however, was still in the dark. He chimed in just before noon. "We have two categories of separated kids: one from the beginning of the fiscal year, the other from May 6, the beginning of zero tolerance," Lloyd emailed Kadlec, Wagner, Wynne, and other HHS officials. "CBP chiefs started separations before the announcement of the zero tolerance policy and we noticed it and started tracking," he continued, neglecting to mention that if it were up to him, that list might be long gone by now.

What he had to report was staggering. As of four days earlier, as I stood outside of the Ursula Central Processing Center, the Department of Health and Human Services "had received 1911 UACs from zero tolerance," and of them, only "114 were discharged," he wrote.

Among the separated children, approximately nine hundred "were unable to contact their parents as of Friday 6/16 because of trouble getting through to the parents," Lloyd admitted. In that group was José, currently wondering if he would ever make it out of Harlingen, and where exactly his father, Juan, was.

The day Lloyd sent his briefing to a group of colleagues, some of whom had no interest in working with him in any capacity, distrustful of his motives and capacity to lead his own organization, Juan was served with a document from the Los Angeles field office of Immigration and Customs Enforcement. The "warning for failure to depart" meant that he was on his way to being deported, regardless of the fact his underaged son was being held in South Texas.

In a tiny room in Washington, D.C., Commander White and his team set to work to try to get them—and thousands of others—back together.

June 23, 2018

On Saturday, as we continued editing our *Dateline* documentary, a career ORR employee walked into the Secretary's Operations Center, the bunker-like facility from where the reunifications of thousands of children forcibly taken from their parents would be run. She was there to get to work, for her name was on Commander Jonathan White's list.

The employee soon found herself standing with Scott Lloyd, who was there despite Commander White's desire that he be nowhere near the facility.

"I'm really glad you're here," Commander White told her as she reported for duty. "This is super important, though I'm sorry you're here."

"You have nothing to be sorry for, Jonathan," she replied to White.

Turning her gaze to Lloyd, she spoke her mind. "Scott, you, however, have something to be sorry for."

Lloyd may not have registered the anger both White and his colleague felt for the way he had heretofore handled the specter of separations, including his unforgivable urge to destroy the list tracking separated children that was being kept by their colleague Jim De La Cruz. Lloyd had repeatedly told them both that he trusted the public denials of the White House and Department of Homeland Security about the existence of a family separation policy.

WHETHER LLOYD CARRYING the Trump administration's water was willful ignorance, negligence, or a coordinated effort to hide the policy, that was the past. There was an urgent mission at hand, one Lloyd would not be able to obstruct. Commander White had begun to direct the dozens of people now reporting to him. Among those who would be under the operational structure headed up by White was a midlevel data analyst at Health and Human Services, a thirty-something taking the initiative to, he thought, match the list of separated children in his possession with what he assumed was a list of separated parents kept by Immigration and Customs Enforcement.

In the midafternoon, Thomas Fitzgerald, who like some of his colleagues physically slept in the Secretary's Operations Center while pouring through the data on all 12,000 children in HHS custody in order to determine who was separated, sent an email directly to Matthew Albence. He was the executive associate director for Enforcement and Removal Operations (ERO), the arm of ICE that transports, arrests, and deports undocumented immigrants. Albence had been in the room on Valentine's Day of 2017, when, in a meeting at the commissioner of Customs and Border Protection's office, the "clear and unambiguous" idea of family separations, as one attendee present put it to me, was first raised as a way to deter migration to the United States. According to the attendees, Albence indicated he supported separations.

Those who worked for Albence at ERO were responsible for taking separated parents to ICE detention after they were split from their children. It was ERO that brought Juan, shackled by his hands and feet, from Arizona to California. In a bizarre twist, these same people were now responsible for physically reuniting separated families.

The subject of Fitzgerald's email to Albence was "UAC Data Request—Parent/Legal Guardian Link."

> Good afternoon,
>
> Attached are two spreadsheets:
>
> 1. UAC_Alien_Numbers23JUN. This is our list of alien numbers of 2,219 unaccompanied alien children (UAC) since 06MAY.
> 2. UAC_ICE_Request23JUN. This spreadsheet is a template for your completion. This spreadsheet contained *two* tabs:
>
> Parent or Legal Guardian information tab
>
> Relationship tab

These spreadsheets, Fitzgerald explained, would be critical to pairing the separated children HHS had in its custody with the parents who had been scattered throughout the United States to dozens of federal, local, and privately run detention centers. Locating "alien numbers"—how ICE identified detainees in its custody—would be key to pairing parents and children, whose alien numbers were already known by HHS.

> On the parent or legal guardian information tab, we need for every parent or legal guardian separated from a child: their alien number, current status (detained, removed, released/ notice to appear, alternative to detention), detention center (if applicable), date released (if applicable), city, state, and country (final destination if not detention center), and case manager information.
>
> On the relationship tab, for each UAC alien number that we provided, we need an alien number, name and relationship type for his/her legal guardian (mother, father, or legal guardian), as well as date of last contact between the parent/legal guardian and UAC. If a UAC has more than one parent/legal guardian, provide information on both.
>
> Thank you for your assistance.

Within twenty minutes, Albence replied to Fitzgerald from his work BlackBerry (talk to any ICE employee and you'll hear complaints about their technology). His email confirmed the worst fears of the HHS staffers hard at work on reunifications.

Tom:

> Are you saying you don't have the alien number for any of the parents? This information should already be in the UAC portal. While I understand that information may be lacking in some instances, for those that you have, it wouldn't be efficient for us to try to run all these.
>
> Further, the type and volume of what you are requesting is not something that we are going to be able to complete in a rapid fashion, and in fact, we may not have some of it.

This would turn out to be an extraordinary understatement. Albence and company had virtually none of the information necessary to reconnect parents and children. Moreover, Albence's feigned shock that HHS didn't have information on separated parents was disingenuous, as was his insistence on the fact that "this information should already be in the UAC portal" (the computer system HHS used to track children). Indeed it was an open secret that the information was not there.

As far back as 2016, when Jim De La Cruz began tracking separations for HHS, and certainly in the summer of 2017, during the separation pilot program in the El Paso sector, Border Patrol agents had not been including detailed information—if any information at all—about the parents of separated children. Often there were no notes at all documenting the fact that the so-called unaccompanied child that HHS was receiving had actually very much been accompanied by his or her parent when they arrived in the United States.

Inside ICE's office of Detention Policy and Planning, Claire Trickler-McNulty had been sounding the alarm, pushing for a technological fix to be able to better track separated families, even if it meant deporting them upon reunification. So had Andrew Lorenzen-Strait, the deputy assistant director for custody management, who worked directly for Albence.

"We are going to have to put these families back together," Lorenzen-Strait realized at the time. But no solutions were put in place to mitigate what would clearly be a spectacular mess if separations ever were carried out on a wide scale. And indeed, it was.

If Fitzgerald correctly understood what Albence was telling him, finding any way to complete the mission was going to be a herculean task. Fitzgerald was frantic. For five hours, he did not reply, and when he did, what he shared with Albence was a nightmare scenario.

> In short, no, we do not have any linkages from parents to UAC, save for a handful in ACF's UAC portal (n of about 60). We have a list of parent alien numbers but no way to link them to children.

Fitzgerald was telling the senior ICE official in charge of reunifications—someone who had been complicit in pushing for the family separation policy—that there were documented connections between separated parents and children for only less than one-half of 1 percent of all children in HHS's custody.

No way to link.

Others were less diplomatic. Among those who had to

deal with the aftermath, there was an immense amount of anger bottled up for those who had allowed systematic family separations to take place. According to an ORR official who was part of the reunification team, "every other word was fuck. Fuck you, fuck that."

At eighteen minutes after ten that evening, the Department of Homeland Security released a "fact sheet" meant to calm the nerves of the still-building protests around the country. The first paragraph alone contained multiple lies:

> Minors come into HHS custody with information provided by DHS regarding how they illegally entered the country and whether or not they were with a parent or adult and, to the extent possible, the parent(s) or guardian(s) information and location. There is a central database which HHS and DHS can access and update when a parent(s) or minor(s) location information changes.

As was by now clear to everyone working on reunifications, not only did most separated children get sent to HHS custody without information indicating "whether or not they were with a parent or adult," there was in no way, shape, or form "a central database which HHS and DHS can access and update." There were only simple spreadsheets that, earlier that day, both ICE and HHS admitted they couldn't complete. Americans were lied to about the existence of a family separation policy. Now they were being lied to about the plan to undo it.

ON SUNDAY MORNING, I was back again at 30 Rock, starting the day speaking with Joy Reid on her program while she was on the border at the Tornillo temporary tent facility, which was attracting protestors like congressional candidate Alexandria Ocasio-Cortez. The balance of the day was spent "crashing" the rest of our *Dateline* hour. That night, "The Dividing Line" debuted on NBC to an audience of nearly three and a half million people.

What started as an exploration of realities of life along both sides of the border became, for me, a lesson in how thirty years of failed border policy led to the present moment, wherein thousands of young children, under the guise of "deterrence," were likely to be permanently traumatized in the pursuit of a political goal. And understanding how separated I was from the realities of bipartisan American border policy was a lesson I learned belatedly, as a journalist and citizen. With thousands of children needlessly taken from their parents, it was too late. The helplessness I felt was an emotion I shared with HHS employees in the Secretary's Operations Center, without ever having met or spoken with them. A feeling that our country, and I, let these children face nightmarish trauma at the hands of President Trump.

That night, Carla Provost, the chief of the Border Patrol, responded to our *Dateline* hour. She tweeted a link to the fact sheet containing lies about the reunification process. "Get the facts on Zero-Tolerance Prosecution and Family Reunification from people in the know," she wrote. If by "people in the know" she meant those who were hiding the government's failure to link separated parents and children, she was absolutely right.

Provost signed off her post "#HonorFirst."

PART THREE

∎ ∎ ∎

On Thursday, June 28, 2018, at 1:54 AM, De La Cruz, James (ACF) wrote:

Dear Case Managers and Clinician,

Please find this message as an update to current events related to children separated from their detained parents.

Please allow me to share that our current primary task is to reconnect every separated child in our network of care to his or her detained parent by the close of business 5:00 PM EST, July 2, 2018.

As many of you know, ORR is currently tasked with reuniting separated children with their parents. During the past weekend some of you worked with ORR staff to focus\prioritize your case management efforts towards reconnecting separated UAC with their detained parents. Since that time we asked some of you to begin tracking information to capture past and present efforts to connect children with his or her parent(s).

The HHS Secretary's Office has identified an improved way to track our efforts to reconnect families. The HHS Secretary's office is designing a database that will eliminate the need to track information on spreadsheets. To prepare for the new tracking system we need your help to prepare to respond in two separate phases . . .

*** Please do not wait for the database to go live to initiate contact with parents! Contact should have already been initiated and should continue. ***

CHAPTER NINE

"Shocks the Conscience"

June 26, 2018

Dead asleep at home in New York City, the lead attorney in the ACLU's case against the Trump administration's family separation policy was running on fumes when his phone rang just after eleven at night. Lee Gelernt had a right to be exhausted that Tuesday evening.

Six days earlier, the day of President Trump's executive order undoing his own policy he denied existed, the federal judge in the case, Dana Sabraw of the Southern District of California, emerged from more than a month of silence to ask both Gelernt and the lawyers defending the Trump administration to answer questions ahead of his ruling on a preliminary injunction that could legally halt separations and force the reunification of separated families.

The landscape had changed significantly since the parties last saw Judge Sabraw. Notably, whereas the government had previously denied the existence of a policy or practice of family separations, the secretary of homeland security had by now signed a decision memo instituting the policy, and the attorney general had announced it. Further, public outrage had reached a boiling point. With thousands of families now separated, the issue had to be addressed urgently.

On Friday, June 22, after the judge heard oral arguments, during which Gelernt told Sabraw he was "pleading" for him to rule as soon as possible, Sabraw requested supplemental briefings from both the ACLU and the government. By Monday, June 25, they were submitted to the court, and Gelernt was now anxiously awaiting a ruling that would have profound implications for the mental health and well-being of the thousands of children taken from their parents.

The phone continued to ring. Gelernt opened his eyes, reached for his phone, and answered it.

"Hello?"

It was one of his co-counsels calling from the West Coast. "We won."

Gelernt shot up, shook off the fog, and dug into the ruling. As John Mitnick, the general counsel from the Department of Homeland Security, had predicted when he gave his legal analysis of the decision memo presented to Secretary Kirstjen Nielsen, the preliminary injunction was granted, mandating the reunifications of separated families, on the grounds that the separations violated their due process rights under the U.S. Constitution.

As Gelernt reviewed the twenty-four-page ruling, I was sitting at my computer in my tiny home office off the kitchen. Earlier that day on a press conference call, Commander White would not tell me nor other reporters that they were still receiving newly separated migrant children despite President Trump's executive order. "Bottom line," I wrote at the computer that night, "we still don't know the total number of kids separated by zero tolerance, don't know when those still in custody will be reunited, nor where they are."

Not until nearly an hour after Gelernt was woken by the late-night phone call did I see the news of the ruling. "Judge bars separation of immigrants from children, orders reunification," a Reuters headline read.

"A federal judge on Tuesday ruled that U.S. immigration agents could no longer separate immigrant parents and children caught crossing the border from Mexico illegally, and must work to reunite those families that had been split up in custody," the wire service wrote. "The ruling by U.S. District Judge Dana Sabraw in San Diego came in a lawsuit filed over the family separations by the American Civil Liberties Union."

The dispatch failed to include the scathing language Judge Sabraw used in his decision. Sabraw characterized the current state of affairs as a "chaotic circumstance of the Government's own making" that "has reached a crisis level," resulting in "the casual, if not deliberate, separation of families." That the Trump administration had "no reunification plan in place" was "a startling reality."

Quoting case law, Judge Sabraw, a George W. Bush appointee, declared that a "practice of this sort implemented in this way is likely to be 'so egregious, so outrageous, that it may fairly be said to shock the contemporary conscience,' interferes with rights 'implicit in the concept of ordered liberty,' and is so 'brutal' and 'offensive' that it [does] not comport with traditional ideas of fair play and decency."

The judge ordered the Trump administration to stop systematic separations of children (except in limited circumstances), and to reunite all currently separated children under the age of five within fourteen days, and all others within thirty days. He ordered Immigration and Customs Enforcement, Customs and Border Protection, the Bureau of Prisons, and the Office of Refugee Resettlement—all of the agencies involved in this man-made disaster—to work together in order to undo it. And perhaps most important, he ordered a stop to deportations of parents without separated children, hundreds of which had already occurred. The judge's countdown had begun, and in detention, children and parents were still clueless about what was happening to them.

June 28, 2018

Around forty-eight hours later I got a phone call from Lindsay Toczylowski, the lawyer who had been attempting to make contact with incarcerated migrant fathers who had been separated. Despite all her work on behalf of separated families, Toczylowski, executive director of Immigrant Defenders Law Center, had only caught my attention a day earlier. In an article in *The Texas Tribune*, she described the extraordinary and heartbreaking experience of standing before an immigration court with her client, a toddler separated from parents. "We were representing a three-year-old in court recently who had been separated from the parents," she said. "And the child—in the middle of the hearing—started climbing up on the table."

Again I thought of my son, not quite three but a table climber nevertheless. The idea of him being anywhere alone and made to fend for himself made me sick. I had been borderline harassing Toczylowski, having showed up unannounced at her office in an art deco building in downtown Los Angeles that dated to the twenties to try to speak with her. I rode the elevator to her floor to try to ask her about the tiny children she was coming across and how Judge Sabraw's order would affect her work on their behalf. Her colleagues politely told me to go away, which I did, and Toczylowski called me back that night. When she did, I pulled out the little blue spiral notebook that I had been holding close since touring Casa Padre.

She explained to me that she had occasionally seen separations before zero tolerance when she was working for Catholic Charities, but the rate of the separations had spiked, by now a surprise to no one. Her firm had a contract to offer legal services to children detained in shelters run by ORR in Southern California.

Toczylowski and I talked about the three-year-old, who she said wasn't alone in being "hysterical and hungry." She was seeing parents "deported almost immediately" after separations. But to my surprise, what she wanted to talk about wasn't children at all—it was separated parents who were being denied the right to an attorney.

She told me about Victorville and the hundreds of migrants, including separated fathers, who were in both the federal prison and the immigration detention center not far away in Adelanto. I had never heard of Adelanto, one of the largest immigration detention facilities in the United States. There, without attorneys, she told me that parents were making decisions not to fight for asylum claims, influenced by the government telling them the quickest way to reunite with their children was to be deported with them.

"If they did have counsel, they could go through with their asylum claim," she told me.

I asked her what the judge's ruling meant for these parents.

"They'll now be able to get a screening" for credible fear, an important step in receiving asylum. Until now "everyone has been told nothing about next steps."

I told her I would be interested in joining her on a trip to the high desert to meet the separated parents she was trying to help, if she was willing. We agreed to speak again, and I wished her good luck.

The next day, June 29, the emergency management staff, working furiously to reunite separated families, made their way into the headquarters of the Department of Health and Human Services in Washington, D.C. Those working in the Secretary's Operations Center (SOC) would enter when it was dark, spend the day in a windowless room, and often emerge again in darkness. On this Saturday, protestors were streaming down Pennsylvania Avenue, a few blocks away, and in hundreds of other cities nationwide, united under the banner Families Belong Together. Inside the SOC, they were doing the very work that the protestors were demanding as they marched toward the White House in scorching heat and heavy humidity.

"These children may never get back to their parents," Commander White was known to say. "If they do it will be because of you. There is no plan B."

After Judge Sabraw's ruling, those hoping to get parents and children back together allowed themselves to crack a smile. They now had backup from the federal courts.

While the protests kept the pressure on President Trump, who tweeted that day in response to the nationwide protests, it couldn't speed up the reunification efforts. Thousands of parents and children waited for the relief so many Americans were hoping they would get.

July 6, 2018

So urgent was the mission to reunite the thousands of children in the custody of the federal government with their parents, that every few days the parties—the ACLU and the Trump administration—would reconvene to update the judge on the government's progress. It wasn't looking good. Four days before all of the children under five years old were to be reunited with their parents, on a Friday afternoon in California, the Trump administration still couldn't say for sure how many kids it had separated, nor where all their parents were.

"I know there was some number that were—at one point were—remained in Marshal Service custody," Trump administration lawyer Sarah Fabian told the judge about separated parents. "I don't have that number for you, if that is part of this. Forty-six are in ICE custody. Nineteen have been removed from the country. And nineteen were released from custody. And I am not sure if that math adds up without my phone."

If what she's saying sounds to you like a complete and total disaster, it's because it was. Shoddy record keeping, poor planning, and a scramble to fix everything made for an unbearably complex situation. But it was one that the ACLU continued to insist was not insurmountable, and one that could be resolved with time and dedicated attention.

The vetting process itself was the most critical issue the government and the ACLU had to agree on. Gelernt argued for an expedited process, emphasizing the urgency of reuniting families. Sabraw seemed to buy the argument, and the government indicated they would likely not fight back.

"I would be prepared to indicate that the ORR, HHS, should not feel obligated to comply with those internal procedures because this case is so different, it involves separation of minor children from parents."

That evening he ordered the government and ACLU to "meet and confer on the ORR policies and procedures in dispute," and to submit a plan to streamline the process.

By Monday, they still had not agreed on the streamlined process even for the less complicated cases. Further, the number of children slated to be reunified by the Tuesday deadline wasn't anywhere near the total number of separated children under five. In other words, the Trump administration was going to miss the deadline the judge set to get toddlers back together with their parents. Part of the problem, as had been suspected all along, is that some of the parents had been deported.

Gelernt interjected, "we think there [are] at least twelve [parents] who have been removed [i.e., deported] and nine have been released into the interior."

It was with this level of granularity that the reunification process had to be dissected in court, every child a soul experiencing added trauma with each passing hour. Further complicating reunifications was the fact that some parents were classified as having a criminal conviction or communicable diseases, two categories exempted from reunification under the judge's order.

On Tuesday, the deadline to reunite 103 children under five came and went, and only a fraction of the children were successfully reunited with their parents. Two days later, the government admitted it had only been able to reunite fifty-seven. The rest, they said, were either deported, locked up, or ineligible to be reunited for reasons including having a communicable disease or criminal history.

The following day, a Friday, the government and ACLU together submitted a status report. On behalf of the Trump administration, Chris Meekins, the chief of staff to the assistant secretary for preparedness and response within HHS, argued against the streamlined unification process, on the grounds that hastily placing an unaccompanied minor with a sponsor would potentially harm children.

"My opinion," he wrote, "is that complying with the Court's orders involves increased risks to child welfare in at least four respects." They were: 1) placing children with adults who were not parents, 2) placing children with an abusive parent, 3) placing children with an abusive person living in the same home, and 4) placing children in a home with an alternative caregiver in the case that a parent has already been deported.

"The court's necessary truncating of the vetting process," Meekins argued, "materially increases the risk of harm to children."

Judge Sabraw excoriated the filing. "I have some very serious concerns about the filing and, frankly speaking, am very disappointed." He continued, saying it was "wholly inadequate."

"The declaration also is clearly written to provide cover for HHS. That's all it is doing. It is explaining a parade of horribles about how under a streamlined process there is a six point eight six percent chance that something is going to happen. That is not going to happen."

"There needs to be a complete readjustment in HHS with how they are going to go about this," Sabraw later concluded.

In an order issued after the hearing, Judge Sabraw wrote, "It is clear from Mr. Meekins's Declaration that HHS either does not understand the Court's orders or is acting in defiance of them. At a minimum, it appears he is attempting to provide cover to Defendants for their own conduct in the practice of family separation, and the lack of foresight and infrastructure necessary to remedy the harms caused by that practice."

Not pulling any punches, Judge Sabraw insisted in his order that the Trump administration "shall have a representative from HHS personally appear" in his courtroom on Monday morning. All the while, efforts to reunify separated parents and children continued into and through the weekend.

July 9, 2018

Under Judge Sabraw's orders, no separated parent was to be deported without having been reunited with their child or children—that is, "unless the Class Member affirmatively, knowingly, and voluntarily declines to be reunited with the child prior to the Class Member's deportation."

Just shy of one month locked up in Adelanto, the immigration detention center in the high desert above Los Angeles, Juan was presented with a form, in English, that contained those exact same words. The "Separated Parent's Removal Form" was given to him in a language he didn't understand despite the fact that when he was apprehended, it was noted he did not speak English. Now he was presented with two options—neither of which, as lawyer Lindsay Toczylowski had warned me, said anything about a right to pursue an asylum claim.

English: I am requesting to reunite with my child(ren) for
the purpose of repatriation to my country of citizenship.

Signature / Firma: _____

   English: I am affirmatively, knowingly, and voluntarily requesting to return to my country of citizenship without my minor child(ren) who I understand will remain in the Untied States to pursue available claims of relief.

Signature / Firma: _____

He signed the second option. Four days later, he signed the same form in Spanish, told by an official inside the detention center he had to because he had signed it already in English. Just as he was pressured to sign forms while he was at the Border Patrol station in Yuma, Juan was unclear about what he was being asked to do. He didn't understand the consequences of his actions.

Intimidated and alone, his only hope would be legal representation that could undo what he had inadvertently done: telling the United States government he wanted to be deported without his son, who was taken from him when they arrived together.

In the meantime, he was stuck in Adelanto. Less than two months earlier, the inspector general of the Department of Homeland Security had conducted a surprise inspection. What they found were conditions suitable for no human being: nooses in detainee cells, migrants improperly subjugated to solitary confinement, and poor-quality medical care. The inspector general noted then, in a report to be released later, that "in about 15 of the approximately 20 male detainee cells we visited within 4 housing units on the west side, we observed braided bedsheets, referred to as 'nooses' by center staff and detainees, hanging from vents. The contract guard escorting us during our visit removed the first noose found in a detainee cell, but stopped after realizing many cells we visited had nooses hanging from the vents. We also heard the guard telling some detainees to take the sheets down."

"One detainee told us," the OIG continued, " 'I've seen a few attempted suicides using the braided sheets by the vents and then the guards laugh at them and call them "suicide failures" once they are back from medical.' "

This was Juan's home for the foreseeable future.

July 15, 2018

One by one their names were called. Thirty-seven separated children were told they would need to pack up and get ready to hop in waiting vans. They were to be taken from the Harlingen shelter for migrant children (operated by BCFS Health and Human Services) to the Port Isabel detention center (run by Immigration and Customs Enforcement), where they would be reunified with their parents. The shelter had twice confirmed by phone with ICE that they would soon be en route with the children. It was all part of the plan, if you could call it that, laid out in court by the Trump administration.

If the thirty-seven were anything like José, who had been in the custody of the shelter for a month with so little exposure to the outside world he didn't even know what the shelter's full exterior looked like, having their names called was a massive relief. After lunch, as they filed out to the passenger vans, hundreds of fellow migrant children were left behind in the shelter. José was one of them, his father nowhere near Port Isabel. Juan was still locked away at another ICE detention center, Adelanto, sixteen hundred miles away.

José would go about his Sunday like he did the previous four. He was not classified as "tender aged"—five to twelve years old—and thus he was over the cutoff age for children who would get to see their parents.

As the younger children pulled out of the facility, the second largest in South Texas behind the Casa Padre shelter, which housed more than five hundred children, they headed toward Los Fresnos, turning left onto East Harrison Avenue. Had they turned right they would have seen the city they had been near but never visited during their detention.

Just beyond the shelter was the Harlingen Soccer Complex, which had been off-limits to them. After likely crossing a yellow vertical lift bridge dating to 1953 that stretches over the Arroyo Colorado, they'd passed through the small city of Rio Hondo. From there it would be just over twenty minutes until they pulled into the detention center. As the crow flies, they were not far from where the Rio Grande meets the Gulf of Mexico, where I thought in April my journey along the border would end.

For these thirty-seven children, the hope that they would soon see, speak with, and touch their parents for the first time in too long must have filled their heads. But as they pulled into the parking lot outside the detention center, that hope withered. The vans began idling in the parking lot at two thirty in the afternoon as staff from the Harlingen shelter brought the children into the ICE facility, designed to detain adults only.

The shelter staff was told paperwork to secure release of the parents in order to reunify them wasn't yet complete, so the kids packed up and headed back into the vans in the parking lot, where they waited. And waited. And waited. Shelter staff called back to colleagues in Harlingen to ask for more vans, to allow the children to stretch out within them, and to have food to eat.

As day turned to night the staff again attempted to jump-start reunifications by bringing the children back inside, but many of the kids were too cold to sit inside the air-conditioned facility and so went back to the vans, where they could rest more comfortably. As Immigration and Customs Enforcement officials inside the facility clocked out and went home for the day, Andrew Carter, the regional director for BCFS, wrote to his boss, Kevin Dinnin, the company's CEO, explaining what had happened.

> It is 22:30 and they are still in the vans and not one of our children has been checked in. In addition, there are other vans with kids from other facilities that are waiting as well. There has to be a better process. I hope as we move forward there can be adjustments so that we don't put tender age kids in this position. If coordinated properly, we can be scheduled for a particular intake time so there are not multiple programs arriving at the same time and overwhelming the intake process at the facility. Any attention you can provide or elevate regarding this issue is appreciated.

Dinnin forwarded the email to his chief operating officer, who almost immediately forwarded it to Commander Jonathan White, the man in charge of the reunification effort who had been holed up in the Washington, D.C., bunker from which he was managing the process. They had sent it to the right guy. Earlier that day, Steven Wagner, the acting assistant secretary at HHS at the Administration for Children and Families, and his direct report, Scott Lloyd, the head of the Office of Refugee Resettlement, had received a stern email from Dr. Robert Kadlec, the assistant secretary in charge of the team managing the emergency response that was the re-unification process.

> Steve and Scott in light of the last 36 hours I am asking that tasking and accountability of ORR personnel involved in reunification operations be given to Don Boyce my overall operational manager and Jonathan White the Federal Health Coordinating Official for this response.
> This request is to ensure the most expeditious management and coordination of what would be ordinarily a difficult mission that as a result of delays and confusion of the last 12 hours [is] now almost impossible. Clear command and control relationships are vital to accelerate what we are doing.

Those two Trump-appointed men, one of whom, Lloyd, had personally supported the destruction of the unofficial list tracking family separations in April, were now officially sidelined, removed from any responsibility having to do with reunifications. Commander White, who had been copied on that email, wrote back to the BCFS leadership the following morning, weighing in.

"You did the right thing," he said. "I am in travel to testify about this mission in court. Thank you."

It was Commander White whom the government had selected to represent Health and Human Services in the San Diego courtroom of Judge Dana Sabraw, who had grown furious with White's colleague Chris Meekins. White had some cleaning up to do. What White didn't say at the time was that, unlike Meekins, he was looking to use streamlined processes in order to get children reunited as quickly as possible.

"This will be chaotic," he told colleagues. "We tolerate chaos and disruption so long as no child is unsafe."

It was White who had given the go-ahead for the BCFS vans to make their way to Port Isabel, knowing that the facility was likely not ready to reunite at the time but that children waiting outside would force the issue.

As White walked into court wearing the dark blue dress uniform to outline the government's new plan, seventeen of the thirty-seven children had been reunified at Port Isabel. But twenty continued to sit in the vans.

At the start of the hearing, Judge Sabraw ordered the government to stop deporting reunited parents and children together. "If space is an issue, the government will have to make space," Sabraw said. He then turned to Commander White, who had been summoned to explain both the government's new plan for reuniting families and what he called the "exasperating" declaration from Chris Meekins on Friday. White explained the reunification process he had devised. Once a parent has been cleared for reunification, "that is the green light to ORR to initiate ORR's administrative process and travel process to move the child.

"It is my planning factor that from that moment—depending on the geographic proximity of the child—anywhere from six to forty-eight hours later the child will be there at that ICE facility for physical reunification," White explained.

After a quick break, Lee Gelernt, the ACLU's lawyer, asked Commander White about the status of reunifications.

"Thank you, Commander, for being here," he began. "Have the reunifications for children five and above already started? Not the process, but have there been actual reunifications?"

"Yes, sir," said Commander White.

After a back-and-forth about the current number of separated children—now officially 2,551—Gelernt returned to questions about the reunification process.

"There has been some concern that reunifications occurred at night for the children under five. Will reunifications occur late at night for the children five to seventeen, as far as you know?"

"Some will occur at night," Commander White said. "It has been operationally necessary for us to ask ICE to extend its hours," he explained. "We understand our operational direction to be to expedite reunification of children, and that's what we are doing." White did not mention that was exactly what was happening, as they spoke, at Port Isabel.

Judge Sabraw, who days earlier was apoplectic at HHS and Chris Meekins, struck an entirely different tune with Commander White.

"The observation I would make is that Commander White is exactly the person that is needed. And I'm very appreciative that you are here, the way you have explained this process. There is no question that you understand the context of this case, the undisputed facts that have led to this difficult situation," the judge surmised. "The responsibility of the government and HHS to make it right through reunification, in a safe and efficient manner. I have every confidence you are the right person to do this. When I hear your testimony and I look at the plan, it provides a great deal of comfort."

What else Commander White did not reveal that morning in court is that he had been trying to stop the family separation policy from happening all along. He and his colleagues within HHS had been sounding the alarm from the earliest days of the administration, for nearly two years, about the damage that the process would do to children. The problem was compounded by the fact that the agencies were not prepared to track and reunite families once the policy started. Indeed there was no plan in place, which is exactly what Commander White was undoing on a daily basis—creating one.

When the hearing ended in San Diego, it was just around lunchtime at Port Isabel. Almost a full day after the vans pulled into Port Isabel from Harlingen with the thirty-seven children on board, thirty-two of them had been reunified. Not until almost six in the morning on Tuesday in South Texas was the last child finally reunited, thirty-nine hours after first arriving in the parking lot. White's system was imperfect, but it was getting the job done.

The next day, José's case manager at the same Harlingen shelter sent notice to ICE that he was ready to be released to his father.

"ORR has determined that the below Juvenile Respondent should be released to a sponsor," the form read. "The Director of the Office of Refugee Resettlement, Department of Health and Human Services requests that the Chief Counsel, Immigration and Customs Enforcement, Department of

Homeland Security notify the Executive Office of Immigration Review of the change of address."

The address listed was the Adelanto ICE Detention Center, where Juan, José's dad, was locked up waiting to see his son. And their waiting would not end anytime soon.

● ● ●

From: National Immigrant Justice Center

To: Salvano-Dunn, Dana

CC: CRCLCompliance

Subject: Urgent: Two children transferred to adult ICE facilities where their parents are not in custody

Date: Tuesday, July 24, 2018 6:04:08 PM

Dear Officer Salvano-Dunn,

Thank you for your time at the stakeholder engagement this evening, and for your willingness to assist in cases of urgently arising rights violation in the context of DHS and HSS's family reunification process.

I am sending this complaint and request for help with regard to two NIJC child clients. In both cases, the children's attorney of record learned this morning via a manifest provided by the ORR shelter that the children would be transferred from ORR custody in Chicago to DHS custody in the Port Isabel Detention Center (PIDC) today for the purpose of reunification with their fathers. We believe both boys are either at or soon arrive at PIDC. In both cases, it is our understanding—verified by the ICE online detainee locator—that the fathers are NOT at PIDC, but are instead in DHS custody at the El Paso Processing Center.

Information regarding both families is below. Our request for remedy in both cases is for DHS to immediately transfer the fathers to PIDC for reunification and release with their sons.

CHAPTER TEN

"Made-for-TV Drama"

July 25, 2018

One of the most powerful Border Patrol officials—the chief of the San Diego sector—was furious at me. Rodney Scott, among the longest-serving members of the Border Patrol at thirty-plus years with the agency, had been stewing about the *Dateline* documentary, which included the interview we did almost half a year earlier while overlooking Tijuana from the United States side of the border.

It had been a full month since the broadcast aired. Izhar Harpaz, the lead producer, had, as a courtesy, sent Chief Scott the documentary on DVD with a thank-you note. Izhar's good intentions didn't land with the chief. Scott pulled out a piece of official Customs and Border Protection letterhead, complete with a giant watermarked eagle in the middle, and typed out a letter.

Dear Jacob and MSNBC Team:

Thank you for the DVD; however, I am returning it. I watched the show when it originally aired and have no reason to view it again.

To be perfectly honest, I was disappointed in the final product. I understand that you have editorial processes and a review cycle through which to clear programming. You also were clear from the beginning that the final storyline could change at the sole discretion of Dateline NBC management. None of that bothered me.

What bothered me was your personal decision to use the extremely inflammatory and emotionally charged description of our processing centers as "cages." That few seconds of video overshadowed and erased any sign of neutral reporting. It became made-for-TV drama and little else.

To be fair, I also queried a number of private citizens who viewed the program in order to get their perspective. They also reiterated that their take away point was that the U.S. Border Patrol separates families and places them in cages. If that was your objective, you were successful.

Regrettably,
Rodney S. Scott
Chief Patrol Agent, San Diego Sector, U.S. Border Patrol

This is the same Rodney Scott who toured President Trump around his border wall prototypes for a bank of cameras. If any of the drama around separations was "made for TV," it was created by the Trump administration itself. Katie Waldman, the Homeland Security spokeswoman, told me on multiple occasions that the policy was designed to play so shockingly in the media that it would force Congress to end it by passing harsh immigration laws, such as permitting indefinite detention of migrant families and the immediate deportation of unaccompanied Central American minors in its place.

As for my use of "cages," the Border Patrol's own officially released photos and video of the detention facilities testify to the accuracy of the description. I am happy the "private citizens" Scott "queried" took away that "the U.S. Border Patrol separates families and places them in cages," as that was exactly what was happening. And, we told him "the final storyline could change at the sole discretion of Dateline NBC management" because nobody knew what Trump would do next along the border. It just so happened he decided to systematically separate thousands of migrant children from their parents at the border, and I ended up seeing it myself.

Maybe Scott was just having a bad day. He slipped the letter in a manila envelope, dropped in the DVD with Izhar's handwritten note attached to it by a paper clip, and sent it to me, care of the *Dateline* NBC team at 30 Rock.

Meanwhile, the government was hours away from a deadline to put all parents and children back together, and it wasn't going well.

July 26, 2018

Deadline day. "The government says every eligible parent will be reunited with their child on this day," I told *Today* show hosts Carson Daly, Craig Melvin, and Hoda Kotb in Studio 1A.

We ran a report about one family I had met, Honduran Maria Gloria and her sons Franklin, eleven, and Byron, seven, who had been reunited in New York. You can't call them the lucky ones, but their good fortune of getting back together earlier than many other families was more than hundreds of others could say.

"Honestly, it's a mess," I said of what was expected to be a large number of parents deported without their children. "The kids may be stranded here forever and not be able to get to their parents because those parents won't be able to get back to the U.S. for reunification."

It wasn't so much that the reunifications themselves were a mess—in fact the emergency management team were completing a herculean task. Rather, the problem was that so many didn't meet the criteria.

Sure enough, in a court filing later that day, the Trump administration admitted that while it had reunited more than 1,400 children with their parents, 711 kids had not been reunited, and of those, 431 had parents who had already been deported.

That night I flew home to Los Angeles. The next day there would be a status hearing in federal court in San Diego to discuss what would happen to those families. I drove down the following morning to be able to see it in person.

I HAD HEARD the voice of Judge Sabraw but never seen him with my own eyes, nor stepped foot inside the courtroom that would touch the lives of virtually every separated child I saw at the epicenter of the policy. As I walked toward the building from where I parked around one in the afternoon, I saw Lee Gelernt, the ACLU lawyer, walking hurriedly across the street with a documentary camera crew in tow. Aarne, who met me down there, and I stayed back to avoid showing up in that footage.

The federal courthouse building, designed by famed architect Richard Meier, was immaculate, sixteen stories of terra cotta tiles and glass and polished metal elevators. Not at all what I had pictured. I walked up the ramp out front, the sunlight reflecting off the windows and blasting me in the face until I made it inside. Upstairs inside the courtroom, I pulled out my blue spiral notebook. There were three blank pages left.

Once the proceedings started, the normal telephone conference line that lets in people from the outside world went dead, leaving us in the courtroom as the only conduits of information. Good timing to be there. Sitting there in person just feet behind Lee Gelernt and Scott Stewart, the government's attorney, I was struck that the interaction between the two felt far chippier than I had anticipated. On the docket was the issue of 120 parents who had signed forms, just like Juan at Adelanto, giving up the right to be reunified with their children. Gelernt was adamant those cases be revisited in some way so that those parents were not immediately deported without their children, as more than four hundred others had already been.

"The trauma that is going on is amazing," Gelernt said of the reports he was getting from the ground. "It would be torturous to have a parent thinking the rest of their lives, I gave away my child because I was confused, and it was my mistake.

"I mean, they are going to go back to their home countries now and people are going to ask, where is your daughter? Where is your son?

"And they are going to be having to say, well, I was confused and didn't understand."

For much of the rest of the hearing, Gelernt continued to

press this issue, and Judge Sabraw attempted to digest it as the Trump administration pushed back.

"I think we never anticipated that people could make the decision requested of them on the form without being with their child, because it is a family decision," Gelernt admitted.

"So this would be a parent in a facility who has a removal order," Judge Sabraw said, describing almost exactly the case of Juan in Adelanto. Gelernt, too, without knowing Juan or his case specifically, described his situation perfectly.

"It was virtually impossible to counsel parents when they were separated because they were constantly being transferred," he said. Juan had been moved from Yuma to Florence to Victorville and finally to Adelanto, where he signed the form after it was presented to the Spanish speaker in English.

The Trump administration's lawyer wasn't buying it.

"The notice form is quite clear. It gives parents the information they need to know," Stewart said. "As with any system, there could be imperfections of operation on the ground."

"Do you agree that with the parents who claim they elected to remove separately but didn't know what they were doing could be carved out," Sabraw inquired of Stewart, "or whatever the term is, so that they can meet with counsel, and then determine whether to reunify and remove together?"

Stewart had a hard time answering the question, saying several times he wanted to "take it back."

"When you say you could take it back, what does that mean?" Sabraw asked.

"Well, I would have to talk to the—just the clients and sort of see, you know, what the, you know, how we, you know, what we can kind of work out, what we might be able to work out there as to that group."

Stewart was floundering. He was unsure of the total number of parents who had signed the form and were now saying they wanted to change their election.

"So, then, whether it is two hundred and six or one hundred and twenty," said Gelernt, "I am not sure exactly I understand what the United States government's legitimate position is in leaving a child behind who the parent doesn't want to leave behind. That seems beyond the pale."

This set off Stewart. I felt like a kid in the room when my parents were arguing. It was intense.

"My legitimate position there, your honor, is that it is one thing if a person here or there says they didn't understand something.

"But my understanding of Mr. Gelernt is that his essential view is that if you elected to be removed without your child, then that somehow, like, presumptively implies coercion or misleading or inadequate information or lack of counseling."

Judge Sabraw interjected like a referee in the ring, sending the two sides back to their corners, leaving the issue to be solved another day. Meanwhile, parents like Juan remained locked up, after the reunification deadline, as his son went through the daily repetitive routine of life in the custody of a shelter.

July 28, 2018

If the judicial branch of the federal government wasn't keeping the Trump administration busy enough as it struggled to undo its family separation policy, the legislative branch had questions about the Trump-made disaster, too. On a summer Saturday, a select group of interagency officials gathered to prepare for a hearing called by the Republican-controlled Senate Judiciary Committee.

The committee had called before it five administration officials: Matthew Albence, the executive associate director of enforcement and removal operations for Immigration and Customs Enforcement, who had advocated for family separations since the earliest days of the administration; Commander Jonathan White, who had done the exact opposite and was now in charge of reunification efforts; Carla Provost, the chief of the Border Patrol, whose agents carried out the separations; James McHenry, the director of the Executive Office for Immigration Review, representing the Department of Justice, which initiated the zero tolerance policy; and Jennifer Higgins, the associate director of the Refugee, Asylum and International Operations Directorate at U.S. Citizenship and Immigration Services, the agency responsible for asylum claims.

They were participating in a "murder board," what they called a practice session in which they would be peppered with hypothetical questions they would hear from senators. The gathering went about as well as you could expect, given the tension among the officials.

Part of the team questioning the soon-to-be witnesses were Katie Waldman, the Department of Homeland Security spokeswoman, and her boss, Jonathan Hoffman, the assistant secretary for public affairs at DHS. Hoffman's counterpart from HHS was also there, Judy Stecker, the assistant secretary for public affairs, as was Brian Stimson, the principal deputy general counsel for the department.

The group walked through the lead-up, implementation, and aftermath of the policy. But one question in particular caused the room to explode: Was separation harmful to children?

Commander Jonathan White, who had long warned of the impacts of separation on children, as had the American Academy of Pediatrics, among others, made it clear he believed it was. If asked, he would stick to the scientific facts.

Waldman suggested a line that was straight out of the Koch brothers' climate denial playbook: "there's no reason to think, or way to know, that separations were harmful to children."

White couldn't believe it.

"I cannot give that answer under oath because it would be perjury."

Stimson, the Health and Human Services lawyer, jumped in. Commander White, he told the DHS flacks, was his "star witness" in the Ms. L. case "and you're pressuring him to give this answer under oath?"

Waldman, Hoffman, Stimson, and Stecker started screaming at one another. After the blowup, Waldman approached Commander White and, as she had done to me on several occasions, used one of her favorite pejoratives.

"I'm sure you're a bleeding heart liberal."

That set Commander White off.

"Ms. Waldman, you should save that attitude for journalists. You literally traumatized these kids. Why don't you go peddle your story to people who don't work in immigration."

Hoffman, looking out for his department and personal interests, interjected.

"Where are your loyalties?" he asked White, using a line that could have come from President Trump.

"I swore to protect the Constitution as a commissioned officer of the U.S. Public Health Service. Under oath I'll answer truthfully," he shot back.

The following Tuesday, he did. At the hearing, ICE's Albence described his agency's family detention facilities as "more like a summer camp," an absurd comparison by any stretch of the imagination.

Senator Richard Blumenthal, the Democrat from Connecticut, asked the five assembled witnesses, sworn under oath, "Did any member of this panel say to anyone, 'maybe this isn't such a good idea'?"

The room sat in silence for four seconds, until Blumenthal looked at Commander White, asking him to speak.

"During the deliberative process over the previous year, we raised a number of concerns in the ORR program about any policy which would result in family separation," White admitted, "due to concerns we had about the best interest of the child as well as about whether that would be operationally supportable with the bed capacity we had."

White leaned back in his chair, his hands folded in his lap as Blumenthal responded slowly.

"Now, I'm gonna translate that into what I would call layman's language. You told the administration that kids would suffer as a result. That pain would be inflicted, correct?"

As he promised Waldman and Hoffman at the murder board, White didn't mince words, and he told the truth.

"Separation of children from their parents entails significant risk of harm to children."

"Well, it's traumatic for any child separated from his or

her parents," Blumenthal said as White nodded. "Am I correct? I say that as a parent of four children."

"There's no question. There's no question that separation of children from parents entails significant potential for traumatic psychological injury to the child."

• • •

From: National Immigrant Justice Center

To: CRCLCompliance

Subject: Complaint | Coercion Against Separated Parents
in DHS Custody

Date: Thursday, August 23, 2018 9:26:02 AM

Over the past several several weeks, we have personally met with dozens of detained men and women whose children were taken from them pursuant to the Trump administration's "zero tolerance" policy. These mothers and fathers shared with us numerous troubling accounts regarding abuse, mistreatment, and coercion by Customs and Border Protection (CBP) and Immigration and Customs Enforcement (ICE) officials.

Please find attached a complaint lifting up thirteen individual cases of parents who describe in detail the explicit coercion they endured at the hands of DHS officials, in addition to the horrific trauma of the separation on the parents and their ability to meaningfully access the asylum process. You will find that in many cases, the parents were coerced into signing documents they simply did not understand, which resulted in the parents ostensibly relinquishing their right to be reunited with their children. We maintain that the government's actions are in direct violation of the U.S. Constitution, federal statute, and regulations.

We ask that your agency investigate DHS policy on the use of coercive tactics against parents to the fullest extent permissible. Further, we ask that you investigate all reports of abuse and coercion against parents and their children and discipline any officer found to have violated parents' rights or any applicable provision of law, regulation or policy.

Chapter Eleven

"It Hurts in My Heart"

August 15, 2018

"We were expecting you."

Those were the words of one of five private security guards in suits employed by the GEO Group, the for-profit private prison company that ran the Adelanto Immigration and Customs Enforcement detention center.

They were waiting for me when I walked outside the facility into 102-degree heat. That they knew I was there wasn't a surprise, since I had told both Katie Waldman, the DHS spokeswoman, and a regional ICE public affairs official that I would be driving up to Adelanto, one of the nation's largest immigration detention facilities, from my house in Los Angeles. It struck me as strange, however, that so many of them were there, hanging around as I tried to visit with a detainee.

That morning, I had met up with Lindsay Toczylowski to make the trek into the high desert. She and I had kept in touch since we first spoke by phone and she tipped me off to the conditions that migrant detainees faced in the Victorville federal prison, a short drive from Adelanto. Since then many of them had been transferred there, including a group of twelve separated fathers who insisted they had been tricked into signing away the right to reunite with their children.

On the ride up in Lindsay's four-door dark gray Ford sedan, we talked about Juan and what he and the others like him were facing.

"You're representing ten people in this facility alone who are fathers that were separated from their kids and signed papers that said basically I don't want to be reunited with my kid."

"Yeah."

"So, Juan, did he want to give up his right to be reunified with his son?"

"Absolutely not. He actually refers to this—him signing this document that he didn't understand—as a sin."

"A sin?"

"Yeah. Because he didn't know what he was signing, and only now that he is working with attorneys does he understand the repercussions of what he signed. And people will sign, because it's an officer in a uniform, you know, telling them that they should sign this."

As we drove from the Los Angeles basin up to the dry desert, the green of irrigated lawns and trees was replaced by the neutral and grainy sand of the Mojave. Toczylowski told me that either she or one of her colleagues was up at Adelanto nearly every day of the week fighting for these separated fathers. She had been looking for Juan and the others like him, but only after months of detention did her associate find him. Alfonso Maldonado Silva, an undocumented immigrant himself, a Dreamer with temporary legal status, who became a lawyer to help others facing challenges worse than his own, had a list compiled with the ACLU of immigrants who had been detained in Victorville and later transferred to Adelanto. He had asked to meet with every person on the list in order to offer pro bono representation. Juan was one of the first people he met with.

At their meeting, despite the fact his son, José, had been cleared for release and transfer in July by ORR, Juan explained what had happened—that he signed a form waiving the right to reunification. It had complicated things not just for him, but for scores of other separated parents who said the government had coerced them into signing.

Only five days before Lindsay and I drove up to Adelanto had Juan first formally requested a "credible fear" interview, with the help of Maldonado Silva, the first step in seeking asylum. (He should have been afforded this right three months earlier, in Arizona.)

"Please refer this case to an asylum officer at your earliest opportunity," read Maldonado Silva's letter on Juan's behalf. The letter highlighted in bold that the government "shall not proceed further with removal of the alien until the alien has been referred for an interview by an asylum officer."

"So this is Adelanto?" I asked Lindsay as we pulled up to the makeshift parking lot across from the facility.

"This is Adelanto. This is the detention facility."

We got out of the car and were met by Maldonado Silva, dressed in shirtsleeves and holding a messenger bag. He had come over from the small office that their firm keeps in the area. We stood together on the road outside the building housing more than one thousand migrants, going through Juan's paperwork together.

"Even though Juan, who I'm hopefully going to meet," I said wishfully, "signed something that says 'I am affirmatively, knowingly, and voluntarily requesting to return to my country of citizenship without my minor children who I understand will remain in the United States to pursue available claims of relief,' they basically say, 'I don't know what that meant.' "

"Yeah. And they say they've been intimidated into signing this," he told me of the ten clients, including Juan, who were in the same boat. Officials told the detainees "that they were going to be deported regardless, and it's up to them to decide whether they want their child deported with them or if they want their child released to some family member here."

"And they said: those are your only options."

"Those are your only options."

"And are those their only options?"

"No," both Alfonso and Lindsay said at the exact same time.

The three of us walked across the street together and inside. We explained to the guard on duty that I had given DHS and ICE both a heads-up that I was coming, and that I wanted to meet with Juan together with his attorneys, which they had the right to do. The guards allowed Lindsay and Alfonso inside, but not me. I waited in the room outside, spending three hours speaking with other assembled attorneys.

From the plastic chairs of the waiting room I saw families coming and going to visit loved ones. The suited private security guards whom I would later speak with outside passed by and glanced at me.

Finally, Juan's lawyers decided that we couldn't wait any longer, and I told them I was disappointed but ready to leave as well. Outside, they told me what happened in the room where they met.

"We talked a little about his son," Alfonso told me.

"You guys talk about the form and that he felt like he signed the form in error?"

"Yeah," Alfonso confirmed.

"He knew that I was here and he would have been cool to talk with me?" I asked.

"Not just cool to talk to you," Lindsay said, "but he really wanted to. He wants people to know the story of what happened with him and his son."

They explained that he had written me a letter in Spanish, which Alfonso read aloud, simultaneously translating it into English as the wind picked up.

"The separation of father and child hurts in my heart. When I asked them to fight my asylum case they didn't allow me. They are deporting me without even knowing. I feel like the government here is treating me really bad. I feel ignored," Juan wrote.

"I'm human. The government is treating me really bad, but I forgive them."

That line, after writing it, was crossed out by Juan. But he continued.

"The separation has affected me a lot. I don't think I will ever be able to forget this. I don't think that will ever be OK and I am going crazy. I am in an inhumane situation. This does not have a name. I just think how somebody of my age, an adult who understands how life works a little more than a child, is suffering so much. I cannot imagine the pain that my son is going through. I just pray and hope that all of this pain is worth it at the end because I fear that even after all this pain, I will still be deported and this trauma will not be worth it and my life will again be in danger. I fear they will deport me. This does not have a name for me."

Juan, like nine other men inside the facility we stood outside of, was losing hope. In the constantly changing numbers coming out of the Secretary's Operations Center in Washington, the government was now saying more than 150 parents were in the same boat.

"This was either the cruelest policy—even more cruel than I think people realize—or it was the most negligent policy of all time," Toczylowski told me about the situation in which the separated parents now found themselves.

I was determined to get inside to meet Juan. A representative from ICE told me by phone that as soon as Monday it would be arranged for me to go and meet him. Alfonso, Lindsay, and I agreed that as soon as we got the green light, we would head back together. I thanked them and hitched a ride back with Aarne, who had been producing the interview, and that night, unlike Juan, had dinner with my wife and son.

August 28, 2018

Family separations were slipping out of the news, even though hundreds of children remained separated from their parents. Part of it was, I felt, my fault. For the *Today* show, I had started on a series that would air ahead of the coming midterm elections where I was visiting some of the congressional districts that were at risk of flipping from Republican control to Democratic, and with them the House of Representatives itself, to figure out what mattered to people in them.

Our first stop was the northern border in Maine, where, to our surprise, we discovered the largest unguarded border on earth. As far as the eye could see the only thing that separated Canada and the United States was a "slash," or what they called a clear cut of the trees dividing Mars Hill and New Brunswick, Canada. But we weren't in Maine's second district to do a story about the border—we were looking at the issues people there cared about, and border security was admittedly not one of them.

"I know they tried and change the laws a lot," a young lobster fisherwoman told me about what was on her mind as we rode on her small boat, her brother at the controls. But she wasn't talking about the laws I might have thought about—how to deal with people illegally entering the United States. "How many traps we fish," she said. "Or when we fish."

Similarly, family separations didn't seem as if they would be a deciding issue when we headed to Florida's 26th Congressional District, despite being home to a large Latino population and the location of the Homestead Temporary Influx Shelter, which was still housing separated children.

"I'm a believer that we should allow a lot of immigrants to come in. But do it the right way, legally," a Cuban American former cop told me as he smoked a cigar, sunglasses on top of his head, hand waving and finger pointing to punctuate his argument. "It's not that I like it. Because you separated families. And it's gotta hurt if you're a family man like me. But as a parent, I would have never put myself in that position."

Carlos Curbelo, the local congressman fighting for his political life, stood beside me. I asked him if he had heard lots of opinions like that one around there.

"We have a big heart for immigrants in this community. But we want our immigration system to be coherent, and legal, and for people to respect our laws."

We decided to stop by Homestead, which on this breezy afternoon was still housing around fifty separated kids of the

528 the Trump administration said was the total (at the time). Homestead was "temporary," but it wasn't anywhere near closing because the factors that were keeping it filled weren't going away—including the slow process of reunifying children taken from their parents. From just across the street, it was easy to see hundreds of the thousand-plus children it was housing outside in the yard, walking single file to and from activities, with no shade from the beating sun.

As I was making my way around South Florida, inside the Adelanto detention center Juan was sitting down for a critical conversation that could potentially reverse his fortunes and win him the right to get his son back. Eighteen days after they first requested it, and eight days after the deadline, he was finally being interviewed by an asylum officer who would determine if his fear of returning to Guatemala was credible. If so, Juan could proceed with an asylum case that could allow him to remain in the United States.

"The purpose of this interview is to determine whether you may be eligible for asylum or protection from removal to a country where you fear persecution or torture," read the asylum officer, a woman conducting the interview by phone from across the country with the help of a telephonic interpreter. "I am going to ask you questions about why you fear returning to your country or any other country you may be removed to. It is very important that you tell the truth during the interview and that you respond to all of my questions. This may be your only opportunity to give such information."

For one hour and fifty-two minutes Juan and the young woman spoke on the phone as he explained the circumstances that drove him to travel from Guatemala to the

Arizona desert and jump over the small international border fence there. The asylum officer had virtually every detail about him and his journey once he reached the United States on the piece of paper in front of her: that he identified as an indigenous Guatemalan who spoke Spanish and Achi, a local dialect; he was an evangelical Christian; his fourteen-year-old son, José, was apprehended on the fourth day of June; and on the seventh he, Juan, was locked up in Florence before he was transferred to California.

Through a series of questions she learned more about why they left. Juan answered "yes" to two critically important questions: "Have you or any member of your family ever been mistreated or threatened by anyone in any country to which you may be returned?" and "Do you have any reason to fear harm from anyone in any country to which you may be returned?"

He told the young woman the story of how on April 15 he had received a phone call in which he learned his life was threatened, as well as that of his fourteen-year-old boy. Within a month they had come up with a plan, and as soon as they were able, they left his pregnant wife and two daughters behind to travel to the United States.

At the end of the nearly two-hour conversation, the asylum officer again read him a statement. "If the Department of Homeland Security determines you have a credible fear of persecution or torture, your case will be referred to an Immigration court, where you will be allowed to seek asylum or withholding of removal based on fear of persecution or withholding of removal under the Convention Against Torture. The Field Office Director in charge of this detention facility will also consider whether you may be released from detention while you are preparing for your hearing."

The officer read back a summary of Juan's claim of fear, and the same day, she made a determination.

"The applicant is found credible," noted the worksheet in which she had made notes about his case. She checked several boxes, including "credible fear of torture established," "applicant does not appear to be subject to a bar(s) to asylum or withholding of removal," and "applicant's identity was determined with a reasonable degree of certainty" based on "applicant's own credible statements."

With the statement signed and dated by the asylum officer and her supervisor on the same day as the interview, Juan, under the law, would now have a chance to be reunited with José. But his time in Adelanto was not yet finished.

August 30, 2018

The woman responsible for instituting a family separation policy with the stroke of her pen, homeland security secretary Kirstjen Nielsen, was in Australia for a meeting with her counterparts from the nations known as the "Five Eyes": the United States, Australia, Canada, New Zealand, and the United Kingdom. Among other issues, she told them about "border security enhancements" in the United States.

Her boss out of town, Katie Waldman, the DHS spokeswoman, took a trip of her own. Waldman was young and brash and often lacking a filter, and she had developed a reputation for ruffling feathers in the department.

The reaction was the same when she made her first trip ever—months after the family separations she defended relentlessly began—to the border. Some in the Border Patrol and CBP felt her messaging was uninformed, and further, that the way she spoke about migrants who were coming to the United States lacked compassion. Her trip, the first of several she would take, was encouraged as a fact-finding mission. In hiking boots, khakis, a black T-shirt, sunglasses, and a Border Patrol hat, Waldman cheesed for pictures next to existing border fencing. She posted a photo to Instagram with the caption "living my best life at the border wall."

The same day, the Trump administration, in a court-ordered filing, claimed that, according to their latest tally, 167 children's parents had "indicated desire against reunification." These families were part of the larger number of 497 children, including twenty-two under five years old, whom the government deemed ineligible to reunite. José, who was still in Harlingen, Texas, was in both categories, and was locked into a daily routine set by his caregivers at the shelter.

On this Thursday his schedule was the same as any other day of the week inside his government shelter for migrant children: wake up at six thirty in the morning, get dressed in clothes given to them by the shelter, and head to breakfast. At eight in the morning school starts inside the shelter, where according to the shelter he would take classes in "science, social studies, math, reading, writing and physical education." He was also being taught English.

After school he would head to lunch, then have "leisure time and participate in large muscle activities." That meant an opportunity to play sports like soccer, which José had grown up playing on the field below his house in Guatemala. This was also the time for him to meet with medical clinicians, his case manager, or attorney, which at the time he did not have.

Dinner was served in the evening followed by "free time to play games, visit, read or watch television." If he wanted, he could attend "voluntary religious services," which were held three times a week. Around eight at night, he would start to get ready for bed, as would the other five-hundred-plus kids there at the time, and at nine it was lights out.

August 31, 2018

The following morning, Friday, in California, José's father, Juan, was going through his own routines, all the while dressed in his orange detention jumpsuit. He was now await-ing release, according to the asylum officer who gave him his credible fear hearing. But there were no signs of that happen-ing yet. That same day, I drove back to Adelanto, where I met Lindsay Toczylowski.

A visitor's pass clipped to the top button of my dark blue button-down, we were escorted by guards through a legal orientation meeting at which a group of largely South Asian detainees—a growing population crossing the south-ern border—were learning their rights. Around the corner, cameraman Dana Roecker, audio engineer Craig Nilson, and Aarne and I were ushered into a tiny room where lawyers were permitted to consult with their clients. We set up our cameras, waiting for Juan to arrive. To my knowledge, it was the first time cameras had been allowed inside ICE detention to film a separated parent.

"Have you ever had a reporter meet with one of your cli-ents in detention like this?" I asked Toczylowski, who was holding a binder filled with legal documents.

"No, and definitely not with cameras."

"Never before?"

"I've never seen this before."

As she was talking, through the glass window behind her one of the contracted security guards in a suit, part of the same group that had greeted me when I was there sixteen days earlier, signaled Juan had arrived from where he was detained and was waiting outside.

"He's here?" I asked.

Juan rounded the corner with a smile on his face, clutching a manila envelope with documents of his own, Lindsay asking him in Spanish how he was doing.

"Bien, mucho gusto," he replied, shaking her hand.

I introduced myself as Jacobo, and shook his hand as he leaned back against the wall. He kept smiling, the gold on one of his top front teeth shining in the fluorescent light of the room. He seemed in good spirits given the circumstances, his hair slicked back, neon plastic identification band strapped to his wrist, dressed in the same orange jumpsuit that he wore every day.

It was amazing to see and meet him in person, after having read his letter, seen the forms he had signed waiving his right to reunification with his son, and following the fact that the government was saying he was one of many parents in the same boat. Craig slipped a microphone under Juan's short-sleeve prison uniform and clipped it to the neckline, then we sat down across from each other at a small table.

I asked him his son's name, and when he said "José," he smiled again.

"What happened when you were separated from your son?"

"They separated us," he told me, "and put us in different

rooms. I could see my son on the other side. It was all so difficult, and I didn't know what was going on. We would ask ourselves, 'What's going on here?'

"There was no chance for us to communicate with each other," he told me of his time in the Yuma Border Patrol station, shooting an occasional glance at Lindsay, who was translating to make sure I understood every last word. "The most difficult part of it all was when they separated us three days later in these cold rooms. I asked the official to give us a chance to say good-bye. Just thirty seconds to hug my son, because there was a bus waiting for us out front," he explained to me of the transport vehicle that would eventually take him to Florence, Arizona.

"And they gave me my backpack," the one he had jumped the wall with. "It's almost like I'm an animal."

"Like an animal?" I asked.

"Yeah," he responded in English.

When the conversation turned to the forms he had signed waiving the right to reunification with José, his face turned more grim, and he looked down at the table, his hands folded together, fingers laced with one another.

"What they say is, look, you signed these papers. These papers say 'I know that I'm requesting to return to my country of citizenship without my child and I understand that he's gonna stay here to pursue the claims of relief.' Explain to me, why would you sign this if you wanted to get back together with your son?

"Because they told me I would not be reunited with my son. If I wanted to be reunited, they would have deported me," he said.

"You thought the only options were be reunited and deported or you be deported and he stays here. So you thought that's the better option."

It was clear to me that Juan understood some English, because again, he nodded along, and responded with "yes."

"But it turns out," I said turning to Toczylowski, "you're his lawyer. Those are not the only two options."

"Those are not his only two options and in fact once he was able to speak with a lawyer we evaluated his case and realized he has a viable claim for asylum, as does his son. And so we were able to make an official request that he get a credible fear interview, which is the first step that allows him to begin the asylum process. He had already been ordered removed by the government," she said, using the legal term for deported. She explained that the day before we were there, his credible fear interview was successful. "Which means now he'll get the chance to see the judge."

The smile began to return to Juan's face.

"Juan, how does it feel now that you know that even though you signed these," I said pointing to the documents on which he waived his reunification right, "working with Lindsay you might have a chance to get back together with José?"

His smile grew bigger.

"I'm happy that there are these people. They're like angels. Working hard, trying to rescue all these people."

"You say you're happy, but you've spent months here in detention in Adelanto. Had you known, and not signed this, you could have been back together with your son much earlier. You're sitting here in your orange jumpsuit, you know? In your prison clothes. With your wristband." I reached out and touched his wrist, his head again dipping as he touched the same plastic identification card strapped to his body.

"Why did they deceive me with this paperwork? They didn't explain exactly what it was. I wouldn't have suffered all this time being separated from my son."

I asked him what he expected if and when he and José got back together. I naïvely thought his answer would be unbridled joy.

"That's something I wonder about myself. How long is it going to take for us to heal from all of the wounds and trauma we've suffered? I have been thinking about this. And I know we need to remain calm."

We stood up from the blue plastic chairs in the attorney-client room and shook hands, and I wished him well, hoping inside that I soon would see him again. I walked back to the front and said good-bye to Lindsay, who headed back to Los Angeles. After she left, an ICE public affairs official took me on a tour of the prison facility that the inspector general had deemed—though it had not yet reported publicly—to be in violation of several Homeland Security policies governing the treatment of inmates.

As we passed through an area of detainees in isolation, I saw one man, lying on the floor in a fetal position, locked behind the glass and metal door of a cell, alone. On bunk beds and in recreation areas, in solitary confinement and within the medical unit, trauma, just as Juan had described, was visible everywhere on my tour.

I drove home again that night, able to see my family, meeting my wife and son, four siblings, and parents for dinner to celebrate my dad's seventieth birthday. Just after seven at night, sparklers lit on his cake, we gathered around my parents' kitchen to sing to him. As we did, I thought about José, who that fall would celebrate his fifteenth birthday. Both he and his father were unsure if it would happen with both of them still in the custody of the United States of America.

■ ■ ■

DHS Office of Inspector General Highlights

*Initial Observations Regarding Family Separation Issues
Under the Zero Tolerance Policy*

September 27, 2018

What We Observed

*DHS was not fully prepared to implement the Administration's
Zero Tolerance Policy or to deal with some of its after-effects. Faced
with resource limitations and other challenges, DHS regulated the
number of asylum-seekers entering the country through ports of
entry at the same time that it encouraged asylum-seekers to come
to the ports. During Zero Tolerance, CBP also held alien children
separated from their parents for extended periods in facilities intended solely for short-term detention.*

*DHS also struggled to identify, track, and reunify families sep-
arated under Zero Tolerance due to limitations with its information technology systems, including a lack of integration between
systems.*

*Finally, DHS provided inconsistent information to aliens who
arrived with children during Zero Tolerance, which resulted in
some parents not understanding that they would be separated from
their children, and being unable to communicate with their children after separation.*

CHAPTER TWELVE

"We Know That He Is a Good Person"

September 6, 2018

As they visited the South Texas border together, the spokeswoman for the secretary of homeland security was pissing off Raul Ortiz, the deputy chief patrol agent in the Rio Grande Valley, the nation's busiest border crossing and the epicenter of family separations. Katie Waldman posted a photo of herself, back in her adventure outfit, standing next to four giant bundles of marijuana, which was still a hot smuggling commodity in Texas, where it was still illegal. In the caption, she explained to her followers that she was "with Border Patrol during a $192,000 seizure of marijuana from five drug mules."

Ortiz shared his frustration about Waldman with others in the department. She would not get off her cell phone to see what was actually going on around her. This was supposed to be a visit to better understand the realities of the border, part of a series of visits meant to address her perceived lack of compassion about separated children.

The same day, the Trump administration upped the number of children whose parents "indicated desire against reunification" to 199, part of the 416 who were still separated. One of those children was José, who had spent the last three-plus months at the BCFS shelter in Harlingen, Texas. His father had been trying relentlessly to get released from Adelanto.

The "separated parents removal form" Juan had signed, waiving the right to reunification with José, had finally been voided, after Juan won a credible fear determination from an asylum officer, putting him back on track to go through proceedings that would allow him and his son, if and when they were reunited, to stay in the United States together. But first he'd have to get out of Adelanto on bond and find his son. The process would start with an appearance before an immigration judge.

As Juan readied his case, the Trump administration and the ACLU announced a settlement: any separated parent and child would be able to redo their asylum interview in order to prove credible fear, and any mental distress a parent was under at the time would be considered if there were inconsistencies in the accounts. On that day, exactly one week after Waldman texted her way through the Rio Grande Valley, the count of still-separated children in the custody of the United States changed again. Two hundred eleven were still separated, now with only twenty-eight waiving the right to reunification.

One week later the government again updated their numbers in a court-ordered filing. Now the number of separated children whose parents had waived reunification was twenty-one. It was unclear to me if José, in his South Texas shelter, was still in that group.

The following morning I was standing outside another Texas shelter run by the same nonprofit, BCFS. I had finally made it to Tornillo, the small desert community where, the day after I first saw separated children with my own eyes, we reported that the tent city I was now standing in front of would be opened to accommodate the surge in separated children being referred to the Department of Health and Human Services.

On this hot fall morning, I jumped on top of a concrete traffic barrier, catching a faraway glimpse of the white tents, where 1,300 unaccompanied minors were still being housed—nearly matching the population of the nearby town of Tornillo itself.

I showed up there to report how immigration policy was (or wasn't) impacting the upcoming midterm elections. The local district, Texas's 23rd, was home to Will Hurd, the Republican who had a thin lead over Gina Ortiz Jones, the Democratic challenger. We wanted to know what residents of the district, which included more of the southwest border than any other area in the United States, would be voting on.

In search of interview subjects, we decided to hang out outside Tornillo's Family Dollar store, the parking lot fishing expedition a favorite journalistic technique of our team. A few locals passed through, but not many who wanted to talk with us. As I stood on the corner of Highland Street and OT Smith Road waiting for someone, anyone, really, to speak with us, Aarne had his camera pointed at a cargo train passing through.

At that moment, a red pickup truck pulled up and a man wearing overalls and a brown wide-brim hat hopped out and stuck one of those flags in the ground you normally see outside a cell phone shop.

"What does this say?" I asked him as he was situating it, the banner flopping around in the wind.

"Pomegranates!" the man excitedly told me.

"Pomegranates?" I asked.

"Yeah! My orchard is right there," he said through an accent that suggested this man also spoke Spanish as well as English.

"Can we go see it?" I wanted to know.

"Yes, sir."

The man told me his name was Marcelino, and I stretched out my hand to shake his, soon realizing he had only two fingers on his right hand: his thumb and index finger. I asked if we could catch a ride with him back to the nursery, which he told me was down the street. He happily obliged, and we hopped into the back of his pickup and flew in reverse down Highland Street until we arrived.

It was a beautiful spot. In the shadow of the giant silver Tornillo water tower, he walked us through the aisle of pomegranate trees, pulling off fruit to show me how to cut it open and how easy it was to knock the seeds out to eat. For a moment I forgot why we came to this tiny desert town. As we stood there surrounded by hundreds of ruby-red pomegranates, I told the farmer why we were there—to better understand what issues mattered to locals on the eve of an election that could flip control of the House of Representatives.

"What do you care about?" I asked him, holding a busted-open pomegranate in my left hand, the tart taste of its seeds still lingering.

"The production of food. Don't forget one thing. I am a farmer."

"So what you're saying is when you go to vote, what you think about is all this," I said as I motioned to his orchard, which he explained to me was the only one in El Paso County.

"Yes, sir."

"I thought you were going to say," as I pointed to the south, "the tents over there with all the kids in them, because it's in your face."

"Well, we need to feed those kids, too. We need to produce food!"

I crunched more pomegranate seeds as he walked us out to the front. I bought a jug of fresh pomegranate juice from him as well, and as I unscrewed the cap and drank the dark purple elixir, I felt our otherwise idyllic interaction sour. Family separations were fading from view, even here, minutes away from the tent city that was at the heart of the protests against the policy.

September 26, 2018

While I was on the border, Juan and his lawyers were preparing to go before the immigration judge who would decide if he could be released on bond in order to be reunited with his son. They were requesting to transfer his case, if he got out, to Virginia, where Juan had previously worked when he had entered the country illegally twice before. He had friends and family there. It would be up to a judge's decision, and in order to go in with the best possible chance of getting a ruling in his favor, Juan had put together two testimonials from people who knew him and would vouch for him.

Dear Immigration Judge,

I am a US citizen and I am writing this letter to express my full support for Juan's release from detention.

I have made all the appropriate arrangements so that Juan can come live with me for the time necessary. I also understand that he is currently separated from his son and I expect for both of them to be under my care. I cannot imagine the pain that Juan is going through being separated from his son, but I hope that this separation can come to an end soon.

I have known Juan for some years and know that he is a responsible and dependable person. I know Juan to be a loving person, especially towards his family. He is also a hard worker and has the determination to be self-sufficient. I know that if allowed, Juan will probably work with my brother doing construction.

Juan can count on me to help him attend all of his immigration hearings. In the event that I am unable to, I know that he has the support of my brother. I know how important resolving this immigration issue is for Juan and I am 100 percent sure that he will see it through, with us there to help him every step of the way. Thank you for your time.

The other letter was equally effusive in its praise for Juan and his character: "I know that if he is realized to fight his immigration case, Juan will do whatever is asked of him. Juan can count on me to help him get to his immigration hearing and comply with any other requirement that you, the judge, may order. I can also help Juan get a job so that he can provide for him and his son. In any event, we are here for him because we know that he is a good person."

In addition to the personal testimonials, two representatives of a group called Immigrant Families Together wrote the judge on behalf of Juan, pledging to "provide ongoing financial support to Juan and his family once he is released from detention. Such support will include, but is not limited to, temporary housing while we arrange for his transportation to reunite with his family."

By the end of the day, the immigration judge at Adelanto had answered Juan's prayers, ordering that "the request be granted" and he be "released from custody under bond of $2,500."

While I worried family separations were slipping away from the American consciousness, I was proven wrong, at least in Juan's case. A group of volunteers came up with the money to pay Juan's bond. He would soon be free.

October 3, 2018

Exactly a week to the day after Juan was ordered released, I met him and Lindsay Toczylowski in downtown Los Angeles. We rendezvoused outside Toczylowski's office, the art deco building to which I had made an unannounced visit earlier that summer while I was trying to track her down. I waited on the street with the rest of our NBC team, excited to see Juan outside of the detention center. Four months earlier, he and José had entered the United States, their lives forever altered.

Juan and Lindsay walked out of her office building together. Juan, released the night before, was sporting a tight haircut, and he had traded his orange jumpsuit for a blue T-shirt with the words "Team Jesus" on the front, tucked into a fresh pair of jeans and dark shoes. We shook hands, and I congratulated him on his release. The same smile I caught glimpses of inside his lockup flashed unrestrained across his face.

Later in the day—immediately after we spoke, in fact— Juan would head to the airport for a flight to Virginia, where the plan was to be reunited with his son within the next few days.

I asked Juan how he felt.

"Good. Happy. Content," he said, folding his hands together in the same way I had seen before while detained, his arms rested on his stomach, his hands intertwined below his waist. As I repeated back in English the words he had said in Spanish, he nodded his head and said "yeah" in English himself.

"The other time I saw you I was sad, because I was locked up," he said, revisiting the weight of the separation.

"I don't have the words," he told me, to describe what it was like to be on the streets of downtown Los Angeles on the verge of seeing his son, his first time in the city.

"What do you think?" I asked him, wanting to know what it was like to be here in the city after so long locked away.

Before Lindsay could translate, he answered.

"Wow! Excellente!"

I asked, even though he was happy, what it was like that he and José were not yet back together.

"I'm happy, but at the same time, I am thinking every moment about the reunification with my son, to be able to hug him. And at the same time, a little sad, because he's still separated from me. I'm sorry he's still locked up, but at the same time I'm happy knowing soon he'll be free too," Juan said of his son, who was still in Texas at the HHS shelter that had been his home for months.

Life on the streets of Los Angeles moved about us as Lindsay told me that it had been ten days since Juan and José last talked. The court had changed Juan's address after he was released from Adelanto to Virginia, where he and José would pursue their asylum claims and live together once they were reunited.

"Life locked up, it's very different," Juan said. It was a life he wouldn't have to experience anymore. His son, however, could not say the same yet. We shook hands, and I wished him well ahead of his flight to the East Coast, where he would soon land in the Washington, D.C., area.

Four days later, Lindsay texted me a picture of Juan and José's reunion at Ronald Reagan Washington National Airport. Juan's arm was around his son, who was nearly as tall as him. José wore a black Spider-Man T-shirt; in Juan's hand was paperwork.

Not long after she sent me the photo, Lindsay posted a message to Twitter, attaching the image.

124 days ago @ImmDef client Juan was separated from his son José at the border. And this morning, after months of fighting for their right to seek asylum together, they were reunited.

I looked at the photo again, this time lingering on the details. They stood, finally, together in Washington, D.C.—the city where the decision to separate them and so many others was made. Neither father nor son was smiling widely, the camera capturing the joy as well as the pain of the moment. Their expressions were almost identical, lips pursed together, their eyes looking firmly ahead. The trauma of the past four months was present, but now, for the first time since agents in green uniforms ushered them into separate cells inside the Yuma Border Patrol Station, they were again side by side. Around them, the sun streamed in through the glass walls of the airport concourse. They were, finally, reunited, and bathed in light.

"The Greatest Human-Rights Catastrophe of My Lifetime"

On March 8, 2019, President Trump, stopping to survey tornado damage in Alabama, told the assembled press corps he couldn't get there "fast enough," about the twister that killed twenty-three in Lee County nearly a week earlier.

"I wanted to come the day it happened," he added about his trip, which he made en route to a previously-scheduled weekend getaway at his Mar-A-Lago resort in Florida.

But while Trump, sporting a dark windbreaker bearing the presidential seal, got a birds-eye view of the damage from Marine One, he had something else on the mind: family separations.

After he ended the administration's practice of systematically ripping apart migrant families in June 2018, the number of those taken into custody crossing the southern border in July dipped slightly—from 43,180 to 40,149—causing some to argue the policy had worked. Toward the end of the year, the number rose back to the levels seen at the end of the Obama administration, and the president was having second thoughts about his decision. By February 2019, the monthly total had skyrocketed to 76,575—a figure not seen since George W. Bush was president, and a sign President Trump's border policies were failing.

"This is something the president gets very emotional about," one former senior administration official told me about his obsession over immigration statistics.

Trump's aerial tour of the natural disaster began at Fort Benning, Georgia, where Air Force One had landed at 10:43 A.M. local time. After deplaning behind him, Housing and Urban Development Secretary Ben Carson, dressed in a long black coat, and Homeland Security Secretary Kirstjen Nielsen, wearing high heels, hustled past a phalanx of aides and ahead of the president and First Lady Melania Trump to board Marine One. They were part of his official entourage touring the devastation.

With all on board, the presidential helicopter took off moments later for a seventeen-minute flight to Auburn University Regional Airport across the state line. Outside their rectangular windows were scenes of flattened trees, destroyed buildings, and wrecked cars. Distracted, the president brought up family separations.

"Kirstjen, we're going to have to reinstitute that," Trump declared while tornado victims awaited him "with open arms and raised cell phones" on the ground, as NBC affiliate KPLC reported.

"Sir," Nielsen began, "I'm not sure I can reinstitute this on my own," she said, attempting to end the conversation.

It wasn't the first occasion the president had brought up restarting family separations since he was forced to end them—and it wouldn't be the last. But this time, the conversation was put to bed not by the president, nor either cabinet secretary on board his chopper.

"We can't do that. We can't do that," Melania Trump cut in, curtailing any debate.

It wasn't the first time the first lady voiced her opposition to family separations. In June 2018, at the height of the outrage over the policy, her spokeswoman said "Mrs. Trump hates to see children separated from their families" and that "she believes we need to be a country that follows all laws, but also a country that governs with heart."

Trump, frustrated, rolled his eyes at the interjection by the sneaker-and-peacoat-clad First Lady, but did not argue back. Instead, the president sighed.

"We'll see. We'll see," he said.

The following morning, the border numbers were still on President Trump's mind. From Mar-a-Lago, he turned to Twitter.

"Border Patrol and Law Enforcement has apprehended (captured) large numbers of illegal immigrants at the Border," Trump wrote. "They won't be coming into the U.S. The Wall is being built and will greatly help us in the future, and now!"

Exactly one month later, Trump fired Nielsen. After my colleagues Julia Ainsley and Geoff Bennett reported their falling out was due in part to Nielsen's reluctance to restart family separations, something Trump had "for months urged his administration to reinstate," Trump responded.

"We're not looking to do that, no," he said at the White

House. Trump then qualified his statement. "When you *don't* do it, it brings a lot more people to the border."

THE NIGHT JUAN arrived in Washington, D.C., to be reunified with José, Katie Waldman, Nielsen's spokeswoman at the Department of Homeland Security who relentlessly defended family separations, enjoyed her birthday dinner at the Trump International Hotel at a table for two. It was October 3, 2018.

Twenty days later, she was on the border again, still mugging for Instagram, this time in Arizona behind a plaque that indicated the boundary between the United States and Mexico. Behind her appeared to be the same corrals that Juan and José passed through and over before they found themselves in the United States.

"The border wall is on the American side," her caption read, a huge smile on her face at the place where Juan's and José's lives changed forever.

Later that year, after Katy Tur and I started filming *American Swamp*, our MSNBC documentary series about corruption in Washington, we met Waldman for dinner in D.C. On an unseasonably warm December night, we sat outside under space heaters.

Katy, who was five months pregnant, asked her about defending zero tolerance on behalf of the Trump administration.

"My family and colleagues told me that when I have kids I'll think about the separations differently. But I don't think so."

It was a line Katie had said to me before—prior to visiting the detention facilities.

"DHS sent me to the border to see the separations for

myself—to try to make me more compassionate—but it didn't work."

"It didn't work? I will never forget what I saw. Seriously. Are you a white nationalist?" I asked, exasperated.

"No, but I believe if you come to America you should assimilate. Why do we need to have 'Little Havana'?"

Waldman, a native of Fort Lauderdale, grew up living side by side with Cuban Americans in South Florida, a group of people whose lives couldn't be more intertwined with the culture and politics of the region.

Neither Katy nor I knew what to say.

Katy, flabbergasted, got up and went to the restroom. When she left, Waldman leaned in, and in a hushed tone asked me a question.

"You know who I'm dating, right?"

"We all know," I told her, about one of the biggest open secrets in D.C.

When Katy returned to the table, I laughed, telling her in front of Waldman that she wanted us to know who she was dating.

"Jacob told me before you got here," Katy deadpanned.

Today, Waldman and her then-boyfriend, Stephen Miller, the architect of the family separation policy and the senior advisor to President Trump, are married.

After leaving DHS, Waldman worked briefly for Arizona senator Martha McSally, and she is now the press secretary to Vice President Mike Pence.

Katy and I ran into Waldman a year later, at a Trump election rally in Hershey, Pennsylvania, as we were shooting another episode of *American Swamp*. Vice President Pence was there to introduce the president on the same day articles of impeachment were introduced against Trump in the House of Representatives. We congratulated her on her engagement and new job, and asked how things were going.

She was elated and told us she was going to meet up backstage with Miller for thirty minutes, the most time they would see each other all week.

Before the rally started, I asked her about a report from the DHS inspector general that had come out just more than two weeks earlier, which confirmed that "DHS did not have the information technology system functionality needed to track separated migrant families during the execution of the *Zero Tolerance Policy*," a surprise to no one.

There was a shocking revelation in the report, however. CBP, which officially separated 2,814 during zero tolerance, then later admitted it separated 1,556 more before the policy officially started, told the Office of Management and Budget: "it [had planned to] separate more than 26,000 children between May and September 2018." If the policy had not been stopped, this would have been a massive increase in the total number of separations and with the report, our understanding of the scale of the tragedy widened. Since the supposed end of family separations, the ACLU alleged, there have been more than one thousand separations, and the practice is still ongoing.

I asked Waldman, as we stood there behind the press riser that President Trump would later point to and ridicule, if she knew about the fact the government was planning to separate five times more children than it had ultimately been able to before the president backed down.

"We had to prepare for all contingencies," she dead-panned.

And with that, she went backstage to see her fiancé.

THE NIGHT AFTER Christmas 2019, I sat down with Juan and José for dinner near their home, the third time I had seen them since I started writing this book. They always asked for updates on my progress (and the first copy). I told them about my attempts to determine and visit exactly where they crossed as I visited the border between San Luis Río Colorado, Mexico, and San Luis, Arizona.

I had spent an entire day driving up and down along the Arizona border looking for what Juan had described to me earlier: white horse corrals and a short border fence. I told the Border Patrol I was going to be there, and they attempted to point me in the right direction. I believe I eventually found the exact area.

Juan and José recounted what it was like to jump over the wall and within a minute have the Border Patrol waiting for them and the rest of the families they crossed with. The vast majority of our conversations were now in English, José's improving particularly fast as he went to school and spent extracurricular time learning the vocational skills of an electrician. Juan showed me the Social Security card and work permit he had received just that day, and we high-fived. We video chatted with María, his wife, and his now three daughters, his wife bottle-feeding the youngest, whom Juan and José had never met.

They freely laughed together. Everything felt loose, and

for the first time I was able to ask them both candid questions about the moment of separation itself. José, who had been reluctant to say anything in our previous conversations, described it almost exactly. Turning away from his son, who was sitting next to him in the booth, both of them across from me about the same distance Juan and I sat across from each other inside the Adelanto migrant prison, Juan started to sob. He hung his head in shame, recalling the particulars of the day they were separated without warning or a chance to say good-bye. José kept a straight face, his fifteen-year-old frame now much bigger than the pictures I had seen of the scrawny kid in his dad's store.

"HARMING CHILDREN MEANS a century of suffering," a government official who was involved in the runification effort told me the following morning at a Starbucks outside of Washington, D.C.

"It's the greatest human rights catastrophe of my lifetime," the official explained, referring to domestic U.S. history, while rocking back and forth.

While there was plenty of blame to go around, the official told me without flinching that former colleague Scott Lloyd is "the most prolific child abuser in modern American history." The official believed Lloyd—head of the agency supposedly responsible for the welfare of migrant children placed in its custody—had abdicated his legal parental authority and custodianship of more than five thousand children. Lloyd was "starry-eyed around Stephen Miller," yet was blind to warnings coming from his own staff.

Lloyd, in a written response, told me he was taken aback by the accusation of child abuse.

"There is nothing anyone can point to that would make that statement true. My job was to take care of the kids and unite them with a sponsor. It's something we did well, and I am proud of the work we did. This person, whoever it is, had the opportunity to air their concerns in person while these events were happening, but instead is choosing to speak anonymously, through the media, two years after the fact. It is a comment that clearly belies everything I have ever done in my professional and personal life. Given all of this, it's impossible for me to take it seriously."

Lloyd was transferred out of ORR into an HHS office overseeing faith-based initiatives in November 2018, after the end of zero tolerance. In February 2019, he was called before the newly-sworn-in Democratic Congress to answer questions about his time at the helm of ORR.

Appearing before the House Judiciary Committee, Lloyd was asked by Texas congresswoman Sheila Jackson Lee about whether he had ordered the destruction of the list tracking separated children, first reported by *Politico*'s Dan Diamond in October 2018.

"It had been reported in the press," Lee began, "that during an internal HHS review of the family separation policy, a top HHS official found that you instructed your staff to stop keeping a spreadsheet tracking separated families. Did you make this decision and if so why? Why in the world would you choose to make a decision like this? As a father yourself can you explain to us how this possibly could have happened?"

Lloyd, dressed in a red tie and now sporting a full beard—

more mountain man than choir boy—sat with his fingers inter-laced on top of the witness table and began to respond.

"Thank you, Congresswoman. That was an incorrect reporting. Um, I did not make that, uh," Lloyd paused and looked down. He searched for his next word, having been sworn in under oath.

"Order," he said.

Before he could continue, Lee moved on, asking Lloyd about proposed shelters in her district.

Lloyd was asked again about the incident, by Diamond in October 2019 after he had left the Trump administration entirely.

"There was a list," Lloyd explained to Diamond. "I knew of the list," he said, contracting what he told his staff. "The list ended up leaking to the media so, really, my direction was about how we communicate about the kids on the list."

Meanwhile, at the Starbucks, for nearly two hours the government official and I discussed the intimate details of the separation policy's development, implementation, and aftermath, the official alternating between anger, remorse, and determination as we ticked through two years of dates and events while I attempted to better understand what I, in the summer of 2018, had seen: hundreds of children, locked up in cages after being taken from their parents, then moved alone, often for months, to shelters.

Though most of the separated children had been reunited with their parents by then, a year and a half after a federal judge ordered the government to put all of the families back together, there were still moms and dads who had been deported without their kids. They had still not been reunited.

Additionally, one final child was still in the custody of the federal government.

THE SAME DAY, after a thirty-minute drive that took me across two rivers, I slid into a booth with a former Department of Homeland Security official who wanted to unburden himself.

"We should have done better to explain what was happening," he said about DHS's response to the public outrage over the crisis. Meanwhile, the White House was putting "impossible pressure" on the agency. Despite that, this person, directly involved not just in the reunifications but the separations themselves, wanted me to know that he regretted being a part of the policy.

"This was the greatest mistake from a law enforcement and human perspective in my career. If I could go back and change it I would. It was wrong." As he spoke, he polished off a bowl of grains topped with salmon.

He had come to this opinion even though he believed data showed "it was working." By this, he meant the separation policy was "deterring families" from coming into the country. That's exactly what President Trump wanted all along, and why he had pressured Kirstjen Nielsen to restart the practice.

It was hard to argue that the shocking cruelty of the Trump administration's separation policy wasn't integral to achieving their objectives.

THE FOLLOWING MONTH, in early January 2020, both Katie Waldman and her former boss, Jonathan Hoffman, now a spokesperson at the Department of Defense, were in the news. They were issuing statements that Iran fired ballistic missiles at a military base in Iraq in response to President Trump's ordered assassination General Qassim Sulemani. The people who were in charge of the most spectacular policy fail of the Trump administration were now in charge of communicating whether or not the nation was about to go to war.

As 2020 continued, Waldman added to her portfolio the government's public relations response to the global pandemic known as COVID-19. She again would find herself working with some of the same public health professionals at the Department of Health and Human Services she repeatedly clashed with during family separations and the court-ordered effort to reunify them.

Waldman's and Hoffman's departures from DHS hadn't moderated the Trump administration's immigration policies. Since zero tolerance, nothing had captured the attention of the nation like that June 2018 did. But the deterrence-based immigration policy championed by the Trump administration since that first meeting on Valentine's Day 2017, and to differing degrees by previous presidential administrations before it, has continued to be deployed at a rapid clip. Some activists argue that what is happening today is as bad if not worse than family separations.

Migrants who make it here and prove a credible fear, like Juan and José did, are now made to wait in Mexico, and tens of thousands of them are doing just that, in some of the most violent cities in one of the most violent countries in the world. Reports of rapes, murders, kidnappings, and families self-separating in order to have the best chance at survival are commonplace. They are the "lucky" ones. Other migrants are being deported immediately to seek asylum in Central America under agreements that place them directly back into harm's way, if not the specific harm they fled. COVID-19 threw the entire immigration system into further chaos, President Trump using it as justification for, amongst other things, his border wall and immediately expelling virtually all asylum seekers, including children. COVID allowed Trump to quickly enact "what DHS was trying to do for three years," a government official quipped to me.

As I write this, I'm watching with the rest of the world as the Trump administration bungles its response to COVID-19. Many of the officials showing up at the once-again daily White House press briefings were names and faces heretofore unfamiliar to most of the American public. Not to me.

Chad Wolf. Alexander Azar. Dr. Robert Kadlec. Katie Waldman. All of them are central figures in the Trump administration's widely criticized response to the ongoing global pandemic. But before that, they were central figures in the Trump administration's family separation policy. Names you've now read and learned about here. Waldman, now Katie Miller, herself tested positive for COVID-19 in May 2020, raising concerns about a potential White House outbreak and sending top officials into self-isolation.

WHILE REPORTING THIS book, and after the height of the family separation policy, I traveled twice to Guatemala to see conditions on the ground there myself. We visited villages where many had picked up and left because of extreme poverty, food insecurity, and violence. Before my trips, I learned from a former government official that the Trump administration had pulled foreign aid to Guatemala despite the fact they knew the aid would slow migration, the Trump administration's goal.

Back in D.C., over breakfast, I told this person and another immigration official about Juan and José, who were from Petén, Guatemala.

They looked at each other and laughed. I was confused.

"What's so funny about Petén?" I asked.

"Nothing, nothing," they both said.

I mentioned that I knew about the narco violence there, the secret airports used by smugglers, and the violence that Juan and José faced before leaving to come here. Before we left the restaurant, I pressed them again about their reaction to my invoking Petén, and they said nothing.

Days later, I saw an article in the *Washington Post,* and it all made sense.

"Asylum seekers rejected by the United States could be transported to a remote airport in the lowland jungles of Guatemala as part of the Central American nation's new migration accord with the Trump administration, according to senior officials from both countries," the *Post*'s Nick Miroff and Kevin Sieff reported. "The plan would have U.S. immigration authorities deliver migrants to Petén's Mundo Maya airport, which is used primarily by tourists visiting the Maya ruins at Tikal."

I texted one of the two officials at breakfast that day.

"No wonder you guys laughed about Petén."

I didn't get a response. Maybe I should have been more explicit about how foul I thought their reaction was— laughing after learning that a separated father and son I was getting to know could be sent back to where they fled death threats.

REPORTING ON FAMILY separations was never the plan, but as the realities on the ground became shockingly clear, my colleagues and I found ourselves consumed by the story. After the media furor died down, we continued our focus on the Trump administration's immigration policies. Julia Ainsley and I kept working closely together, breaking several stories that exposed the hypocrisy and brutality of the administration's policies.

After family separation, at least seven migrant children died in the custody of Customs and Border Protection. No child had perished in the previous ten years. A sadly predictable outcome to a punitive Border Patrol enforcement strategy based around "consequence delivery," or "prevention through deterrence." It was an outcome that an activist with No More Deaths, a humanitarian group that leaves water bottles for migrants in the Arizona desert, told me had happened before and would happen again so long as the border was militarized.

Later in the year—as family separation ended and cartels exploited the perceived weakness of President Trump, who had backed down from the policy—a record number of families and unaccompanied children entered the United States, overflowing Border Patrol stations. Reports emerged of horrid conditions including children locked up for days, as José was, far beyond the seventy-two-hour limit.

Julia and I broke a story about the badly overcrowded Yuma, Arizona, Border Patrol station—the same one Juan and

José were separated in. We were leaked more than thirty reports of alleged abuse of minors in custody there—including a sexual assault and retribution for protesting conditions. To this day, Customs and Border Protection has not released the result of the investigations it opened into those allegations based on our reporting.

When I went to Yuma to look into where Juan and José had crossed, I also asked the Border Patrol for an official interview with the sector chief, who had promised to investigate the claims we had revealed in our reporting. At first, it looked promising. The local public information officer told me that he was going to run it up the flagpole to headquarters in Washington, and he would let me know a time to come back.

I checked in after having not heard anything.

Good morning Mr. Soboroff,

We will not be able to accommodate your request for any engagements until further notice. We appreciate you reaching out. Thank you.

At least on this trip, as I worked to excavate details from the separation of Juan and José and follow up about abuse in the Border Patrol station in which they were held, I wasn't so welcome in Yuma after all.

But in January 2020, when Kevin McAleenan, who had succeeded Kirstjen Nielsen as acting homeland security secretary, was himself succeeded as acting secretary by Chad Wolf, who had authored an early version of the justification for family separations, I would finally be invited to officially visit Yuma. The trip, however, would be to watch Wolf discuss how President Trump was, finally, building stretches of his "big, beautiful border wall." I didn't go.

Following Wolf's visit to Yuma, the Border Patrol named a new chief, Rodney Scott, the same Rodney Scott who had penned me a letter accusing me and our network of covering family separations as a "made-for-TV drama." Today he is the man in charge of the nation's border force and its thousands of agents who were tasked with the unprecedented mission of separating thousands of migrant families, the same agents now responsible for a suffering so profound it will last a lifetime.

A MONTH AFTER Scott's appointment as Border Patrol chief, Physicians for Human Rights, a nonprofit group that shared the 1997 Nobel Peace Prize for its efforts to ban land mines, issued a scathing report about the Trump administration's family separation policy. In it, the group declares the "government's forcible separation of asylum-seeking families constitutes cruel, inhuman, or degrading treatment and, in all cases PHR evaluated, meets criteria for torture."

Torture.

Despite the warnings, the evidence, the journalism, and the public outcry, "torture" was not a word I had used to describe what I had seen with my own eyes. But that's exactly what it was.

"U.S. officials," the group wrote, "intentionally carried out discriminatory actions that caused severe pain and suffering, in order to punish, coerce, and intimidate Central American asylum seekers to give up their asylum claims."

By their measure, the Trump administration succeeded

in one respect—the act of separations and the damage it caused to thousands of parents and children. But where they failed, and will continue to fail, was to quash the determination, perseverance, and love that those they tortured share. Look no further than Juan and José, who, on the contrary, didn't give up their asylum claims once they were separated and reunited. They only fought harder.

Their claims are now being adjudicated separately by the United States government. Once they're able to clear the massive backlog of cases and if President Trump's new policies don't stop them again, Juan and José hope to achieve their dream of becoming legal permanent residents, and then citizens, of the United States. If and when that happens—likely no sooner than within the next three years because of the massive case backlog—the father and son dream of having their family join them here. They dream of holding the newest, youngest member of their family—a baby girl—for the first time.

Here, in the country that represented safety and opportunity, only to give way to immeasurable pain and unexpected suffering. Now, once again, at the dawn of a new beginning, the United States is home to what they had hoped it would be when they approached the international boundary in Arizona: the possibility of a better future, and life together, for them all.

"It's Criminal"

The Trump administration would have separated far more children if they could have. Even more than we knew when the first edition of this book was published.

But it wouldn't be long after that before I found out.

In July 2020, as I was publicizing the book, an unknown number appeared on the screen on my cell phone.

It was from an area code I didn't recognize, so I double clicked the button on the side of my iPhone and sent the call to voicemail.

The caller didn't leave a message.

Wrong number?

The phone rang again. Same number. Same drill. I put the call to voicemail. No message.

Eventually, I was curious who was behind the mystery red digits left by the missed calls, so I scrolled down and tapped the number.

On the other end of the line was someone who wanted me to know she had quickly devoured this book and offered praise. As I stood in my front yard, I expressed my appreciation to the caller, whom I assumed was a loyal MSNBC viewer.

But this person politely and nervously let me know they had a secondary reason for getting in touch: a critique of the book. Oh. Okay, I said, go for it.

"You missed some things," she said, as I recall. "Some really important key events."

"Like what?" I asked, self-consciously acknowledging that for all the things I had seen firsthand and research and reporting I did after the fact, there were definitely black holes in what I knew about the lead-up to the policy.

The caller paused. And then, in the next moment, she became a source.

The source offered a tip, which set me and my NBC News colleague Julia Ainsley on a month-long quest to chase down new, shocking details about the Trump administration's family separation policy.

What we learned was that while one separation of a parent from a child is unconscionable and creates, as the official involved in the reunifications told me, "a century of suffering," the Trump administration's plans were even more extensive than we thought.

Beyond the more than five thousand cases of "torture," as Physicians for Human Rights put it, and "government-sanctioned child abuse," as Colleen Kraft from the American Academy of Pediatrics claimed.

Here's what the source wanted us to know: if Stephen Miller, Attorney General Jeff Sessions, and their allies had their way, tens of thousands of families—even more than the number referenced in the DHS Inspector General report from December 2019—might have been separated during zero tolerance alone. What's more: the claim could be proven.

For all the talk of prosecuting law breakers and the indignation about the illegality of crossing the border, charging migrants with a crime was not the goal, the source said. Rather, the Trump administration saw family separations as a means of punishing them.

We know this because our reporting that sprang from the source's call led us to a previously unknown May 3, 2018, cabinet-level meeting in the White House Situation Room.

May 3 had been a busy news day, which helped explain why the meeting had gone under the radar. That day the media were focused on Trump repaying his lawyer Michael Cohen for hush money he sent to porn star Stormy Daniels to cover up their affair. And the president hiring Clinton impeachment lawyer Emmet T. Flood to represent him in the Justice Department's Russia investigation. And House Republicans threatening impeachment of Deputy Attorney General Rod Rosenstein over his handling of that Russia investigation.

Invited to be in the Situation Room that same day were Rosenstein's boss, Sessions; Homeland Security Secretary Kirstjen Nielsen; Health and Human Services Secretary Alex Azar; Secretary of State Mike Pompeo; and National Security Advisor John Bolton, amongst others.

Sessions was prepared for the meeting and the high tensions around moving forward with family separations. The talking points prepared for him to use at that meeting by Gene Hamilton, his counselor and Miller's ally, made clear that "zero tolerance" was the backup plan.

> DHS should consider—separately—whether the requirements of the Flores consent decree and the general inability to detain entire family units for the duration of immigration court proceedings justifies administrative separation of family units.

I had heard the term "administrative separations" before, at the Christmastime meal in D.C. with the former homeland security official who expressed remorse over his role. At the time, I didn't fully get it. I came to understand, after this book was published, that it was the version of family separations proposed in the Chad Wolf and Gene Hamilton memo in late 2017, which would have separated every parent and child without charging anyone with a crime.

It was an option that, throughout late 2017 and early 2018, Nielsen refused to entertain. So Miller pivoted to their first option: "zero tolerance" prosecutions, which Sessions had announced nearly a month before the Situation Room meeting. And they wanted Nielsen to stop stalling because they needed her support to start separating and sending parents for prosecution. On her desk sat the decision memo that would begin the referrals that would exponentially increase separations.

In the Situation Room, Miller, Trump's virulently anti-immigrant advisor, was furious the wide-scale family separation plan had not yet been put into place.

Justice Department officials had started increasing prosecutions, but Nielsen had not yet signed the decision memo increasing referrals DOJ. Waiting any longer would be un-American, Miller claimed.

"If we don't enforce this, it is the end of our country as we know it," he said, according to officials who were with him inside one of the White House's most secure rooms, normally associated with operations to save lives, not destroy them.

He called for a show-of-hands vote on moving forward with family separations.

"A sea" of hands went up, but Nielsen kept hers down, concerned about the same logistical considerations Commander Jonathan White had flagged for CBP Commissioner Kevin McAleenan late the previous year. Outvoted, the following day Nielsen, bullied and overwhelmed, went along with the plan and signed the decision memo, starting the process of separating thousands of families.

The final day of the 2020 Democratic National Convention, Thursday, August 20, we finally were ready and able to publish what we had learned.

"Trump Cabinet officials voted in 2018 White House meeting to separate migrant children, say officials," our headline read.

LESS THAN TWO months later, October 7, the *New York Times* dropped a bombshell report: the Department of Justice's inspector general was conducting an investigation into the origins of the separation policy, and they had received a draft.

Their headline: "We need to take away the children," a quote attributed to Attorney General Sessions, whose department, the draft report indicated, had played a "driving role" in the planning and implementation of the separation policy.

Julia and I followed up with a report of our own, about

an item we had noticed in the report, which we had also obtained, but the *Times* left out: DOJ prosecutors had developed a maturity test for separations, after realizing that some of the kids they had taken from their parents were too young.

The 2020 Presidential election was around the corner. And even closer—at the end of the month—would be an enormous opportunity to press President Trump on family separations. The final debate, before one of the biggest television audiences of his presidency, would be moderated by my colleague, *Weekend Today* anchor and White House correspondent Kristen Welker.

Two days out, news broke in a regular joint court filing from the Trump administration and the ACLU.

Parents of 545 kids separated still had not been reached by the government.

545.

Just shy of three years since the pilot program that ripped parents and children apart was revealed by Lomi Kriel in the *Houston Chronicle,* nearly six hundred parents were still missing—either still separated and deported, or purposely avoiding contact with the United States government because of the terror that was inflicted upon them.

Onstage at the debate in Nashville, Kristen masterfully asked President Trump about the systematic separation of thousands of migrant children from their parents. An estimated 63 million people were watching.

"Mr. President, your administration separated children from their parents at the border, at least four thousand kids. You've since reversed your zero tolerance policy, but the

United States can't locate the parents of more than five hundred children. So how will these families ever be reunited?"

President Trump pivoted to blaming "coyotes and lots of bad people, cartels," just as he did at the height of the policy.

Kristen asked again.

"But how will you reunite these kids with their families?"

Another dodge by the president, who blamed Biden for building the cages, accurately, as some separated children were housed in during his Vice Presidency. But Trump did not acknowledge his "torture" program, as Physicians for Human Rights put it.

Once again, she persisted.

"Do you have a plan to reunite the kids?"

"Yes, we're working on a very—we're trying very hard," Trump told her, before going back to his lies about the children he separated. "But a lot of these kids come up without the parents, they come over through cartels and the coyotes and through gangs."

Turning to former vice president Biden, Welker asked for his thoughts, who started with a fact-check of his own.

"These five hundred plus kids came with parents. They separated them at the border to make it a disincentive to come to begin with. Big real tough, really strong. And guess what? They cannot—it's not coyotes that bring them over, their parents were with them. They got separated from their parents. And it makes us a laughingstock and violates every judge of who we are as a nation."

Biden continued, after Trump attempted to interject: "Let's talk about what we're talking about. What happened? Parents were ripped—their kids were ripped from their arms and separated. And now they cannot find over five hundred sets of those parents and those kids are alone."

Biden's voice continued to rise.

"Nowhere to go, nowhere to go. It's criminal. It's criminal."

JOE BIDEN WAS elected the 46th President of the United States on November 3, 2020. He was declared the victor of the election by NBC News and other outlets on Saturday, November 7.

That morning, as I drove home to Los Angeles from covering the post-election disinformation effort by Trump allies to reverse or overturn the election outcome in Nevada, Juan, still living with José in the Washington, D.C., area, sent me a WhatsApp message.

It was a GIF of an ebullient man dressed as Uncle Sam, celebrating in a looping victory dance.

"Hahah," I texted back.

"Gracias a dios," he replied.

Thank God.

Another time, when Juan and I video chatted to catch up, we both had our masks on. It struck me that not only had he fled home and family, only to be ripped apart for five months by the U.S. government. As if the separations weren't enough, next came the once-in-a-century global pandemic.

COVID had affected José, too; he, like most teenagers, had been going to school remotely. His dad sent me a photo of the certification he got from his electrician schooling before the lockdown began.

José's mom and sister remain in Guatemala. All of them

are waiting to find out what type of relief, if any, they'll get from the Biden administration.

For now, they're eligible for mental health services based on a fourteen-million-dollar deal struck in another court case brought on behalf of all the separated families—one we reported at the end of 2020 that Stephen Miller tried to block.

Six days before the inauguration of President-Elect Biden, the Department of Justice released the inspector general's report we had obtained earlier.

The department, the final report said, was the "driving force" behind Trump's family separations. In it, the level of care or concern for the children and parents ripped from one another—or lack thereof—was clear.

"Whether it took twenty-four hours, or twenty-four days, the point is that there would be a reunification on the back end," said Gene Hamilton, counselor to then attorney general Jeff Sessions.

Part of candidate Biden's closing argument in the campaign was a TV advertisement featuring his debate remark about the criminality of family separations, and in it he promised a task force to reunite separated parents and children "on the first day of his presidency."

He did, ultimately, a couple weeks in, on February 2021.

Alejandro Mayorkas, the first Latino and immigrant to head the Department of Homeland Security, was announced as its leader.

He and the task force will take on the responsibility of determining restitution, remaining reunifications of separated parents, and interagency coordination so, like Juan and José and I all wanted in cooperating on this project, nothing like this ever happens again.

"We're going to undo the moral and national shame of the previous administration that literally, not figuratively, ripped children from the arms of their families, their mothers, and fathers, at the border, and with no plan—none whatsoever—to reunify," Biden said in the Oval Office, flanked by Vice President Harris and Secretary Mayorkas as he signed the executive order creating the task force. He said he believed doing so would "remove the stain on the reputation" of the United States.

Secretary Mayorkas announced his task force would reunite all of the hundreds of remaining separated families in the United States. He also appointed Michelle Brané, who while working for the Women's Refugee Commission, was part of the group that issued the "Betraying Family Values" report in early 2017 that warned of family separations even before President Trump took office—a promising sign to advocates hoping to not only right the wrong of family separations, but to reform or reconstitute the decades-old deterrence-based immigration enforcement system in the United States.

The Biden administration promised a "a safe, orderly, and fair process" for asylum seekers and a new approach to immigration. And, indeed, Trump is gone, but the system that allowed him to rip apart families in an instant remains.

As I type, deportation flights continue despite a promised moratorium that was jammed by a Trump-appointed judge. Families remain incarcerated in detention centers activists call "baby jails," though in an early March 2021 exclusive interview for NBC News, Mayorkas also told me "a detention facility is not where a family belongs." Trump's COVID-19 health restrictions continue to be used to immediately expel migrant families across the border without access to lawyers. Wall construction merely is "paused." A record number of migrant children crowd Border Patrol facilities because of backed-up Health and Human Services shelters, a repeat of 2011, 2014, 2016, 2018, and 2019. And even righting the wrongs of family separations, with as much public support and blazing spotlight as the families have received, will not be as easy as a debate-stage quip, a campaign commercial, or what can be said in a television interview.

During the transition, President-Elect Biden told my colleague Geoff Bennett his DOJ would conduct a "thorough, thorough investigation" of the separations to determine responsibility and potential criminality.

When I spoke with Secretary Mayorkas, what President Biden's words about the family separation policy being "criminal" remained top of mind.

"Mr. Secretary, the Attorney General is a member of the task force as well, or when he is confirmed will be a member of the task force," I pointed out to him, Merrick Garland's confirmation still not a done deal. "Will his role be to look at the potential criminality of members of the Trump administration?"

"I think we are focused right now, Jacob, on reuniting the families and restoring them to the best of our abilities," Mayorkas responded. "This will be an all-of-government effort. It is not just the Department of Homeland Security and the Department of Justice. It's also the Department of State working with our international partners, the Department of Health and Human Services to bring whatever health relief we can to the families, and we're going to work, as I mentioned, with international organizations, our international partners, and the private sector, this is all of America effort."

Mayorkas hadn't answered the question. I tried again.

"How is it possible that the task force can issue a report so that it never happens again, if there is not a holistic investigation into potential criminality of the Trump administration?"

"Well, I—I haven't excluded anything but what I'm focused on right now is reuniting the families. And in terms of not happening again, our intention, also, in the task force, after the reunification of the families, after restoration of the families, to the best of our abilities, and as fully as the law permits, is to build institutional safeguards to make sure it does not happen again."

He hadn't excluded anything.

The door remained open to a criminal investigation of the American tragedy of the Trump administration's family separation policy.

ACKNOWLEDGMENTS

There's no question who deserves my deepest gratitude: Juan and José. Through their unimaginable trauma, and the ongoing separation from the rest of their nuclear family, they chose to allow me to drop into their lives on a regular basis. They always had one selfless goal: to figure out, together, how what happened to them did, so that it would not happen to anyone ever again. I thank them for their selflessness, and friendship. Rest assured my promise will be kept and they'll get the first copy of this book.

I would not have met Juan and José were it not for the indefatigable Lindsay Toczylowski, who by simply letting me watch her and her colleagues work on Juan's behalf, taught me that immigration attorneys are as important as any first responder on any front line.

Peter Hubbard, vice president and editorial director at HarperCollins's Custom House (formerly an executive editor at William Morrow), is the man responsible for this book. He has been an extraordinary guide, partner, and friend. The magic he worked on this text and his constant encouragement to focus on the people in this story, not the politics or process of separations, has helped me tackle a challenge I would have never known how to start let alone complete. I'm profoundly grateful to him, as well to his phenomenal HarperCollins/Custom House colleagues, including but not limited to Liate Stehlik, Maureen Cole, Molly Gendell, Kayleigh George, Suzanne Franco Mitchell, Andrea Molitor, and Kelly Rudolph. Anwesha Basu deserves extra credit and gratitude for expertly guiding the promotional rollout of the book.

I would not be in the position to write this story were it not for my teammates at NBC News and MSNBC. Phil Griffin took a chance on a guy with zero broadcast news experience in 2015, offering me a job as an MSNBC correspondent. Andy Lack made it official. Noah Oppenheim welcomed me to the network with open arms. I've had many bosses in my nearly five years at 30 Rock who have all enabled and empowered me to color outside the lines. Special thanks is due to Janelle Rodriguez and Betsy Korona, who adroitly and affectionately shepherded our team through the period I write about here.

Another one of my early bosses was Rashida Jones, who now leads all of us at MSNBC as our president. I have always been grateful for her leadership, and especially when it comes to her and the network's unequivocal support for the updated edition of this book and our continued reporting on the separation policy years after it began. As the then-head of NBC News Specials, Rashida also oversaw the 2020 presidential debate in which my colleague Kristen Welker's masterful work quite literally put family separations front and center again. I'm still in awe of Kristen's performance, grateful to her for thinking of and ultimately including the question, and to Benjy Sarlin for including me in the process.

My aforementioned "team" is the small reporting unit built

together with producers Aarne Heikkila and Mitch Koss. Mitch came with me to MSNBC and has been my journalism guru as long as I've reported on TV. Aarne jumped on board whole-heartedly, with more than a decade of institutional knowledge of NBC News under his belt, and is the glue that keeps us together. Our team also includes some of the best in the business behind the camera at NBC News: Dana Roecker, who shoots as beautifully as any Hollywood DP often without the opportunity to do a retake, and Robert Colvill and Craig Nilson, who are able to pick up the tiniest of sounds to make the biggest of emotional impacts. And all of them would say thanks, I'm sure, to Mariana Martínez Esténs, who was by our side sharing her journalistic expertise for much of our early reporting in Mexico.

We are all supported relentlessly by the NBC News Los Angeles bureau, led by the steady hands and compassionate hearts of Polly Powell and Zoya Taylor. Thank you, as well, to the lengthy list of top-notch NBC News and MSNBC writers, reporters, producers, editors and crew members we collaborated with as we reported this story. Our work would not have made it on-air were it not for the the uniquely talented and supportive people behind the scenes at *Today, Nightly, Morning Joe, AM Joy*, MSNBC dayside and MSNBC primetime—especially *All In With Chris Hayes*. I'm deeply appreciative to them all for sharing their air time with us for original reporting. Special thanks, too, to David Verdi and his team for keeping a watchful eye over us in the field.

Whatever we were reporting on, I could always count on Mark Kornblau, Ali Zelenko, Errol Cockfield, Lorie Acio, Hollie Tracz, and their teammates to help us get the word out. Same goes for the amazingly talented marketing group, led by Aaron Taylor.

Julia Ainsley was and still is my partner in my border coverage, tag teaming from Washington during the separation crisis and on the twists and turns since. She broke the separation story and several other huge pieces of news I write about here. Julia taught me how to actually report, that is, work sources to get to the bottom of what it was I was seeing on the ground. She's dogged, intrepid, and couldn't be a kinder, more generous person. I'm so lucky to know and work with her and her fellow members of our investigative unit. To Rich Greenberg and Mark Schone: thank you for letting me contribute and supporting the work.

The *Dateline* team, led by Liz Cole and David Corvo, inexplicably turned to this still-green correspondent to tackle the giant issue of border politics. Paul Ryan, Izhar Harpaz, and Simon Dolittle trusted me to tell a story they conceived. I'll never forget our experience together on *The Dividing Line*, nor everyone who assembled the hour on paper and in the edit room. A double thank you to Liz who (along with Phil Griffin) asked me to pair up with Katy Tur and a superb team for our MSNBC documentary series *American Swamp*.

Katy has not only been a cohost and friend since we were teenagers growing up together in Los Angeles, but a mentor as I wrote this book, never hesitating to share the lessons she learned in writing *Unbelievable*. She also introduced me to Ben Phelan, who helped me fact check what you've read here. Thank you, as well, to Richard Chacon of the NBC News standards team for his thoughtful reading of the text. Any errors which slipped through the cracks are on me.

I'm grateful as well to Alan Berger and Jonathan Lyons, whose advice and counsel I relied on as I embarked on this project. R.

ACKNOWLEDGMENTS

Andrew Free skillfully consulted as I attempted to navigate the labyrinth of pulling documents out of the government.

Each and every source who provided even a single detail for this book are the real tellers of this story. Everyone from ranger Kelly Cummins at the Resaca de la Palma State Park in Brownsville (who helped me identify a bird call), to those who could not go on the record: thank you for the countless hours you spent with me going over, and over, and over what happened and where to look to understand why.

To the Soboroffs: mom, dad, Miles, Molly, Hannah, Leah (plus their families), my in-laws the Caris, Rosa and everyone else in my little family's universe: we would be lost without you. To Nicole, Noah, and Lucia—who watched me write this book through a pregnancy and then global pandemic—I love you more than you'll ever know. Thank you for sacrificing your husband and dad for hours on end to the writing vortex of the home office laundry room. Now that I'm done, I'll still be in here, just washing clothes.

385

NOTES ON SOURCING

As I recount in my author's note, this book grew out of my real-time reporting for NBC News and MSNBC about immigration policy on both sides of the U.S.–Mexico border. When I set out to tell the story of family separations—what happened, and how—in the breadth and depth a book affords, the first thing I did was go back to that material, including, but not limited to, reports I filed on-air and online, and the pen-and-paper notes I took during zero tolerance.

Next, I circled back with people I met that critical week in June 2018 and in its wake. Most were eager to introduce me to other key players I might have heard of but had never met or spoken with at length. I went through the timeline of events with each of them. They pointed me to other sources, who pointed me to documents, transcripts, recordings, and places to visit. What it became was an exercise in reporting on what I had already reported on, and realizing how much more of a story there was to tell.

Were it not for those who decided to step forward (most on the condition of anonymity to protect themselves and others) over a year after President Trump's man-made disaster—to recount to me, in great and specific detail, private conversations about the planning, execution and reversal of the family separation policy—understanding my own blind spots and giving you as full and complete a picture as I have attempted to would not have been possible.

More often than not, I was surprised to learn, sources who were battling each other at the time recalled events similarly, and instead disputes were about the underlying motivation for actions, not debating what actually occurred. It's hard to argue with documented evidence, and there was plenty of it. But when what I was hearing from sources did conflict, I've noted that here.

I relied, too, on the incredible work of so many other journalists and organizations for background information and details I did not know, which I attempted to cite within the text as much as possible. You'll find details of what I did not or could not in what follows. If any errors are contained in these pages, they're mine and mine alone.

Prologue

This is a story about a policy, but also about people. Juan and José could not have been more generous with their time, including the details that make up the prologue. When I reached out to Juan for the first time after starting the book to ask him if he would participate, he didn't think twice. While I was researching and writing, the three of us shared delicious meals together—laughing, learning, and sometimes crying—but he was always clear about his motivation for our time together: to make sure what happened to him and his son never happened to anyone ever again.

Juan was an open book, helping me paint the picture of

his life in Guatemala over those meals by sharing private photographs, text messages, documents about his and José's ordeal, and introducing me to their new lawyers working to win their asylum cases. I ended up traveling to his country while writing the book on assignment for NBC. But while I was there he and his wife María decided it would be too dangerous for them to have me visit her, so instead we met virtually, via video conference, during one of our meals.

Chapter One: "I Just Couldn't Do That"

Obama administration officials faced their own crises at the border, and while the administration rejected any attempts to systematically separate families, the way they responded set the stage for what the Trump administration carried out. Nevertheless, many of them, including former homeland security secretary Jeh Johnson and Domestic Policy Council chair Cecilia Muñoz, were more than willing to tell me about how family separations were specifically considered and rejected during their tenure in the White House.

As they were grappling with what to do on the border, I was an inexperienced campaign reporter. To piece together the day I came face to face with Stephen Miller, whom Muñoz would later sit side by side with in a transitional meeting, I relied on the reporting of my NBC News colleague Benjy Sarlin as well as a live blog of the event by Jennifer Kerns at ColoradoPolitics.com.

The email from James "Jim" De La Cruz, the Office of Refugee Resettlement employee, warning of family separations at the end of the Obama administration was first reported by the Center for Public Integrity in December 2019 and obtained in a freedom of information request, according to CIR, "submitted to Health and Human Services by the American Immigration Council, the National Immigrant Justice Center, Kids in Need of Defense, the Women's Refugee Commission, and the Florence Immigrant and Refugee Rights Project."

Chapter Two: "I Don't Have Those Numbers"

This chapter documents the confusion around early family separations during the Trump administration. As I was reporting from the inauguration, then on drugs at the border and the specter of deportations, discussion of family separations began almost immediately. My now-colleague Julia Ainsley reported on March 3, 2017, in her Reuters piece "Trump administration considering separating women, children at Mexico border" that as early as February 2, 2017, it was being discussed. The details I learned about the February 14, 2017, Valentine's Day meeting, which was publicly confirmed by Commander Jonathan White in congressional testimony before the Democratically controlled House Energy and Commerce Committee on February 7, 2019, were from multiple officials present.

Statistics in this chapter about migration came from the Pew Research Center, and the quotes from Jeff Sessions and Steve Bannon's 2015 conversation about U.S. immigration were reported by Brian Tashman for Right Wing Watch (a project of People For The American Way) in an article called "Jeff Sessions Also Misled The Senate About His Civil Rights Record."

Commander White's July 4, 2017, memo warning of potential family separations was obtained by the Energy and Commerce Committee (to whom I am grateful for spending an afternoon on Capitol Hill going through a binder full of these emails with me), as was the August 15, 2017 email he received about a rise in separations over the summer, which turned out to be the El Paso pilot program.

Chapter Three: "A Significant Increase"

When the first clues about widespread family separations started to emerge, details were hard to come by. My characterizations of Commander White's attempts to stop a wide scale family separation policy are based on interviews with multiple people who knew or worked with him personally, but also on primary source material that shows clearly what he was up to. His email to Scott Lloyd, his Trump-appointed boss, flagging what he learned about Operation Mega (which came from Julia Ainsley's exclusive piece with our colleague Andrew Blankstein on September 7, 2017, "Homeland Security Plans Massive Roundups of Undocumented Immigrants") was obtained by House Energy and Commerce.

The fascinating details revealed by Chris Meekins, the then-Chief of Staff to the Assistant Secretary for Preparedness and Response at Health and Human Services, about what the agency is supposed to be preparing for (including a COVID-19-like pandemic, *not* family separations) were from a January 2019 episode of Dan Diamond's Politico Pulse podcast. What was happening in HHS Secretary's Operations Center during preparations for Hurricane Irma came from government press releases and handout photos. The details about how Homestead, Florida, was bracing for the storm, and how it had fared during Hurricane Andrew, came from the *Miami Herald* and the *South Dade News Leader*.

Scott Lloyd's memo to Steve Wagner about keeping open

the temporary ORR shelter in Homestead, was a House Energy and Commerce document, as was Commander White's November email to acting CBP Commissioner McAleenan about an increase in referrals of separated children. The follow-up emails sent by McAleenan, acting Border Patrol Chief Carla Provost and Deputy Chief Gloria Chavez were obtained by the watchdog group American Oversight.

President Trump's quote about working on a plan for DACA was reported by Sheryl Gay Stolberg and Yamiche Alcindor in the *New York Times* article "Trump's Support for Law to Protect 'Dreamers' Lifts Its Chances."

It was KQED's Alexandra Hall who, in haunting detail, described in her report "Seeking Asylum at the California Border: In the Basement Cells at San Ysidro Port of Entry," what Ms. L. and her daughter likely went through.

Details of the funeral of an El Paso Border Patrol agent were reported by the Associated Press, and images of it were taken by Ivan Pierre Aguirre and published by the *San Antonio Express News*. Lomi Kriel's reporting about the existence of the El Paso pilot program was game-changing, and its importance cannot be overstated. Her piece "Trump Moves to End 'Catch and Release,' Prosecuting Parents and Removing Children Who Cross Border" on November 25, 2017, was groundbreaking.

The December conversation between the Border Patrol's Gloria Chavez and an ORR staffer was documented in an email, and details of the after-action report about what she was discussing were revealed in a report by the Department of Homeland Security's Office of Inspector General on December 1, 2019.

Senator Kamala Harris's back-and-forth with Kirstjen Nielsen when she was nominated to become homeland security secretary was published by the Senate Homeland Security and Governmental Affairs Committee, and I'm grateful to her staff for answering questions I had about it.

Gene Hamilton and Chad Wolf's emails planning for a family separation policy were first reported on January 17, 2019, by Julia Ainsley in the report "Trump admin weighed targeting migrant families, speeding up deportation of children." She followed up on that report in October, 2019 with another one: "Trump admin considering Chad Wolf, an author of family separation policy, for DHS chief."

Chapter Four: "Very, Very Worried"

As more people became aware of family separations occurring, concern mounted behind the scenes. I've never been inside Health and Human Services Headquarters, but the U.S. General Services Administration, which maintains the building for the federal government, has more information than you could ever imagine about it online. I learned of the stakeholder meeting held there by the Office of Refugee Resettlement in the batch of documents published by House Energy and Commerce, and contacted one of the organizations on the list to find out more. KIND, Kids in Need of Defense, was in the room, and their representative, Jennifer Podkul, shared extensive details with me about the meeting, as did ORR sources who were present.

It was Melissa del Bosque's reporting about the Trump administration's plans to build border wall on a wildlife refuge in South Texas that brought us there, particularly her November 10, 2017, report "Records Show Where Trump Plans to Build Texas Border Wall."

The Border Patrol email from Gloria Chavez to Commander White was a House Energy and Commerce production, as was his reply.

Lee Gelernt, the ACLU lawyer, has always been generous with his time, and provided context for me around what was publicly known and reported about his *Ms. L.* lawsuit.

I learned about the phone call in which a critical IT glitch was discussed that would prevent reunifications of separated families from House Energy and Commerce, but it was Claire Trickler-McNulty and Andrew Lorenzen Strait, two former ICE officials, who helped fill in the details about what it meant. So, too, did the DHS OIG report "DHS Lacked Technology Needed to Successfully Account for Separated Migrant Families," published in November 2019. Emails between DHS Secretary Nielsen and her staff were uncovered by American Oversight.

Statistics about migrant deaths in Arizona came from the Colibri Center for Human Rights, No More Deaths, and La Coalición de Derechos Humanos.

Chapter Five: "Get Rid of the List"

Trump political appointees and career government officials approached family separations completely differently. The extraordinary back and forth between HHS and *New York Times* reporter Caitlin Dickerson was revealed in a lengthy email exchange produced by House Energy and Commerce. Its timing squared with what I had heard from multiple sources about then-ORR director Scott Lloyd's desire for a subordinate to destroy the list of separated children he was keeping. Nailing down what happened there was a challenge, and key details about what was said in the ORR coordinating meeting were confirmed by several officials who were present. Neither HHS nor ACF would issue an official statement for the record about the meeting nor its aftermath.

The existence of the decision memo presented to Secretary Nielsen was first reported by the *Washington Post*'s Maria Sacchetti on April 26, 2018, in her piece "Top Homeland Security officials urge criminal prosecution of parents crossing border with children." Nielsen ultimately signed it, instituting family separations, on May 5, 2018. But the document itself was not published until September 25, 2018, by the Project for Government Oversight. I obtained a copy from a source who had received it, too, while writing, and the same source gave me a copy of the legal memo authored by John Mitnick, the general counsel of the Department of Homeland Security, the details of which had never been previously revealed.

The briefing document Secretary Nielsen received about the interview I was going to do with her the same day as the cabinet meeting in which she was eviscerated by President Trump was obtained by *BuzzFeed*'s Jason Leopold, my former colleague at *The Huffington Post*, who shared it with me. Details I reported about that cabinet meeting came from an administration official who was present. Trump's berating of Nielsen in the meeting was first reported by *The New York Times* in an article by Michael D. Shear and Nicole Perlroth, "Kirstjen Nielsen, Chief of Homeland Security, Almost Resigned After Trump Tirade."

Data about capacity issues within border facilities came from the aforementioned November 2019 DHS OIG report. The warning sent about family separations occuring in Arizona was uncovered by the Center for Public Integrity's FOIA request to HHS.

Chapter Six: "These Kids Are Incarcerated"

This chapter was a pivotal moment for Juan and José, and myself; it's when we all learned painful truths about family separations firsthand. Their crossing into the United States was based on details they described to me, a trip I took to the United States side of the border in Yuma and San Luis, Arizona, to investigate in November 2019, and reviewing of Google Maps images of the area with them personally. The number of migrants dying on the Barry Goldwater Air Force bombing range were reported on August 15, 2018, by investigative journalist John Carlos Frey on the independent television news program *Democracy Now!* (which I've been watching since my college professor Bertell Ollman told me to start in 2002).

Details of Juan and José's apprehension and detention were culled from documents obtained via freedom of information act requests to the Department of Homeland Security, which I would have never been able to figure out were it not for the Nashville immigration attorney R. Andrew Free, who fought as doggedly for details about Juan and José's case as he does for his clients. The email from Jim De La Cruz to his colleagues, the night of Juan and José's apprehension, was part of the batch the Center for Public Integrity obtained via FOIA. I have never been to the Florence Detention Center, where Juan was sent from Yuma, but The Florence Project and attorney Laura St. John helped me understand how it works. VICE's reporting, particularly the June 27, 2018, piece by Taylor Dolven, "Five federal prisons are being asked to accept hundreds of migrants under the 'zero tolerance' immigration policy," provided important details about the federal prison in Victorville where Juan ended up next.

Details of my tour of Casa Padre in Brownsville came directly from my "little blue notebook," and were all observations I made in real time while touring on June 13, 2018.

The email sent by Commander White to the Office for the Assistant Secretary of Health on June 15, 2018, came from House Energy and Commerce.

Chapter Seven: "They're Cages"

Even though I was getting a look for myself at life inside detention for separated children, the conditions of adults taken from their children were far from the headlines. Eva Bitran from the ACLU of Los Angeles, the first immigration attorney to get inside Victorville during family separations, helped me track down and understand the declaration of attorney Munmeeth Kaur Soni from the Immigrant Defenders Law Center, filed on July 23, 2017, describing attempts to get inside the Victorville prison where Juan was detained. It was in those documents I learned of Toczylowski's attempts to gain access to the facility, long before I met her.

Before I toured the Ursula Border Patrol Processing Station, my conversations with Border Patrol Chief Padilla and his press attaché Robert Rodriguez were transcribed from a livestream video that picked up what was said by CBS Austin. Details of my tour of Ursula were, like details of my tour of Casa Padre, straight from my notebook.

Oprah Winfrey's voicemail to Dr. Colleen Kraft was shared with me by the American Academy of Pediatrics, which had been long advocating against family separations.

I'm grateful to the organization, particularly Jamie Poslosky, for arranging a briefing for me at their Washington, D.C., offices about their work on family separations.

Chapter Eight: "No Way to Link"

Once public pressure and opposition to family separations in Washington reached a boiling point, the Trump administration was forced to act. But it wasn't just those outside the White House. Details of Ivanka Trump's direct advocacy against the policy to her father, specifically for him to sign an executive order ending it, were conveyed to me by a Trump administration official. Same goes for President Trump's phone call to Secretary Nielsen about ending the policy, and the Oval Office meeting that followed.

Once the president ended separations by executive order, the reunification effort began almost immediately within the office of the HHS Assistant Secretary for Preparedness and Response, and multiple sources with knowledge of the planning in those meetings described them to me. On the verge of being pushed out of the effort, Scott Lloyd sent an email about separation statistics to the group that would replace him, which was produced by House Energy and Commerce. The scene in the Secretary's Operations Center between Scott Lloyd, Commander White, and a third ORR employee, in which tensions ran high, was described and corroborated by multiple sources with knowledge of what occurred.

I first reported about the email from HHS analyst Thomas Fitzgerald to Matt Albence at ICE on May 1, 2019, for NBC News in an article entitled "Emails show Trump admin had 'no way to link' separated migrant children to parents," and obtained the email from the House Judiciary Committee.

Chapter Nine: "Shocks the Conscience"

President Trump's ending systematic family separations by executive order was critical to ending the policy, but the decision by Judge Dana Sabraw was even more consequential. Lee Gelernt of the ACLU described the moment he learned he and his colleagues had prevailed over the Trump administration in the case, stopping the policy and ordering reunifications. The courtroom conversations between the Trump administration, Judge Sabraw, and the ACLU are from official court transcripts accessed online via PACER.

Details of the conditions inside Adelanto, the ICE detention center outside of Los Angeles where Juan was transferred after Victorville, were described in the October 2018 DHS OIG report "Management Alert—Issues Requiring Action at the Adelanto ICE Processing Center in Adelanto, California."

The July 15, 2018, incident in which separated children were made to wait overnight in vans outside the Port Isabel detention center were first reported by myself and Julia Ainsley on June 3, 2019, in our story for NBC News titled "Botched family reunifications left migrant children waiting in vans overnight." Details of what José experienced in the "care and custody" of BCFS Harlingen were described to me by him, and, generally, by a representative for BCFS, who explained what a day in the life of a child housed there would look like.

Chapter Ten: "Made-for-TV Drama"

Tensions were running high inside the Trump administration, and that was evident during the pressure-field reunification process. The letter San Diego Sector Border Patrol Chief

Rodney Scott (who is now leading the entire agency) sent to me ended up on my desk at the NBC News bureau at Universal Studios. I packed it away, deciding not to publish it at the time, but dug it out to paint a more complete picture of what was happening at the time for this book.

I was personally present for the dialogue from the scene inside the San Diego courtroom of Judge Sabraw, but it, too, was based on court transcripts. The contentious "murder board" that took place on July 28, 2018, was recounted to me by multiple people present at the session.

Chapter Eleven: "It Hurts in My Heart"

As summer 2018 wound down and deadlines for reunifications passed, the number of remaining cases began to shrink—that's when I first attempted to meet Juan with his attorney Lindsay Toczylowski and Alfonso Maldonado Silva. Both of them worked with me then, and again as I wrote this book, to understand details of what occurred to their client and what it took for them to make contact with him.

Details of Juan's asylum interview were based on the form filled out by his asylum officer which, like other documents referenced in the book, were obtained with his permission.

DHS spokeswoman Katie Waldman's trip to the border was described to me at the time by her personally, and was also documented on her Instagram feed.

Chapter Twelve: "We Know That He Is a Good Person"

Juan and José's reunification happened four months after their separation, thanks to the dogged work of his attorneys. The letters sent vouching for him were also a part of his case file I obtained with his permission, and other details of the bittersweet reunion were described to me by father and son.

Epilogue: "The Greatest Human Rights Catastrophe of My Lifetime"

The "end" of family separations was not the end of family separations, which I did not understand at the time. President Trump attempted on multiple occasions to restart family separations, first reported by my colleagues Julia Ainsley and Geoff Bennett in April 2019, after Trump fired Nielsen, in a piece titled "Trump's support of renewed child separation policy led to collision with Nielsen." The scene in which Trump, the First Lady and Nielsen discussed restarting the policy was described by a source with knowledge of the conversation. The president's remarks about the Alabama trip and details of his movements were documented in a live blog by the *Auburn Plainsman,* WSFA, in their report "Alabama welcomes Trump days after tornado devastation," and the U.S. Army's Fort Benning Facebook page. Asked to respond to the exchange between the First Lady and President Trump, a spokeswoman for Mrs. Trump declined.

Interstitials

I included the interstitials that appear in between each chapter of the book to take a step back and show how family separations unfolded in primary source material. The story of "Ana" in 2016 was from a Lutheran Immigration and Refugee Service testimonial within the *Betraying Family Values* report assembled by KIND, the Women's Refugee Commission, and LIRS.

The declarations of Ms. C, Mr. U, Mr. A, and Ms. M.M.A.L.

were submitted by the ACLU as part of their *Ms. L v. ICE* lawsuit.

The "Significant Incident Reports" about the separated five-year-old from Guatemala and nine-year-old from El Salvador were uncovered through the aforementioned Freedom of Information Act request by the Center for Public Integrity, as was James De La Cruz's email to case managers on June 28, 2018, and the two complaints filed by the National Immigrant Justice Center to DHS's department of Civil Rights and Civil Liberties about separated children and parents.

Scott Lloyd's email on June 22, 2018, was part of the documents shared with me by the House Energy and Commerce Committee.

The DHS OIG report "Initial Observations Regarding Family Separation Issues" was released publicly in September 2018.

INDEX

Abortion, 54, 62, 147
ACLU. *See* American Civil Liberties Union
Adelanto ICE Detention Center, 265, 273, 289, 294–96, 303, 321–26, 328–30, 332–36, 347
Administration for Children and Families (ACF), 97–98, 150
Administrative Procedure Act (APA), 31, 166
Aeropuerto Internacional Mundo Maya, 2
Ainsley, Julia Edwards, 222
  breaking the story on family separations, 37, 53–54, 55–56, 76, 124
  overcrowding at Yuma Border Patrol Station, 365–66
  Trump's firing of Nielsen, 353–54
Aki, Sidney, 34–35, 93–94, 172, 175
AK-47s, 148
Albence, Matthew, 275–77, 314–17
"Alien numbers," 276–77
American Academy of Pediatrics, 221, 245–46

American Civil Liberties Union (ACLU), xviii–xix, xx. See also *Ms. L v. ICE*
  Immigrants' Rights Project, 123–27
  Reno v. Flores, 21
American identity, 3
American Swamp (TV series), 354, 355–56
Ana, 9
Anzalduas Bridge, 127–29, 168, 177, 261
Arctic warming, 140–41
Arivaca, 148, 260
Army Corps of Engineers, 109–10
Arnie's Point, 112, 119, 172
Arpaio, Joe, 17
ASPR (Assistant Secretary for Preparedness and Response), 57
Associated Press, 262–63
Asylum interview. *See* "Credible fear" interview
Asylum seekers, 25, 66, 74–75, 91, 129, 137
Atencio, Mariana, 257
Auburn University Regional Airport, 352

Azar, Alexander "Alex," 269–70, 271, 363

Bannon, Steve, 20, 45
Barry M. Goldwater Air Force Range, 194
BCFS Health and Human Services, 212–13, 296, 298–300, 342–43
Bed space, 116–17
Begnaud, David, 240
Bennett, Geoff, 353–54
"Betraying Family Values" (report), 98–100
Big Bend sector, 80–81
Blitzer, Wolf, 36–39
Blue spiral notebook of author, xiv–xvii, 203, 207, 214–15, 238–39, 289, 311
Blumenthal, Richard, 316–17
Boca Chica State Park, 168
Border fencing
    Bush and, 108, 111, 112, 113
    Clinton and, 64, 77, 112, 119–20
Border Patrol
    author's patrols with, 82–83, 105–11, 118–23, 127–29, 131–34, 167–70
    Bush's expansion of, 77
    death of Martinez, 75–76, 79, 82–83
    IT systems, 130, 134
    Migration Crisis Action Team (MCAT), 115–17
    strategy of "technology, infrastructure, and manpower," 194
    Trump's hiring push, 79–80
Border Patrol Union, 12
"Border Security and Immigration Enforcement Improvements" (directive), 30–31
Border wall, 15–16, 28, 34, 104–14, 118, 179
    author's visits to, 63–66, 82–83, 105–11, 118–23
    eminent domain issues, 111
    funding and budget deal, 70–71, 105, 112, 122
    President Bush and, 108, 111, 112, 113
    prototypes of, 63–65, 81–82, 308
Border Wars (Davis and Shear), 180
Boutte, Lucy, 41–42, 43
Boyce, Don, 272, 299
Breitbart News, 20
Brownsville South Padre Island International Airport, xiii–xiv
Brzezinski, Mika, 27, 112–13
Burnett, John, 171, 184
Bush, George W., 54, 61, 164, 287
    border wall and fencing, 108, 111, 112, 113
    expansion of Border Patrol, 77
    Hurricane Katrina, 85
    immigration policy, 77, 120, 143, 352
Bush, Laura, 247–48, 253
BuzzFeed, 69–70

"Cages," xvi, xvii, 207–8, 242, 247, 248, 309
California Adult Use of Marijuana Act, 93
Cameron County Child Advocacy Center, 209
Carson, Ben, 352
Carson, Johnny, 96
Carter, Andrew, 298–99
Casa del Migrante, 19

Casa Padre
    author's invitation to tour, xiv,
        203–5
    author's notebook, xiv–xvii,
        203, 214–15, 289
    author's reporting on, xvi–
        xvii, xix, 213–14, 216–23,
        231
    author's tour of, xiv–xvii, 202,
        205–12
    author's tweeting about,
        214–16, 218
    Senator Merkley's visit, 202–3,
        204, 207, 215, 216–17, 220
"Catch and release," 16, 21,
    166–67
    ending, 29–33, 44–45, 115,
        141–44, 147
        memorandum, ix, 141–44,
            147
Cathedral of Our Lady of the
    Angels, 43–44
Cathedral of Saint Vibiana, 43
Catholic Charities, 289
Catholic Church, 40–44, 231–32
CBS This Morning (TV show),
    256–57
Central American Dry Corridor
    (CADC), 141
Channel One, 18
Chavez, Gloria, 70, 83, 84, 115–17
Child abuse allegations, 134,
    163–64, 245–46, 271, 319,
    358–59, 366
Cissna, L. Francis, 89
    family separation decision
        memo, 163–67, 169–70, 174
Citizenship and Immigration
    Services, U.S. (USCIS), 30, 37,
    89, 126, 163, 314
Climate change, 18, 140–41,
    144–45, 315

Clinton, Bill
    border fencing, 64, 77, 112,
        119–20
    immigration policy, 119–20,
        131–32, 261
Clinton, Hillary, 12, 13, 17
CNN, 40, 77, 245–46
    Kelly's announcement of
        family separation policy, ix,
        36–39, 44, 77, 86–87
Colonia Libertad, 112, 172
Colorado Republican presidential
    caucuses of 2016, 11–15
Colvill, Rob, 82
Comcast, 111
"Consequence delivery," 99–100,
    365
Cooper, Anderson, 40
Corden, James, 220
Cordova, Anna, 42–43
COVID-19 pandemic, 57–58, 225,
    362, 363
Crank, Joel, 13
"Credible fear" interview, 25, 51,
    91, 200, 290, 362–63
    Juan's, 323, 328–30, 335,
        342
Cruz, Ted, 14
Curbelo, Carlos, 327
Current TV, 18
Customs and Border Protection,
    U.S. (CBP), 9, 28–29
    Air and Marine Unit, 167–70
    El Paso pilot program, ix, 70,
        83–84, 277
    IT systems, 130, 134

DACA. See Dreamers
Daly, Carson, 94–95, 309
Dateline (TV show), 104–5,
    118–19, 122, 147–48, 175, 181,
    269, 307–8

Dateline (continued)
  author's Black Hawk helicopter
    ride, 167–70
  author's Nielsen interview,
    170–73, 181–85, 203–4,
    260–61
  author's purchase of dried
    shrimp on Rio Grande,
    161–63
Davis, Julie Hirschfeld, 180
Deaths. *See* Migrant deaths along
  border
Deferred Action for Childhood
  Arrivals (DACA). *See* Dreamers
De La Cruz, James "Jim"
  family separations, 22–23,
    29–30, 76, 152, 225, 277–78,
    283
    tracking parents and
      children, 23, 67–68, 154,
      159–61, 195–97, 209, 274,
      277–78
  migrant surge of 2016,
    22–23
Deportations (deportation
  policy), 40–44
  George's story, 72–74, 94,
    95–97
  under Obama, 17–19, 77, 81,
    120
  Operation Mega, 54–56
Deterrence-based immigration
  policy, 38, 47–48, 261, 280, 361,
  362, 365
  under Bush, 77, 120
  under Clinton, 77, 119–20,
    131–32, 261
  drug smuggling rationale,
    33–36, 115
  history of, 77–78, 119–20
  under Obama, 21–22, 77,
    120

  under Trump, 33–36, 38,
    47–48, 361, 362, 365. *See also*
    Zero tolerance policy
Devil's Highway, The (Urrea), 132
DHS (Department of Homeland
  Security)
  creation of, 77
  Dickerson's reporting on
    family separations, 147,
    149–59, 195
  El Paso pilot program, ix, 70,
    83–84, 277
  ending "catch and release,"
    29–33, 44–45, 141–44
  Kelly's announcement of
    family separation policy, ix,
    36–39, 44, 77, 86–87
  Kelly's appointment, 30
  Kelly's departure, 84–85
  Nielsen's confirmation, 84–90
  Office of Civil Rights and Civil
    Liberties, 124
  Sessions' public
    announcement of
    implementation of policy, x,
    174–77
  use of "family unit," 55
"DHS Deterrence" model, 47–48
Diamond, Dan, 57–58, 359–60
Dickerson, Caitlin, 147, 149–58
Dinnin, Kevin, 298–99
Doolittle, Simon, 104–5, 118–19
Downs, Jim, 18–19
Dreamers, 17, 20, 70–71, 105
  George's story, 72–74, 94,
    95–97
Drug cartels, 3–5, 5, 121, 145, 146,
  193, 265, 365
Drug smuggling, 3–4, 33–36,
  93–94, 172–73, 341
  Galvez Tunnel, 118–19,
    120–23, 172

Dry Corridor, 141
Duke, Elaine, 88

Edwin, 128–29, 168
Edwin Jr., 128–29, 168
Election of 2016, 11–16, 82
    Colorado Republican
      presidential caucuses, 11–15
    Texas Republican presidential
      caucuses, 15–16
Election of 2018, 326–27, 343–45
El Niño, 141
Eloy Detention Center, 137
El Paso pilot program, ix, 70,
    83–84, 277
El Paso Processing Center, 25–26
Eminent domain, 111
Enforcement and Removal
    Operations (ERO), 275–77
Enforcement and Removal
    Operations Law Division
    (EROLD), 129–31, 133–34
Epiphany Catholic Church, 40–43
Executive Office of Immigration
    Review (EOIR), 30, 102, 303, 314

Fabian, Sarah, xviii–xix, 174, 291
Family reunifications, 134, 155,
    271–79, 291–94, 296–303,
    309–10, 360–61
    court order ruling, 285–94,
      299–302, 310–13, 360–61
    deadline day, 309–10
    of Juan and José, 349–50, 354
    Kriel's reporting, 78, 223
    migration surge of 2016, 22
    timeline of key events, i–xi
    tracking children and parents,
      xix–xx, 195–97, 277–78
    "UAC Data Request-Parent/
      Legal Guardian Link,"
      276–79

Family separations
    Ainsley's reporting on, 37,
      53–54, 55–56, 76, 124
    "Betraying Family Values"
      (report), 98–100
    child abuse allegations, 134,
      163–64, 245–46, 271, 319,
      358–59, 366
    congressional hearings,
      314–17, 358–60
    DHHS Office of the Inspector
      General reports, 295–96,
      339, 356
    Dickerson's reporting on, 147,
      149–58, 195
    El Paso pilot program, ix, 9,
      70, 83–84, 277
    EROLD, 129–31, 133–34
    Ivanka Trump and, 255–56,
      258–60, 266, 267
    Kelly's announcement of, ix,
      37–39, 44, 77, 86–87
    Kriel's reporting on, 76–77,
      78–79, 83, 88, 98, 124, 223
    leaked list of seven-hundred
      separated children, 152–54,
      157–58, 173–74
    Melania Trump's opposition
      to, 352–53
    Nielsen's decision memo,
      88–90, 163–67, 169–70,
      174–75
    number of children, x, xix–xx,
      152–57, 160–61, 273, 286–87,
      291, 301, 331, 341–42,
      351–52, 353, 356
    under Obama, 21–22, 37, 67,
      99–100, 152, 160, 163–64
    ProPublica audio tape, 255
    public outrage over, 245–49,
      253–55, 256–57, 260,
      262–63

Senate hearing, 314–17

Sessions' public announcement of implementation, x, 174–77

seven deaths of children in custody, 365

timeline of key events, ix–x

tracking parents and children, 66–68, 157–61, 181, 195–97, 209

Trump's executive order ending, x, 259, 266–69, 285, 286–87

Trump's justifications for, 231–34

Father's Day, xvii, 2, 35, 237, 238, 248, 261

FBI (Federal Bureau of Investigation), 76

Fifth Amendment, 166

Fingerprinting, 117, 197, 212

Fitzgerald, Thomas, 275–79

Five Eyes (FVEY), 330

Florence Detention Center, 199, 329

Florence Immigrant & Refugee Rights Project, 124

Flores, Pete, 35–36

Flores v. Reno, 21

Florida Air National Guard, 60

Food insecurity, 141, 144, 145

Fort Benning, Georgia, 352

Fort Wayne Rotary Club, 231–32

Fox & Friends (TV show), 232

Francis, Pope, 81

Franco, Maureen, 78

Fresno Yosemite International Airport, 255

Friendship Park, 175

Fuentes, David, 106–9

Galvez Tunnel, 118–19, 120–23, 172

Gangs. *See* MS-13

GAO (Government Accountability Office), xix

Garamendi, John, 219

Garcia, Jaime, 207

Garcia, Olga, 207, 208

Garcia, Ramon, 106–9

Gaslighting, 248, 257

Gatorade, xv, 131

Gelernt, Lee, 123–27, 135, 166, 285–86, 291–92, 301, 310–13

GEO Group, 321

Georgia State Senate, 164

Gloria, Maria, 309–10

Gomez, José H., 43–44

Gore, Al, 18

"Gran Marchas," 81

Great Recession, 19

Greenland, 139–41

Griffin, Phil, 257

Guatemala, 363–65

climate change's effects, 141, 144–45

Juan and José's life in, 1–2, 3–4, 69, 145–46, 185–86

Gulf of Mexico, 161–62, 297

Gura, David, 244–45

Guthrie, Savannah, 94–95, 96

Gutierrez, Gabe, 257

Haberman, Maggie, 259

Hamilton, Gene, 88–90, 135

Hardball (TV show), 223

Harlingen shelter, 202, 212–13, 264–65, 296, 331–32, 342

Harlingen Soccer Complex, 297

Harpaz, Izhar, 104–5, 118–19, 181, 254, 271, 307–8, 309

Harris, Kamala, 85–88, 156–57

Harrison, Brian, 251

Hayes, Chris, 204–5, 257
  author's Casa Padre report,
    xvi–xvii, 214, 215, 216–20
Haynie, Susan, 56
Heikkila, Aarne, 113–14, 205,
  236, 269
  border visits, 65, 79, 80, 82,
    107–8, 111, 237, 244
  Casa Padre visit, xiv–zv, 214,
    219, 220, 223–24, 229
  courtroom visit, 310–11
  election of 2016, 11
  Greenland visit, 139, 140
  Juan's interview, 326, 332–33,
    343
  surfing, 174
Heritage Foundation, 165
Heroin, 34, 35
HHS (Health and Human
  Services), 20, 28, 29, 48, 58–59,
  224–26. See also ORR
  memorandum of
    understanding, 116–17
"Hieleras," 197–98
Higgins, Jennifer, 314–15
Hinojosa, Martin, 206–8
Hoffman, Jonathan, 170, 181, 185,
  314–17, 361–62
Holt, Lester, 257
Homan, Thomas, 21, 66–67, 89,
  158
  family separations decision
    memo, 163–67, 169–70, 174
Homeland Security Department,
  U.S. See DHS
Homestead, Florida, 60–61
Homestead Air Reserve Base,
  60–61
Homestead Temporary Influx
  Shelter, 60–63, 327–28
Hood, John, 114
Hotel Internacional, 193

Hotel Saint George, 82
Houlton, Tyler, 134–35
House Judiciary Committee,
  359–60
Houston Chronicle, 76–77, 78–79,
  83, 88, 98, 124
Huazano, Carlos "Cao," 107–8
Human rights, xiii, 358–60,
  367–68
Hunt, Kasie, 246–47
Hurd, Will, 343
Hurricane Andrew, 60
Hurricane Harvey, 56
Hurricane Irma, 56–57, 60, 63,
  141, 270
Hurricane Katrina, 85

ICE (Immigration and Customs
  Enforcement, U.S.)
  deportation policy, 40–44,
    130
    Operation Mega, 54–56
  ending "catch and release,"
    31–32, 44–45, 141–44
  EROLD, 129–31, 133–34
  the "glitch" with ORR,
    155–56, 258
  IT systems, 130, 134
  Ms. L v. ICE. See Ms. L v. ICE
ICE Health Service Corps, 199
Illegal border crossing numbers,
  19–20, 61, 142, 143
Immigrant Defenders Law Center,
  229–30, 264, 288–89
Immigration Act of 1924, 45
Immigration policy
  under Bush, 77, 120, 143,
    352
  "catch and release." See "Catch
    and release"
  under Clinton, 119–20,
    131–32, 261

Immigration policy (continued)
deterrence-based. *See*
Deterrence-based
immigration policy
family separations. *See* Family
separations
indefinite detention, 21–22,
269, 308
migrant deaths along border,
83, 119, 132–33, 194, 365
under Obama. *See* Obama,
Barack, immigration policy
under Trump. *See* Trump,
Donald, immigration policy;
Zero tolerance policy
Inauguration of President Donald
Trump, 27–28
Inconvenient Truth, An
(documentary), 18
Influenza A virus subtype H7N9,
58
"Interior removals," 44
Iran, Operation Martyr
Soleimani, 362

Johnson, Jeh, 20–23
Jolie, Angelina, 98
Jones, Gina Ortiz, 343
José, xviii, xxi–xxii
author's interviews, 357–58
border crossing, 193–95,
357–58
declaring asylum, 197, 199
at Harlingen shelter, 202,
212–13, 264–65, 296, 331–32,
342
the journey, 4–5, 186, 187
life in Guatemala, 1–2, 3–4, 69,
146, 185–86
at Port Isabel Detention
Center, 296–97, 302–3

reunion with father, 349–50,
354
separation from father,
196–202, 212
Juan, xviii, xxi–xxii
at Adelanto ICE Detention
Center, 265, 273, 275, 294–
96, 303, 312, 321, 322–26,
328–30, 332–36, 347
author's interviews with, 2–3,
332–36, 347–50, 357–58
border crossings, 2–3, 193–95,
357–58
"credible fear" interview, 323,
328–30, 335, 342
declaration of asylum, 197, 199
the journey, 4–5, 186, 187
life in Guatemala, 1–2, 3–4, 69,
145–46, 185–86
release from custody, 347–50
reunion with son, 349–50, 354
Separated Parent's Removal
Form, xviii, 294–95, 322,
323–25, 334–36, 342
separation from son, 196–97,
213, 333–34
taken into custody, 196–200
testimonials for, 345–47
at Victorville Federal
Correctional Institution,
200, 229, 237, 264, 265
Juan Bosco Migrant Shelter, 148

Kadlec, Robert, 56–57, 58, 251,
270, 363
family reunifications, 271–73,
299
Kay, Tom, 148
Kelly, John, 256
ending "catch and release,"
30, 44

family separation policy, 53, 58–59, 139, 177, 178–79, 184
    announcement of, ix, 37–39, 44, 77, 86–87
    promotion to chief of staff, 53, 84–85, 88
Kerlikowske, Gil, 21
Kim Jong Un, 233
KIND (Kids in Need of Defense), 98–104, 124
King, Gayle, 256–57
Knights of Columbus, 54
Kornacki, Steve, 15
Korona, Betsy, 111, 205
Koss, Mitch, xxi, 18, 19, 40–41, 71–72, 111
Kotb, Hoda, 94–95, 96, 221, 309
Kraft, Colleen, 245–48
Kriel, Lomi, 76–77, 78–79, 86, 98, 124, 223
Kube, Courtney, 222

Lafferty, John, 37
Las Americas Premium Outlets, 75
Las Palomas Wildlife Management Area, 161–62
Late Late Show, The (TV show), 220
Latino voters, 20
Lee, Sheila Jackson, 359–60
Lee, Wendi, 17, 118
LeNoir, Lance, 118–19, 120–21
LeNoir, Robert "Lance," 172
Ling, Lisa, 40
Lloyd, Scott
    abortion issue, 54, 62, 147
    child abuse allegation, 358–59
    family reunifications, 270, 272–75, 299

family separations, 61–63, 146–47, 251, 257–58, 358–60
    Dickerson's reporting on, 150–51, 153, 155, 157–59, 195
    "let's get rid of the list," 158–61, 359–60
    tracking parents and children, 66–67, 158–61, 181, 195
    White's informal email, 224–26
    House hearing, 359–60
    Operation Mega, 54–56
Lockheed C-130 Hercules, 139
Lockheed P-3 Orion, 140
Lopez, John, 241–44
Lorenzen-Strait, Andrew, 278
Los Angeles International Airport, 232
Los Angeles Times, 114, 245–46
Los Zetas, 193
Lutheran Immigration and Refugee Service (LIRS), 9, 98–99, 100–104

McAleenan, Kevin, 366–67
    ending "catch and release," 29–30, 144
    family separations, 66–67, 69–70, 83, 144, 158, 238, 243, 266
        decision memos, 89, 163–67, 169–70, 174
        El Paso pilot program, ix, 70, 83–84
    migrant surge of 2014, 21
McAllen, Texas. See Ursula Border Patrol Central Processing Station
McCarthy, Kevin, 255–56

McGahn, Don, 266–67
McGarry, Erin, 140
McGuire Air Force Base, 139–40
McHenry, James, 314–15
McSally, Martha, 355
Maddow, Rachel, 13–14, 262–63
Maldonado Silva, Alfonso, 322–26
Mar-a-Lago Resort, 351, 353
Marcelino, 344–45
Marfa Border Patrol Station,
  82–83
María, 1–2, 4, 69, 146, 186, 213,
  237, 357
Mariana, 72, 74
Maricopa County Sheriff's
  Department, 17
Marijuana, 93–94, 341
Marine One, 71, 351, 352
Marriott, Brian, 206, 208
Martinez, Rogelio, 75–76, 79,
  82–83
Mary E. Switzer Federal Building,
  97–98
Matthews, Chris, 223
Maya Biosphere Reserve, 145
Mayans, 2, 364
Meadows, Mark, 215, 219
Meekins, Chris, 270, 271–73,
  293–94, 300
Meier, Richard, 311
Melvin, Craig, 94–95, 257, 309
Merkley, Jeff, 202–3, 204, 207, 215,
  216–17, 220, 247
Methamphetamine, 34, 35
Mexican-American War, 109
Mexico-United States barrier. *See*
  Border wall
Mexico-United States border,
  16–17, 80–81, 82–83
  author's visits to, 104–14,
  118–23

Galvez Tunnel, 118–19,
  120–23, 172
  migrant deaths along, 83, 119,
  132–33, 194, 365
Microsoft, 98
Migrant deaths along border, 83,
  119, 132–33, 194, 365
Migrant surge of 2011, 20, 46
Migrant surge of 2014, 20–21,
  46, 77
Migrant surge of 2016, 20, 22–23,
  46
Migration Crisis Action Team
  (MCAT), 116
Miller, Stephen
  election of 2016 and, 11–12,
  14–15
  family separation and
  immigration policy, 44–45,
  89, 266, 358
  Trump rally, 355–57
Miroff, Nick, 364
Mitchell, Andrea, 269–70
Mitnick, John, 164–66, 286
Mixed-status families, 94–97
  George's story, 72–74, 94,
  95–97
Moana (film), 210, 216, 218
Morning Joe (TV show), 27–28,
  44, 111, 112–13, 256
Ms. L v. ICE, xviii–xix, 134–35,
  166, 285–94
  background on, 122–26
  bars family separations and
  orders family reunifications,
  286–94, 299–302, 310–13
  declarations, 25–26, 51–52,
  91–92, 137
  filing, ix, 126–27, 166
  oral arguments, 173–74,
  286–87

pending agreement, 342
timeline of key events, ix–xi
MSNBC, 56, 57, 81, 112–13,
204–5, 234–35, 279–80
author's Casa Padre report,
xvi–xvii, xix, 213–14, 216–20
election of 2016, 12–13
MS-13 (gang), 115, 214, 261–62
Mueller, Robert, 113, 233
Muñoz, Cecilia, 22
"Murder board," 314–15
Muslim ban, 28, 36–38, 123, 256

Narcos aterrizando en peten, 3–4
NASA (National Aeronautics and
Space Administration), 140
National Defense Commission, 98
National Immigrant Justice
Center, 305, 319
NBC News, 14, 53–54, 111, 257
Nebraska Avenue Complex
(NAC), 21–22
New Brunswick, Canada, 327
New York Review of Books, 125
New York Times, 124, 147, 149–58,
173, 180, 195, 259
Nicaragua, 148–49, 177
Nielsen, Kirstjen
in Australia, 330
author's Dateline interview
with, 170–73, 181–85, 203–4,
260–61
border wall, 106, 108, 258
DHS confirmation, 84–88,
156–57
family reunifications, 286
family separations, 85–90, 135,
178–80, 238, 249, 259, 260
decision memos, 88–90,
163–67, 169–70, 174–75
press conference, 255, 260

Trump's desire to restart,
352–53, 361–62
Trump's executive order
ending, 259, 266, 268
NPR interview, 170–71. 184
Trump's confrontation with,
179–80, 184
Trump's firing of, 353–54, 366
Nilson, Craig, 332–33
Nogales Port of Entry, 148–49
Northern border in Maine,
326–27
North Korea, 178, 233
Northridge Earthquake of 1994,
43

Obama, Barack
immigration policy, 17–23,
60–61, 143
deportations under, 17–19,
77, 81, 120
family separations, 21–22,
37, 67, 99–100, 152, 160,
163–64
illegal border crossing
numbers, 19–20, 142
nickname of "Deporter in
Chief," 120
surge of 2014, 20–21, 46, 77
surge of 2016, 20, 22–23,
152
unaccompanied children,
55, 61, 67
inauguration of, 27
Obama, Michelle, 248, 253
Ocasio-Cortez, Alexandria, 280
Odalys, 9
O'Donnell, Lawrence, 219–20,
257, 263
OFO (Office of Field Operations),
22–23

Old Hidalgo Pumphouse, 106, 107
Operation IceBridge, 140–41
Operation Mega, 54–56
Organ Pipe Cactus National
   Monument, 131–33
ORR (Office of Refugee
Resettlement)
   ending "catch and release," 29,
      31, 32–33
   family separations, 9, 29–30,
      37, 58–60, 61–63, 66–69,
      83–84, 91–92, 137, 224–26
      announcement of, ix, 37–39
      Dickerson's reporting on,
         147, 149–59, 195
      KIND/LIRS and, 98–104
      leaked list of seven-
         hundred separated
         children, 152–54, 157–58,
         173–74
      tracking parents and
         children, 66–68, 158–61,
         181, 195–97, 209
   the "glitch" with ICE, 155–56,
      258
   migrant surge of 2016, 22–23
   UAC. See UAC
   White's resignation, 147, 160,
      224, 257–58
Ortiz, Raul, 341–42
Otay Mesa border fence, 63–66,
   118–23
Otay Mesa Detention Facility, 51
Otay Mesa Port of Entry, 120–23,
   127, 172–73
Our Lady of Guadalupe Church,
   75–76

PACER, xx
Padilla, Manuel "Manny," 172,
   173, 238–41, 261–62
Peace Corps, 98

Pence, Mike, 30, 178, 266, 268,
   355–56
Perry, Cal, 257
Petén, Guatemala, 1–2, 3–4, 69,
   145–46, 185–86, 364–65
Petermann Glacier, 140–41
Physicians for Human Rights,
   367–68
Pivot, 18, 19, 81
Podkul, Jennifer, 97–104, 134, 210
Politico, 57–58, 359–60
Pomegranates, 344–45
Port Isabel Service Detention
   Center, 227, 296–97, 300, 302–3,
   305
Presidential election of 2016. See
   Election of 2016
Prevention Through Deterrence.
   See Deterrence-based
   immigration policy
Price, Tom, 32, 56–57, 269
Prieto, Javier, 82–83
ProBAR Children's Project, 209
ProPublica audio tape, 255
Provost, Carla, 70, 83, 280,
   314–15
Public Health Service
   Commissioned Corps (PHSCC),
   29, 225, 272, 316

Qualia, Carmen, 241
Quicken Loans Arena, 15

Rachel Maddow Show, 13–14,
   262–63
Raytheon, 165
Reid, Joy, 234–35, 257, 279–80
Reno v. Flores, 21
Republican National Convention
   (2016), 21
Reunifications. See Family
   reunifications

Rio Grande, 82–83, 109, 110, 168, 297
  author's purchase of dried shrimp, 161–63
Rio Hondo, 297
Rodriguez, Alexia, 206–8
Rodriguez, Janelle, 105, 111, 204, 235–36, 237
Rodriguez, Robert, 127–29, 240, 261
Rodriguez, Sarah, 56
Roecker, Dana, 82, 168–69, 332–33
Roker, Al, 94–95
Ronald Reagan Building and International Trade Center, 29, 32, 180–81, 233
Ronald Reagan Washington National Airport, 349–50
Rosie, 9
Rotary Club, 231–32
Ruhle, Stephanie, 232–34, 257, 265–68
Russia investigation, 113, 179, 233
Ryan, Paul, 13, 104–5

Sabraw, Dana, 285–94
  bars family separations and orders family reunifications, 286–94, 299–302, 310–13
  oral arguments, 173–74, 286–87
Salvano-Dunn, Dana, 305
Sanchez, Juan, 205–6, 211–12, 222
Sanders, Bernie, 12, 13, 17
Sanders, Sarah Huckabee, 232, 234, 239
San Diego Union-Tribune, 114
San Luis Río Colorado, 193–94, 213, 357
Santa Ana Wildlife Refuge, 109–10

San Ysidro Port of Entry, 34–36, 51, 74, 93–94, 166
Schepel, Elizabeth, 206–8
Scott, Rodney, 118–19, 172, 175, 307–9, 367
Sea level rise, 140–41
Senate Appropriations Subcommittee on Homeland Security, 170
Senate Committee on Homeland Security and Governmental Affairs, Nielsen DHS confirmation, 85–88, 156–57
Senate Committee on the Judiciary, 314–17
Separations. See Family separations
Sessions, Jeff
  family separations policy, 88, 135
    biblical justification for, 231–32
    public announcement implementing, x, 174–77
  memorandum prioritizing prosecution of immigration offenses, ix, 44–45
  zero tolerance policy announcement of, 174–77, 208
    memorandum instituting, ix, 142–44
Shanahan, Patrick, 178
Shear, Michael, 180
Sieff, Kevin, 364
Sierra Club, 109–10, 113
Significant Incident Reports, 191, 227
Sikorsky UH-60 Black Hawks, 167–70, 177, 236
"Slash," 326–27
Smuggler (coyote), 2

Social media, xix, 214–16, 253–55
Social Security, 357
Sonoran Desert, 131, 133, 194
Sontag, John, 140–41
South El Monte, 39–43
South Texas Detention Center, 91–92
Southwest Key, 203, 205–6, 210, 212
Stecker, Judy, 314–15
Steinle, Kate, 12
Stewart, Scott, 311–13
Stimson, Brian, 314–15
Sualog, Jallyn, 160–61
Sulemani, Qassim, 362
Sullivan, John, 178
Supreme Court, U.S.
    Muslim ban and, 123
    Reno v. Flores, 21
Surf Fence, 172

Tax Cuts and Jobs Act of 2017, 70–71, 105, 110, 122
Taylor, Miles, 170
"Tear sheet," 243
"Tender aged" children, 68, 265–66
Texas Republican presidential caucuses of 2016, 15–16
Texas Tribune, 288
Thomas, Debra, 186
Thule Air Base, 140
Tijuana, 17, 19, 71–72, 127–28
Timeline of key events, ix–xi
Toczylowski, Lindsay
    at Adelanto ICE Detention Center, 321–26, 332–36
    author's phone interview, xvii–xviii, 288–90
    Juan and José, xviii, 229–31, 294–95, 322–26, 332–36, 347–49

    at Victorville Federal Correctional Institution, 229–31, 234, 264, 265, 321–22
Today (TV show), 40, 94–95, 256, 309, 326–27
    author's Casa Padre report, 220–21
Tornado outbreak of March 2019, 351–52
Tornillo, 343–45. *See also* Casa Padre
Tornillo Land Port of Entry, 222–23
Tornillo tent city, 280
Torres, Miguel, 78
"Torture," 367–68
Trafficking Victims Protection Reauthorization Act (TVPRA), 87
"Treated us like animals, like dogs," xviii
Treviño, Jackelin, 109–11, 113
Trickler-McNulty, Claire
    family reunifications, 258, 278
    family separations, 129–31, 134, 155, 163–64, 210
Trump, Donald
    border wall, 15–16, 28, 34, 70–71, 105–6, 108–15, 118, 179
        prototypes, 63–65, 81–82, 308
    budget deal, 70–71, 105, 110, 122
    election of 2016, 17–18, 21
        announcement, 81
        Colorado delegates, 11–15
        Texas delegates, 15–16
    foreign aid policy, 145

impeachment of, 355–56
inauguration of, 27–28
on leakers, 157
Muslim ban, 28, 36–38, 123, 256
press availability, 232–34
Russia investigation, 113, 179, 233
State of the Union Address, 105, 112, 114–15, 122
surveying tornado damage of March 2019, 351–52
Trump, Donald, family
separation policy, 47–50, 58–59, 76–77
Ainsley's reporting on, 37, 53–54, 55–56, 76, 124
confrontation with Nielsen, 179–80, 184
congressional hearings, 314–17, 358–60
desire to restart, 352–53, 361–63
DHHS Office of the Inspector General reports, 295–96, 339, 356
Dickerson's reporting on, 147, 149–58, 195
El Paso pilot program, ix, 9, 70, 83–84, 277
executive order ending, x, xv, 259, 266–69, 285, 286–87
Ivanka Trump and, 255–56, 258–60, 266, 267
justifications for, 231–34
Kelly's announcement of, ix, 37–39, 44, 77, 86–87
Melania Trump's opposition to, 352–53
public outrage over, 28, 245–49, 253–55, 256–57, 260, 262–63

Senate hearing, 314–17
Sessions' public announcement of, x, 174–77
Trump, Donald, immigration policy, 17, 28, 81–82, 365–67. See also Zero tolerance policy
death of agent Martinez, 75–76
deportation policy, 40–44
deterrence-based, 33–36, 38, 47–48, 361, 362, 365
Dreamers and, 70–71, 105
drug smuggling rationale, 33–36
ending "catch and release," 29–33, 44–45, 115, 141–44, 147
memorandum, ix, 141–44, 147
executive orders, x, xv, 30, 44, 259, 266–67, 266–69, 286–87
fingerprinting, 117, 197, 212
firing of Nielsen, 353–54
Trump, Ivanka, 255–56, 258–60, 266, 267
Trump, Melania, 253
border visit, 269–71
opposition to family separations, 352–53
"Trump effect," 61, 142
Trump International Hotel, 354
Trump rallies, 355–57
Trump travel ban (Muslim ban), 28, 36–38, 123, 256
Trump v. Hawaii, 123
Tunnel Rats, 120–23
Tur, Katy, 222–23, 354–55
Twitter, 214–16, 218

UAC (Unaccompanied Alien Children), xvi–xviii, 9, 29, 46–50, 53–54, 66–69, 89–90, 186–87, 195

UAC (continued)
tracking children, 67–68,
159–61, 195–97, 277–78
"UAC Data Request-Parent/Legal
Guardian Link," 276–79
United Nations Convention
against Torture, 329–30
United States Agency for
International Development
(USAID), 145
United States Conference of
Catholic Bishops (USCCB),
231–32
Universal Studios Hollywood,
111
University of Nevada, Las Vegas,
17
Unruh, Kendal, 13
Urbanowicz, Peter, 251
Urrea, Luís Alberto, 132
Ursula Border Patrol Central
Processing Station, 235–49, 273
author's invitation to tour,
235–36
author's tour and reporting,
xvii–xviii, 238–49

Valley Baptists Medical Center,
209
Victorville Federal Correctional
Institution, 200, 229–31, 234,
237, 264, 265, 321–22
Vietnam War, 64
Villareal, Roy, 63–65

Wagner, Steven, 61–62, 159–60,
251, 272–73
Waldman, Katie, 354–57, 361–63
author's interview with
Nielsen, 181, 184–85, 203–4
border visits, 330–31, 341,
354–55

Casa Padre invitation, 203–5
family separations, 258, 308–9,
341–42, 356–57, 362–63
leaked list, 157, 158, 181
McAllen invitation, 235, 237
Senate hearing, 314–17
Trump rally, 355–57
Walgreens, spiral notebook,
xiv–xix, 203
Walmart, xii, 202, 217
Washington Monument, 27
Washington Post, 124, 134–35,
238, 247, 364
Welker, Kristen, 267
West Texas Detention Facility
(Sierra Blanca), 25–26
White, Jonathan
abortion issue, 54, 62, 147
ending "catch and release,"
29–30, 31–33
family reunifications, 271–75,
299–303
family separations and UAC,
53–54, 55, 58, 59–60,
66–69, 103, 146–47, 196, 210,
224–26, 290
Chavez request, 115–17
deterrence model and,
46–50
El Paso pilot program, ix,
70, 83–84
email to Lloyd, 224–26
tracking surge in, 46–50,
66–67, 83, 158, 248
Homestead Temporary Influx
Shelter, 60–63
resignation from ORR, 147,
160, 224, 257–58
Senate hearing, 314–17
White nationalism, 355
Winfrey, Oprah, 246, 257
Witt, Alex, 239

Wolf, Chad, 85, 88–90, 135, 170–71, 363, 366–67
Women's March, 28, 256
Women's Refugee Commission, 98–99, 124
World Birding Center, 106
Wynne, Maggie, 251, 272–73

Yuma Border Patrol Station, 197–99, 200–201, 213, 334, 350, 365–66
"Yuma 14," 132, 133

Zero tolerance policy, 198, 239, 253, 259–60, 359, 362

DHS implementation of, x, 174–80, 339
Kraft on, 245–46
Sessions' announcement of, 174–77, 208
Sessions' memorandum instituting, ix, 142–44
Trump's announcement of, 177–80
Trump's executive order ending, x, 259, 266–69, 285, 286–87
Waldman's defense of, 354–55